M

AFTER *BROWN*

✳

AFTER *BROWN*

THE RISE AND RETREAT OF
SCHOOL DESEGREGATION

*

Charles T. Clotfelter

PRINCETON UNIVERSITY PRESS

PRINCETON AND OXFORD

Library of Congress Cataloging-in-Publication Data

Clotfelter, Charles T.
After Brown : the rise and retreat of school desegregation / Charles T. Clotfelter.
p.   cm.
Includes bibliographical references (p.) and index.
ISBN 0-691-11911-2 (cl : alk. paper)
1. School integration—United States.   2. Segregation in education—United States.
3. Education and state—United States.   I. Title: Rise and retreat of school desegregation.
II. Title.
LC214.2.C56 2004
379.2'63'0973—dc22   2003066382

British Library Cataloging-in-Publication Data is available

This book has been composed in Minion

Printed on acid-free paper. ∞

www.pupress.princeton.edu

Printed in the United States of America

1   3   5   7   9   10   8   6   4   2

FOR THERESA

*

✳ *Contents* ✳

* Illustrations *

* Tables *

✱ Preface ✱

I<small>N SEVERAL RECENT YEARS</small>, I have taught a seminar at Duke on the subject of school desegregation. When I have asked my students why they wanted to take the course, more than a few gave a reason that surprised me. They said their parents had experienced desegregation, and my students were curious to find out what it had been all about. That school desegregation would be for many Americans something that existed only in the distant past had not occurred to me, though on reflection this made perfect sense. For most of my students, the concept of an officially sanctioned policy of racial separation—such as existed in some twenty states before 1954—was so foreign to their own experience as to be nearly unimaginable. Only as the class viewed film footage of the desegregation of Central High School in Little Rock in 1957 and South Boston High School in 1974 did they seem to appreciate the intensity of white resistance or the magnitude of the change that this policy brought about in the lives of ordinary citizens.

As the fiftieth anniversary of the *Brown v. Board of Education* decision approached, I came to believe that the time could not be better for a renewed assessment of school desegregation. It seemed especially important to address this subject in light of the growing indications that, as a policy, it was losing some of the pillars of support that had sustained it through decades of determined resistance, both loud and quiet. How could the changes wrought by desegregation, or the warnings that schools were becoming "resegregated," be appreciated without a fuller understanding of what was at stake in the *Brown* decision? I resolved therefore to build upon some earlier research I had done to put together a factual chronicle of school desegregation. I decided to use as my indicator changes in interracial contact in schools, a concept for which social science has developed several mathematical measures. Using data for as long a period as possible, I applied these measures to document the changes that have occurred over the five decades since the *Brown* decision. Thus the study contained in this book can be viewed as a sort of arithmetical history.

In conducting the research, I have benefited enormously from the combined assistance of able research assistants, insightful colleagues, and generous institutions. Robert Malme provided the bulk of the data management and programming necessary to the analysis of the many data sets used in the project. I also relied on the research assistance of these students: Roger Aliaga Diaz, Janeil Belle, Shawn Brandt, Reid Chisholm, Jane Cooley, Ben Dalton, Ryan Fleenor, Megan Fotheringham, Aneil Lala, Sarah Levin, Faye Miller, Abiskar Mitra, Amanda Nybro, Jasmina Radeva, Vanessa Rousso, Martin Steinmeyer, and Jianguo Xu, and on the invaluable library reference services at the Duke Law School, particularly those of Jim Ruwaldt.

Of my faculty colleagues at Duke, Helen Ladd and Jacob Vigdor were especially important to me, as we coauthored one of the studies on which I report in detail in chapter 5. I also received helpful comments and suggestions from Ronald Ehrenberg and James Hearn and long-standing encouragement from Martin Feldstein. Others provided me with data and other assistance: Angel Beza of the University of North Carolina, Stephen Broughman and Michael Ross of the National Center for Education Statistics, Elizabeth Glennie of the North Carolina Education Resource Data Center, Cara Nakamura of the Andrew W. Mellon Foundation, Sarah Reber of Harvard University, and Franklin Wilson of the University of Wisconsin. Tables 5.2 and 5.3 are reproduced from *Urban Review* 34, no. 1, by agreement with Kluwer Academic / Human Sciences Press. Figure 5.2 and tables 5.1 and A5.1 are derived from an article previously published in the *North Carolina Law Review* 81, no. 4, and reprinted with permission. The Spencer Foundation and Duke University provided financial support. The views in the book are mine, however, and do not necessarily reflect those of any institution.

AFTER *BROWN*

*

Introduction

> Our decision, therefore, cannot turn on merely a
> comparison of these tangible factors in the Negro and white
> schools involved in each of the cases. We must look instead
> to the effect of segregation itself on public education.
> *Earl Warren,* Brown v. Board of Education, *1954*[1]

THE CHANGES wrought by school desegregation since the 1954 *Brown
v. Board of Education* decision have been at times dramatic, uneven, and
subject to reversal. As illustration, consider two school districts in the
formerly segregated South.

The first is Taylor County, Georgia, situated between Macon and Columbus, some ninety miles south of Atlanta. A news item that appeared
on the national wires in the spring of 2003 reported on a practice there
that seemed to bespeak a bygone era: racially segregated proms. Following the desegregation of the county's public schools in the fall of 1971,
school officials at Taylor County High, like those in many other districts
in the South, decided to discontinue the tradition of holding a spring-
time prom, allowing instead separate, privately sponsored proms for
white and black students. This practice continued until 2002, when, for
the first time, a single, integrated prom was held. The next year, however, most white students voted to revert to their all-white prom. Another prom, open to blacks and whites, was held at nearby Fort Valley
State University.[2] Thus, five decades after the landmark *Brown* decision,
in a high school evenly split between white and black students, this one
part of high school life remained every bit as segregated as it had been in
the days of de jure segregation.[3]

A second school district is the Winston-Salem / Forsyth Schools, located in the western piedmont of North Carolina. This district illustrates
the sweeping change that desegregation brought to the formerly segregated South, as well as its vulnerability to reversal. In 1969, after a decade of minimalist steps taken by reluctant school officials, very few of
the district's students attended racially mixed schools. Although 28 percent of its students were nonwhite, all but ten of its sixty-eight schools

had enrollments that were 90–100 percent white or nonwhite. Suddenly, in 1970, as a result of a desegregation order, the district's schools became nearly racially balanced, with only two schools in either 90-plus percent category by 1971.[4] Between 1969 and 1971, the percentage of black students attending 90-plus percent nonwhite schools fell from 84 percent to 3 percent. And for the next twenty-three years the district's schools remained racially balanced. Then, in 1995, a newly elected school board, freed by the courts from continuing its racial balance plan, instituted a new "controlled choice" plan that allowed parents to express their preferences for schools within their part of the district, guaranteeing them one of their top three choices. Although school administrators expressed the hope that the resulting school assignments would produce schools that departed from the systemwide racial composition by no more than 20 percent, this limitation was not enforced, in spite of complaints of growing racial disparities among the district's schools.[5] Indeed, the district's schools steadily became racially imbalanced. The percentage of black students attending 90-plus percent nonwhite schools increased from 0 in the fall of 1994, to 6 percent in 1996, 13 percent in 1998, 21 percent in 2000, and 22 percent in 2002.[6] Thus, during the fifth decade after the *Brown* decision, Winston-Salem's schools were gradually resegregating.

Whatever else might be said about racial patterns in these two school districts, the degree of interracial contact their students experienced in 2004 was far more extensive than it had been a half-century before. Even the most cursory glance backward in time reveals change in the racial makeup of American public schools that is little short of breathtaking. Consider what schools looked like before 1954. As a result of the official segregation that existed in more than twenty states, some 40 percent of the nation's students attended schools that were segregated by law.[7] Tens of thousands more students attended schools that were every bit as segregated, but by virtue of starkly uneven residential patterns rather than by legal sanction. In the ensuing decades schools that had been under the regime of de jure segregation experienced marked increases in interracial contact, and so did many others where segregation had not been enforced by law. As impressive as it was, however, this general increase in interracial contact was diminished by two contrary tendencies. One was the stubborn continuation of pockets of segregation, such as Taylor County's all-white prom. The other was an unmistakable trend in the direction of resegregation, as illustrated by the Winston-Salem / Forsyth district.

The purpose of this book is to document the course of school desegregation over the half-century since the *Brown* decision. It uses as its basic marker of change the degree of interracial contact in schools. It measures the extent of that contact in schools, both public and private, over as much of the half-century since the *Brown* decision as available data allow. It compares patterns of interracial contact across regions in the country, in communities both inside and outside metropolitan areas.[8]

Why the focus on contact? The most obvious reason to do so is its central importance to state-sponsored segregation. The fact at the heart of both the apartheid practiced in the American South and the *Brown* decision that ruled it unconstitutional was the physical separation of the races. In a legal leap based in part on social science research, the Supreme Court concluded that separate schools were "inherently unequal," making unnecessary further comparison of the school facilities available to students of different races. Left unsettled by *Brown*, however, was whether racial segregation in schools brought about by segregated residential patterns—so-called de facto segregation—might not also be vulnerable to constitutional challenge. Ultimately, the court would reject this interpretation, making state action to segregate schools the necessary condition for federal intervention.

One might argue that, in assessing a policy such as school desegregation, the dimensions of interest should be the quality of resources available to students or socially significant outcomes such as its effects on academic achievement, self-esteem, attitudes, interracial friendships, or long-term social and economic success. Although these considerations are undeniably important, even crucial, in any full assessment of desegregation, no one study can do justice to all of them. Instead, I focus on an aspect that is a necessary intermediary for virtually all potential effects of desegregation—interracial contact. Contact lies at the heart of some theories about how desegregation might affect young people. Psychologist Gordon Allport's "contact theory," for example, asserts that contact is a necessary, but not sufficient, condition for the reduction of racial prejudice. To have this beneficial effect, the contact must embody equal status and a common objective, and it must enjoy official approval.[9] Theories of labor market success based on information and social connections also require contact. Any number of theories of academic achievement also factor in the effects of peers. And some models of political economy imply that the distribution of resources depends on the distribution of students, that blacks would not receive equal educational facilities until they attended the same schools as whites. Thus, while interracial contact is by no means the whole story nor the only metric by which effects might be measured, it does represent a significant aspect of schools and a necessary ingredient for important potential processes that social scientists have identified.

Interracial contact in schools also has direct relevance to several important issues in education policy. Most obviously, it relates to the policy of school desegregation itself. How the federal courts have come to interpret *Brown* and refine its constitutional mandate is a question of undiminished importance to both constitutional lawyers and local school boards. The Supreme Court's growing reluctance to require racial balance has been blamed for the resegregation noted by observers of public schools.[10] It is not too much to suggest that some observers believe the era of school desegregation may be drawing to a close.[11] Given the widely acknowledged importance of school desegregation as a component of social policy, a shift of this significance surely deserves careful documentation. Fears of increased racial segregation have also helped drive discussions of school vouchers and school choice proposals; detractors worry that such policies would make it easier for middle-class white families to choose predominantly white schools.[12]

Interracial contact also has direct relevance to the use of ability grouping or academic tracking. These policies are employed widely at all levels of education, particularly in high schools. Justified on the basis that homogeneous classes make for more effective instruction, tracking policies have been decried by critics who argue that their criteria for grouping are often capricious, the assignments they create are usually irreversible, and their educational benefits are dubious.[13] Since these policies tend to decrease the amount of interracial contact within schools, especially when assignment to groups is subject to racial bias, their use quite clearly bears on interracial contact in schools.

Ultimately, patterns of interracial contact have the potential to influence educational outcomes. Consider the distribution of resources in the schools. If whites and nonwhites tend to be in different schools, the possibility exists that students in these racial groups will be exposed to different levels of resources or teachers of different quality. As an illustration that segregation may have this effect, two recent studies suggest that nonwhites are more likely than whites to be taught by inexperienced teachers.[14] If schools are racially balanced, however, such differences simply cannot arise except between classrooms; and if classrooms are racially balanced, they cannot arise at all.

Quite apart from its implications for the distribution of school resources, interracial contact may bring about outcomes of considerable social value. Consider three sets of possible outcomes: academic achieve-

4

ment, job market success, and racial tolerance. First, from at least the days of the Coleman Report in 1966, some researchers have held out the possibility that interracial contact in schools may itself have a positive impact on the achievement gains of minority students, without causing any offsetting losses among whites. Second, some evidence has suggested that integration may improve the life prospects of minority students by giving them access to social networks formerly open primarily to whites. A third potential benefit of interracial contact is that suggested by Allport's contact theory: under the right conditions, contact can lead to productive interracial relations and thereby enhance racial tolerance. More broadly, interracial contact is important simply because of the significance of racial and ethnic diversity itself. Whatever else its effects may be, interracial contact in schools offers students from all racial and ethnic groups the chance to learn about living in a diverse society. In his study of American race relations a decade before the *Brown* decision, Gunnar Myrdal observed: "One of the effects of social segregation is isolation of Negroes and whites. The major effects of isolation are, of course, on Negroes. Contrary to popular opinion, however, there are bad effects on whites also, and these are increasing as the level of Negro cultural attainment is rising. . . . Whether they know it or not, white people are dwarfing their minds to a certain extent by avoiding contacts with colored people."[15] In light of the society's growing racial and ethnic diversity, the force of this statement with regard to schools has surely grown since Myrdal wrote it. For all of these reasons, there can be little doubt that interracial contact holds considerable policy significance.

How Much Did Interracial Contact Change after 1954?

A primary aim of this book is to document changes in interracial contact over time. One of the best illustrations of the results of judicial and executive branch measures to desegregate formerly segregated schools remains Gary Orfield's *Public School Desegregation in the United States, 1968–1980*, which presents a summary by region of the percentage of black students who attended schools that were 90–100 percent nonwhite in enrollment. He shows that by this measure black students were more racially isolated in the South than in any other region in 1968. Whereas 78 percent of the South's black students attended such schools, the corresponding percentage in all other regions was 60 percent or less. To be sure, this measure is not a perfect indicator of segregation, as it reflects in part the overall racial makeup of regions.[16] Nevertheless, it provides an easily comprehended metric and is an illuminating marker of changes over time for a given region. As a result of the federal government's vigorous pursuit of desegregation beginning in 1968, racial isolation measured in this way declined precipitously in the South, transforming its schools from the most to the least segregated in the country. The percentage of black students in the South who attended 90–100 percent minority schools fell between 1968 and 1972 from 78 percent to 25 percent. By 1972, the region with the next lowest corresponding percentage was the West, where 43 percent of its black students attended such schools.

As compelling as it may be, this statistical record of changes wrought after 1968 still misses what went before. One of the aims of the present study is to extend the historical field of view to cover as much of the period since 1954 as possible. Thus I use unpublished data from the period before 1968 to chart the trends in interracial contact for selected districts and by region. Not only does this analysis provide new evidence on the degree of school segregation outside the South in the 1950s and early 1960s, it also allows for an assessment of changes in segregation over a longer period in all regions. And, in light of the steady relaxation of judicial oversight of desegregation orders beginning in the 1990s and the prospect of resegregation observed in previously desegregated school districts, it is necessary to extend the measurement of interracial contact into the new century.

Documenting changes in interracial contact over the last fifty years is one thing. Assigning causation is another. Did *Brown* bring about the well-documented reductions in segregation? I believe it is virtually impossible to isolate the effect of the 1954 decision or indeed the subsequent major Supreme Court decisions in light of the other powerful forces at work during the same period. For one thing, the 1964 Civil Rights Act gave to the executive branch a powerful lever—funding—to use to encourage school districts to comply with court decrees and other federal law. In addition, the manifold changes brought about by the civil rights movement, not the least of which was the Voting Rights Act of 1965 but also including actions in state legislatures and local school boards and changing attitudes on the part of ordinary citizens, surely influenced the direction of change as well. For these reasons, I generally sidestep the question of causation. Rather, I focus on documenting measurable changes in interracial contact, noting where appropriate the coincident events of the time.

The Blunting of School Desegregation

Using the yardstick of interracial contact, one is tempted to ask whether school desegregation has been a "success." To what extent did desegregation measures break down the barriers of racial separation that previously existed? In light of the large declines in racial isolation, one is almost compelled to judge the policy a success, perhaps a great success, for the changes accomplished in its wake were undeniably significant. Yet that judgment inevitably will be tempered by the failure of school desegregation to achieve *more*. Owing to the very nature of the process, the success of school desegregation would ultimately depend, in part, on the reaction of private citizens, as well as the actions of local school officials. In the end, the federal authorities empowered to employ their considerable policy tools to transform interracial contact found themselves in the position of squeezing a balloon: pressure in one place caused bulges to appear elsewhere. Some amount of change in interracial contact could be accomplished quickly and easily, some change was possible only with difficulty or only temporarily, and some change could not be accomplished at all.

The campaign for school desegregation—for many it was nothing less than a crusade—was launched by a judicial decision of extraordinary simplicity and moral clarity, and it soon received the backing of all three branches of the federal government. But it faced resistance in the country. Most obviously, it confronted an entire social system of racial separation in the American South, enforced by both the power of the state and informal intimidation, and elaborately codified in law, custom, and myth. The ferocity of the immediate reaction to the *Brown* decision made clear that the states of the former Confederacy, at least, would not stand idly by while an imperial federal government sought to destroy a central pillar of its social order. Nor was opposition confined to the South. Many whites outside the South had enjoyed privileged treatment in their public school systems as well. Public schools had been segregated by law in the District of Columbia and the six Border states (Delaware, Kentucky, Maryland, Missouri, Oklahoma, and West Virginia) as well as in parts of three other states (Arizona, Kansas, and New Mexico).[17] More significantly, public schools in much of the urban North were characterized by pronounced de facto segregation, owing to the highly fragmented jurisdictional landscape in most metropolitan areas. Thus, when later judicial decisions extended the logic of *Brown* to urban school dis-

7

tricts outside of the South, resistance to integration that had previously lain beneath the surface became increasingly evident.

Hence the execution of the policy of desegregation was frustrated, and ultimately blunted, by four factors: apparent white aversion to interracial contact, the multiplicity of means by which whites could sidestep the effects of the policy, the willingness of state and local governments to accommodate white resistance, and the faltering resolve of the prime movers of the policy. Apparent white aversion to interracial contact was widespread, and certainly not confined to the South, although it was most visible in that region. To be sure, it was neither universal nor uniform. Nor was it exclusive to whites, although it was surely more common in whites than among other major racial and ethnic groups. And it undoubtedly sprang from more than one source. For some, it surely grew out of pure racial antipathy. For others, however, it arose from inclinations common to most parents of any group: the desire to send children to well-appointed schools, staffed with skilled and experienced teachers, in safe neighborhoods, and with students from economically advantaged families. These preferences simply tended to correspond to a preference for schools with higher proportions of white students.[18] For the sake of understanding the decisions of white parents, the origin of the preference matters less than the preference itself.

The second factor frustrating desegregation was the multiplicity of escape routes open to many families wishing to reduce the level of interracial contact in their children's schools. Three main avoidance options existed. First, suburban school districts were the most obvious alternative to city school districts with high or rising proportions of minority students. Where they were conveniently located and predominantly white, these suburban districts offered a ready alternative to central city schools. They offered an especially ready option for newly formed households or families moving into a metropolitan area for the first time, because choosing to live there did not require the cost of an additional move. It turned out that these conditions differed markedly by region. In the Northeast and Midwest, it was not unusual for suburban school districts to be very small, so small that families moving into or living in some of the largest metropolitan areas in the country had dozens of school districts from which to choose. In the South and the West, however, school districts historically covered much larger areas, leaving families fewer districts from which to choose. A second avoidance option was, of course, private schools. Not for everyone, owing to their cost, private schools remained a safety valve for whites who were unhappy with the public schools. Although there is good reason to believe that race was not the only or even primary reason why many parents sent their children to private school, the pertinent fact with respect to interracial contact is that, by and large, the private schools had smaller shares of minority students than the public schools. Extracurricular activities provided a third avoidance option, admittedly less effective than the first two. By participating in predominantly white activities in school and after school, whites could reduce their rate of contact with nonwhites.

The third factor that frustrated desegregation efforts was the willingness of state and local government officials ranging from legislators who shaped state curricula to principals and counselors who determined classroom assignments—to accommodate white parents' wishes to minimize interracial contact. School officials in various parts of the country followed policies that had the effect of keeping schools racially identifiable. These included such well-documented practices as building new schools in predominantly white or nonwhite neighborhoods, adjusting school attendance boundaries to minimize racially mixed schools, and allowing whites to transfer out of racially changing schools. More important and longer lasting was the policy of academic tracking and other forms of ability grouping, which created racial disparities within schools. Other public policies not obviously related to education, including the creation of small local government jurisdictions and segregation of public housing projects, also had the effect of maintaining segregation in public schools whose attendance zones were based on residential neighborhoods.

Finally, desegregation efforts were constrained by faltering resolve on the part of the federal government and erstwhile proponents of integration. Beginning with the *Milliken* decision in 1974, the Supreme Court steadily backed away from its aggressive attack on racial imbalance. Limiting desegregation efforts to what could be accomplished within school districts necessarily left open the possibility that segregation caused by racial disparities between districts could continue to grow. In addition, federal courts, led by the Supreme Court, began to deem local school districts as "unitary" after they fulfilled certain requirements, thereafter allowing or mandating that they back away from explicit efforts to balance schools racially. Following *Milliken*, enthusiasm for integrated schools among spokespersons for minority groups visibly waned.

While acknowledging that these barriers reduced the impact of desegregation policies on the extent of interracial contact, we must not lose sight of the increases in interracial contact that did occur over this half-century. The extent of change can be seen by tracing the trend in the percentage of black students attending schools that were 90–100 percent minority. This share went down sharply in the early 1970s, especially in the South, and then increased modestly, remaining well below where it stood in 1954. Interracial contact in school has also increased for whites. Today, most white students attend schools with some racial diversity, and in the South they attend schools whose numbers of black students could not have been imagined in 1954. To be sure, interracial friendships remain the exception rather than the rule, but the "loose ties" of association routinely bridge the color line. Thousands of integrated football and wrestling teams, bands, and school clubs give students in middle school and high school opportunities to know those from other racial and ethnic groups as individuals rather than as stereotypes. So, while school desegregation has been an imperfect revolution, falling far short of what some of its original proponents had dreamed it might have become, it has been a revolution nonetheless.

Yet these achievements are by no means secure. As the example of Winston-Salem / Forsyth illustrates emphatically, the process of desegregation is potentially reversible. Thus, after fifty years, it remains important to assess this policy, warts and all.

Outline of the Book

The book's first chapter provides a brief historical narrative context for the study. It begins by describing official policies governing interracial contact in public schools on the eve of the *Brown* decision as well as other social forces affecting racial patterns of school enrollment. It then briefly summarizes the court decisions and other government actions relevant to school desegregation in the period. It also discusses differences in resources available in schools attended by students of different races.

Chapter 2 describes, using numeric indices, changes in interracial contact and segregation over the fifty-year period following the *Brown* decision. Focusing first on data for school districts, it extends backward to earlier years the trend analysis developed by Gary Orfield, using previously unpublished statistics from the 1950s and early 1960s collected from individual school districts, and other previously unutilized data. Together with newly calculated measures for more recent years, these calculations for earlier years provide the longest time series picture of interracial contact in public schools so far available. The chapter then examines school desegregation measured for metropolitan areas. For the shorter 1970 to 2000 period, it decomposes segregation into three components and shows how each has changed over that period. Like most previous research on school segregation, the numerical analyses presented in the book focus on racial disparities in school enrollment. Owing to the paucity of relevant data, no attempt is made to measure segregation by social or economic class, nor is attention given to the distribution of teachers by race.

Chapter 3 discusses the connection between school desegregation and residential location. It considers, first, how residential patterns affect the segregation of schools. Second, it examines the effect of school desegregation on the residential choices of whites. In particular, it assesses the hypothesis that whites seek to avoid racially mixed schools. The chapter begins with a selective review of the previous research on this subject. It then presents two new empirical tests relevant to the question of what independent effect school desegregation has had on residential patterns. Finally, it considers the motivations that underlie white behavior.

Chapter 4 focuses on private schools and their role in school segregation. It begins by examining trends and patterns in private school enrollment. It then incorporates private school enrollment in a comprehensive decomposition of school segregation. Unlike conventional measures that are based on public schools in districts, this comprehensive approach accounts for both public and private students and groups students by metropolitan area rather than by district. Although they enroll only one-tenth of all K–12 students, private schools are sufficiently distinctive in terms of racial composition, in most communities, to contribute to overall racial segregation. How much they contribute to segregation is another question, and one that is examined in this chapter.

Almost all studies of school segregation have used school-level data, measuring segregation by looking at racial disparities among schools. Yet there is ample reason to pay attention to disparities that arise within schools, creating segregation across classrooms. Chapter 5 draws on research using otherwise unavailable data. First, it analyzes classroom-level data for North Carolina, which allows the measuring of segregation within schools as well as between them. Second, it discusses findings based on interracial contact in high school clubs and sports teams.

Chapter 6 is devoted exclusively to higher education. Using similar methodology on the unfamiliar application of colleges and universities, it develops measures to give a longitudinal perspective on interracial contact, calculated at the campus level, for colleges that are roughly comparable to those used for elementary and secondary schools. The picture that emerges is one of tremendous change in previously white colleges and universities but remarkably little change in historically black institutions. Applying the conventional exposure and segregation measures at this level produces an unusual perspective from which to view developments in American higher education over the last several decades.

The last chapter summarizes the book's findings and assesses their importance for educational, social, and economic outcomes. Drawing from empirical research on the effects of interracial contact, it discusses the likely effect of the changes that have accompanied school desegregation. Finally, it notes policy questions related to interracial contact that remain pertinent as desegregation enters its second half-century.

✳ CHAPTER ONE ✳

Walls Came Tumbling Down

I draw the line in the dust and toss the gauntlet before the
feet of tyranny and I say segregation now, segregation
tomorrow, segregation forever.
Alabama Governor George Wallace, 1963[1]

THE DECISION that Chief Justice Earl Warren read aloud in a hushed
Supreme Court on May 17, 1954, is justly celebrated as one of the signal
events of American legal history. In its wake, the public schools of a
region would be transformed. The decision challenged one of the linch-
pins of Southern custom and law, the separation of the races in public
schools. Unlike many events whose implications become evident only
with the passage of time, most of the likely consequences of *Brown v.
Board of Education* were appreciated immediately. The front pages of
Southern newspapers featured defiant statements by elected officials,
plus a few voices of resigned acceptance, but most observers seemed to
understand, or at least to suspect, that the days of segregation were
numbered. The decision itself anticipated resistance, of course. As testament to the delicate process of negotiation and revision that allowed him
to obtain a unanimous vote, Warren crafted a decision full of moral
weight but lacking any reference to enforcement. In fact, it would be
another fourteen years (in the 1968 *Green v. County School Board of New
Kent County* decision) before the court came to the aid of beleaguered
federal district judges with an unambiguous order finally putting to an
end state-sanctioned separate school systems.[2] As a piece of American
social policy, few would doubt that it ranks among the most important,
if it is not the most important policy of its century. For one large region,
it brought about a change that few could have imagined would be possible, but its effects were felt throughout the country.

The purpose of this chapter is to lay out, in brief, the events, the
public acts and decisions, that marked the formation and evolution of
this policy, as a way of providing the institutional background to the
quantitative descriptions of patterns and changes that follow. To students
of education policy or constitutional law, much of this history is quite

familiar, for it has been well covered in admirably thorough studies.[3] Most readers, however, may find it helpful to preface their assessment of the quantitative aspects covered in the following chapters with a consideration of the major historical markers that punctuate the period under study. And to better appreciate the changes over this period, it is helpful to consider the state of education at the time the Supreme Court was considering the segregation cases before it in the early 1950s.

This chapter begins with a description of the policies regarding racial segregation of the schools both in and outside the regions ruled by de jure segregation. It then reviews the significant government actions over the following five decades, noting three distinct periods. To the chronicle of policies and events in these sections is added descriptions of disparities in resources, where they existed, between schools attended by whites and those attended by blacks. Such disparities are important to document because they emphasize one consequence of interracial contact or the lack thereof. Not only does segregation keep students of different races apart, it also has the effect of exposing students of different races to different levels of school resources if resource levels differ systematically by race.

De Jure Segregation

If one knows nothing else about public education at the time of the *Brown* decision, the one fact that is probably most familiar is that schools were segregated by law in the South. Although this much is true, it is not the entire story. For one thing, "the South," for purposes of describing the extent of such segregation, included not only the eleven states of the former Confederacy, but also the six Border states and the District of Columbia. In addition, racial segregation in schools was official policy in a surprisingly large number of districts elsewhere in the country. Before documenting the events that provide the historical backdrop to changes in interracial contact after 1954, it is essential to describe the starting point.

Before May 1954 public schools in both the South and the Border states were segregated by law, but it was the South that would cling most resolutely to this system after *Brown*. What gave school segregation such importance in the South? Segregation in the public schools was merely one part of a vast and elaborate superstructure that was the segregated South. In his classic *An American Dilemma*, published in 1944, Gunnar Myrdal described the various aspects of the system. School segregation

14

in the South was just one, though an important, manifestation of an elaborate social structure at the center of which was separation between whites and blacks. There existed numerous taboos against contact, or more exactly, an elaborate working out of the ways in which contact could occur. Except for otherwise unavoidable contact in the workplace, the market, the criminal justice system, and the home (an outgrowth of personal service work), contact between the races was minimized or otherwise highly structured so as to maintain the unequal social standing of the two races.[4] Supporting all this was a belief system that justified behavior that would otherwise have been readily recognized as inconsistent with the moral sensibilities of whites—a belief on the part of whites in the inferiority of blacks. As Myrdal points out, this separation, plus the multifarious forms of discrimination on economic and political dimensions, helped to create conditions consistent with that belief.[5] Behind the curtain of etiquette that circumscribed interaction between the races, to be sure, lurked the real threat of violence to enforce the system's strictures.

As unjust, unproductive, and, frankly, bizarre as this system of apartheid sounds to the twenty-first century American, it must be emphasized that this was the only system that much of the South knew or could comprehend. Although from the perspective of fifty years the demise of segregated schools may look inevitable and natural, from the perspective of Southern whites, desegregation was an almost unimaginable evil. In a spirited defense of segregation in schools, North Carolina Senator Sam Ervin wrote in 1956: "Racial segregation is not the offspring of racial bigotry or racial prejudice. It results from the exercise of a fundamental American freedom—the freedom to select one's associates. . . . This freedom is bottomed on a basic law of nature—the law that like seeks like. It is one of the most precious of human rights, because man finds his greatest happiness when he is among people of similar cultural, historical and social background."[6] Ervin maintained that segregation benefited both races, and warned that school integration would be disastrous. Although the white caste may have been, in Myrdal's words, "enslaved in its prejudices by its short-range interests," it was wedded to the principle of segregation.[7] What would happen after 1954 was therefore truly earthshaking.

Separation was only one of two important elements that defined segregated public education in the South. The other was inequality in resources. Belying the "separate but equal" standard by which the segregated South purported to operate its public schools, the Southern states had historically spent vastly more on white schools than on black schools. Annual spending rates were decidedly unequal (see table 1.1). In an early

TABLE 1.1
Per-Pupil Spending for Public Schools by Race, Eight Southern States,
1940 and 1952, 2000 Dollars

State	1940			1952		
	White	Black	Black as percent of white (%)	White	Black	Black as percent of white (%)
Alabama	$509	$170	33	$830	$665	80
Arkansas	370	160	43	663	440	66
Florida	772	337	44	1,268	996	79
Georgia	574	180	31	1,064	719	68
Louisiana	782	250	32	NA	NA	—
Mississippi	513	89	17	763	229	30
North Carolina	513	336	65	989	836	85
South Carolina	625	186	30	1,036	622	60

Sources: Ashmore (1954, p. 153); Consumer Price Index, U.S. Bureau of the Census, *Statistical Abstract of the United States*, 2001, table 692; U.S. Council of Economic Advisers, *Economic Report of the President* (Washington, DC: Government Printing Office, 1996), p. 343; U.S. Bureau of the Census (1975, p. 125).

study of spending patterns, Horace Mann Bond demonstrated not only that spending differences were large but also that they were greatest in counties where the proportion of blacks was the highest, a pattern made possible by the practice of white-controlled school boards of taking equal capitation state grants and using them primarily on white schools.[8]

These disparities showed up as differences in class sizes and course offerings. They also manifested themselves in disparities in the facilities offered in white and black schools. The state of Mississippi at the end of World War II was a stark example of such disparities. In 1944–1945, the state had 2,120 one-room, one-teacher schools; although slightly less than half the state's students were black, 95 percent of these schools were used for blacks. And, whereas 54 percent of the teachers in white schools were college graduates, only 10 percent of those teaching in black schools were.[9] A detailed study of Durham, North Carolina, public schools in 1950 lends detail to the differences in resources suggested by the statistics on expenditures. Not only did the buildings for the white schools have higher valuations per pupil, they were better outfitted. White schools had more drinking fountains relative to the number of students. Six white schools had gymnasiums, while none of the black schools did. All of the white schools had auditoriums, which three of the black schools lacked. All the white schools had at least one room for music and art, while no black school did. Class sizes were smaller on average in the white schools; for example, the average-size classes for whites and blacks were 24 and 30 in English IV, and 34 and 36 in Algebra II. And large disparities existed in the equipment in science labs, as revealed in a detailed comparison of labs in the white Durham High with those in the black Hillside High. Consideration of the pieces of lab equipment used to study electricity and magnetism reveals a preposterous contrast: Durham High had 136 of the enumerated pieces of equipment, while Hillside had only 21.[10]

In the years leading up to 1954, such differences were shrinking. Southern states appeared to be headed in the direction of equalizing resources for black and white schools (see table 1.1). From about 1940 on, racial gaps in such indicators as length of the school year and class size, as well as per-pupil expenditures, narrowed across the region.[11] Thus, although the South honored the "equal" part of the separate-but-equal principle mainly in the breach, it was moving in that direction when the *Brown* decision was handed down.

Schools and Segregation in the North
on the Eve of *Brown*

Although the extent of school segregation in the South and the Border states in 1954 is well understood—because the segregation there was unambiguous, universal, and unabashedly documented in official records—surprisingly little is known about the degree to which schools in the country's other regions were racially segregated. As will become clearer in chapter 2, the general absence of data on enrollment patterns for the 1950s makes it impossible to give a precise answer to this question.[12] But enough documentation does exist to suggest that schools in many parts of the North were substantially segregated in the years leading up to 1954, as they would continue to be in the following decades. To be sure, most of this segregation was of the de facto variety, aided by the generally small size of many school districts, which had the effect of guaranteeing that residential segregation would be translated into school segregation as long as districts could not be required to move students across jurisdictional lines.

In some Northern districts, however, segregation carried the imprimatur of official policy. Three states—Arizona, New Mexico, and Kansas—permitted districts to operate segregated schools. Arizona actually required segregated schools until 1951, after which it made the policy optional. Phoenix began to desegregate its schools, using voluntary transfers, in 1953.[13] And in New Mexico, elementary schools in six cities and high schools in two cities were segregated.[14] As late as 1952, Kansas had nine city districts with segregated elementary schools, and in Kansas City and Topeka the junior high and high schools were segregated as well. Wichita began desegregating its elementary schools in the fall of 1952, and Topeka took the step in 1953.[15] Wyoming also permitted segregation where black enrollment was large, but the numbers were evidently not large enough for this provision to be used.[16] Until 1949 Indiana had given its local boards the option to segregate.[17] One of the last Northern states to outlaw segregation was New Jersey, which did so by amending its state constitution in 1947. Still, a survey in the following year found that de jure segregation remained in forty-three districts, or roughly one of every thirteen school districts in the state. By 1951, forty of those districts had integrated their schools and the remaining three had pledged to do so.[18] The remaining states either prohibited segregation or made no reference to it in their laws, which is not to say that those states had never operated segregated schools.

Despite the official policy of these and other states in the North, some renegade districts managed to operate entirely segregated schools into the early 1950s. In Illinois, despite a state prohibition dating from 1874 and legislation in 1948 cutting funds to districts that practiced segregation, local school boards in at least eleven counties maintained separate schools for blacks.[19] Located in the southern part of the state, districts including Cairo and East St. Louis continued to mandate segregation into the early 1950s, mostly at the elementary level.[20] In Centerville, another district in southern Illinois, the public schools had been operated on double sessions, with whites attending in the morning and blacks in the afternoon.[21] Some Illinois districts simply had no schools where black students could attend—even though blacks lived in the district.[22] Districts in other states routinely gerrymandered school districts to maintain segregated schools. Columbus, Ohio, engaged in this practice in the two decades before the end of World War II so as to maintain five all-black schools. One critical report described the district's attendance zones as "skipping about as capriciously as a young child at play."[23] The Hillsboro, Ohio, school district successfully segregated a much smaller black enrollment into one school as late as 1954.[24] Districts in other states, including Indiana, Pennsylvania, and New York, operated segregated schools, often in defiance of state law.[25]

More frequently, high degrees of segregation, falling short of complete separation, were maintained in more than a few Northern districts, owing to housing patterns. Fueled by racial discrimination among homeowners, real estate brokers, and banks, residential segregation was bolstered by government action and inaction. In its most active mode, government enforced residential segregation through legislation, such as the ordinance in Stockton, California, requiring all Chinese to live south of Main Street.[26] But one of the most potent tools for maintaining residential segregation, a California innovation of the 1890s that was approved by the Supreme Court in 1926 and used widely following World War II, was the restrictive covenant, the insertion into deeds the promise not to sell a property to blacks or members of other specified groups.[27] Although ultimately declared unenforceable in 1948, its effects were solidified in the segregated patterns of residential development in the large cities of the North.[28] More extreme was the practice of some suburban communities to exclude blacks altogether, including Dearborn in the Detroit area and Cicero, Illinois.[29] Combined with other policies, in particular the selective location of public housing projects and the largely unchecked discrimination in the housing market, many of the urban areas of the North became highly segregated. Perhaps the epitome of such segregation was Detroit, which as late as 1970 had fourteen suburban communities with populations of 36,000 or more, none of which had more than fifty blacks.[30] Such residential patterns led quite naturally to substantially segregated schools. A 1952 analysis concluded, "The vast majority of white school children in the metropolitan centers like Chicago attend schools where only white children are enrolled."[31] Sociologist Milton Yinger's unpublished report on Cincinnati, written as part of Harry Ashmore's project examining school segregation in the North, provides a telling example. Because virtually all blacks in the city lived in one of a handful of neighborhoods, including the "basin" area in the city's downtown, most blacks attended schools where most of their classmates were also black, despite the district's official policy of integration. He estimated that 85 to 90 percent of blacks attended schools where at least three-quarters of the students were black.[32]

Beyond the de facto segregation arising from residential patterns, many Northern districts engaged in practices designed to strengthen patterns of segregation, including gerrymandered attendance zones, crowding

19

black schools, the judicious placement of newly constructed schools, and liberal transfer policies, described in more detail below. Cincinnati exemplifies just one approach. It mandated, and then allowed, one form of segregation within schools: until 1950 all high schools required swimming but separated classes by race; but when classes were integrated, the swimming requirement was dropped.[33] Yinger concluded his report with this summary: "Communities have a way, of course, of making changes gradually, even when a legal pattern seems to require an abrupt shift. With regard to schools, residential segregation, informal or formal gerrymandering, social and extra-curricular segregation *within* schools, growth of private schools, etc. are techniques for postponing integration that one can expect to find, especially if the obstacles to integration are stronger than those in Cincinnati."[34]

As for the resources provided to predominantly nonwhite schools in the North at the time of the *Brown* decision, little evidence exists. One contemporary observer, decrying the lack of detailed data on school facilities, maintained that facilities for schools attended by blacks were older and less adequate than those for white schools, a disparity maintained by inadequate spending on improvements.[35] Some information, however, is provided by a study undertaken on behalf of the New York City public schools in 1955. The study included a detailed audit comparing the facilities, teacher corps, and expenditures for a sample of seventy-five predominantly white and fifty-one predominantly nonwhite elementary and junior high schools. The first group of schools had enrollments between 90 and 100 percent white, and the second had enrollments between 90 and 100 percent black and Puerto Rican. Although no differences were found in per-pupil spending, the study concluded that the buildings used by the predominantly nonwhite schools were older, less adequate, and less well maintained than those of the predominantly white schools. In addition, the teachers in the nonwhite schools were "not as competent" as those in the white schools, as evidenced by the smaller proportions who were tenured and the larger proportions who had probationary or substitute status. Some of the specific comparisons for the elementary schools in the sample are shown in table 1.2, which reveals that the predominantly nonwhite schools in the comparison had older buildings, less space per student, and a smaller share of tenured teachers. Based on the availability of four specialized facilities—auditorium, gymnasium, library, and science room—there was no clear advantage either way. The report notes that the explanation for the dis-

TABLE 1.2
Comparison of Facilities in Predominantly White and Predominantly
Nonwhite Public Elementary Schools, New York City, 1955

	Predominantly white[a]	Predominantly nonwhite[b]
Average age of building (years)	31	43
Available space per pupil (square feet)		
Site	103.1	46.2
Floor	88.9	59.0
Playground	3.8	2.2
Percentage of schools with:		
Auditorium	83	78
Gymnasium	61	68
Library	68	71
Science room	51	36
Percentage of teachers		
On tenure	78.2	50.3
On probation	13.5	31.6
Permanent substitutes	8.3	18.1
Total	100.0	100.0

Source: New York Public Education Association (1955).
[a]Less than 10 percent Negro and Puerto Rican. N = 60.
[b]90 percent or more Negro and Puerto Rican. N = 42.

parities in facilities was probably the fact that minority groups tended to live in "the older, well-established areas of the city."[36]

In sum, on the eve of the *Brown* decision, the Border and Southern states maintained totally separate schools for blacks and whites. Although the resources offered in the two systems were becoming more comparable, neither the facilities nor the level of services offered to black and white students had achieved equality. In the North, segregation was much more of a mixed bag, with some districts offering education on an entirely integrated basis, some districts operating schools segregated in whole or in part owing to residential segregation, and some districts holding on to vestiges of officially sanctioned segregation. What little information exists suggests that the resources available likewise differed by race, though it seems unlikely the differences were as great as they

21

were in the South. One observer summarized, "The North[,] like the South, practices segregation; like the South, uses the schools to perpetuate it as a way of thinking about race, but the North, unlike the South, needs no laws to achieve this result."[37]

SEGREGATION OF HISPANIC STUDENTS

Often overlooked in assessments of school segregation was the treatment of the minority group that would, by century's end, outnumber African Americans. In parts of California and Texas, Mexican American students were subjected to systematic segregation of varying degrees in public schools in the decades before *Brown*, although no state prescribed this segregation in law. One study estimated that in 1930 some 85 percent of Mexican American students in the Southwest attended separate classrooms or separate schools.[38] A number of sizable districts in California had designated "Mexican" schools in that year, a practice that continued in some districts through World War II.[39] While separate schools were common in larger districts, in districts where their numbers were smaller Mexican Americans attended schools with non-Hispanic whites.[40] The practice of establishing separate "Mexican" schools in several school districts in Orange County was challenged in a 1945 suit in federal court (*Mendez v. Westminster School District*), resulting in an order to cease the practice.[41] One of the challenged districts, Santa Ana, had for more than three decades maintained largely separate schools for Mexican Americans by means of judiciously drawn attendance areas, liberal transfers granted to whites who wanted to transfer out of predominantly Hispanic schools, and a prohibition against Hispanic students attending Anglo schools. As a result of the *Mendez* decision, that district opened up white schools on a space-available basis.[42] In Riverside, California, a virtually 100 percent Hispanic elementary school was maintained up until 1967, a year after that district instituted one of the first thoroughgoing desegregation efforts outside the South.[43] In contrast to these examples, the schools of Arizona and New Mexico did not practice segregation against Hispanic students, only blacks.[44]

Hispanic students were subjected to officially sanctioned segregation in some Texas districts in the years leading up to *Brown*, particularly in the communities in the south and central part of the state. Although a federal court had also ruled against segregated schools for Mexican Americans, such schools were slow to disappear.[45] Surveys in 1949 and

1950 found numerous districts practicing various forms of segregation, many segregating Hispanic students in early grades and allowing mixed classes in later grades. Most of the sampled districts also segregated students in extracurricular activities.[46]

DELIBERATE SPEED, 1954–1964

As it is usually told, the history of the first years following the Supreme Court's historic decision of May 17, 1954, is one of resistance and foot-dragging on the part of states and districts of the South. The Court's follow-up *Brown II* decision in 1955, with its admonition to desegregate with "all deliberate speed," has been viewed, alternatively, as weak-kneed failure of will or pragmatic recognition of the enormity of the change and the limits of judicial power. In any case, it was taken in the South as permission to proceed slowly, an interpretation bolstered by a U.S. district court decision in the South Carolina case *Briggs v. Elliott* (1955) to the effect that the Supreme Court meant only to forbid discrimination, not to require integration.[47] Nor did President Eisenhower take any action to bolster desegregation. Apparently harboring personal doubts about the Supreme Court's frontal attack on segregation, he consistently sidestepped opportunities to endorse desegregation orders and was reluctant to send federal troops where such orders met violent resistance.[48]

All the same, reaction in the South was defiant. Although there were voices of philosophical resignation, the region's predominant attitude was horror and hysterical jeremiad. Governors stood adamant, and most of the region's elected members of Congress signed on to a "Southern Manifesto," denouncing the decision in the most trenchant terms.[49] So vigorous was the opposition and so slow were the workings of the justice system that actual change in racial patterns of enrollment came only gradually. Reminiscent of the "phony war" in the first months of World War I, nothing much happened to Southern segregation in these first years. To be sure, the color line was broken in a few places, and in fact it was broken first in 1953, in the west Texas town of Friona. Following the 1954 decision, two Arkansas districts with few blacks, Charleston and Fayetteville, immediately decided to end segregation, with several other districts in Arkansas and Tennessee following suit the next year. In 1957 three North Carolina districts desegregated previously white schools while the world watched the infamous desegregation of Central High School in Little Rock. Districts in Florida and Virginia began desegregation in 1959. Except where the numbers of blacks were small, "token integration" aptly described all of these initial forays. A common tactic adopted by Southern districts during these years was to institute a policy of "freedom-of-choice," by which students could apply to any school. In practice, however, the procedures were complicated, the criteria were vague, and the usual (and intended) result was denial of transfers. By 1959–1960 only 0.2 percent of the region's black public school students were attending schools with whites.[50]

The next three years saw desegregation plans initiated in two big city districts, New Orleans and Atlanta, but by 1963–1964 the numbers were still minuscule, with only 1.2 percent of blacks attending schools with whites.[51] In Atlanta, the school district slowed desegregation by crowding black students into black schools while leaving nearby white schools only partially filled. And in 1964 when judicial pressure and protests by black parents made it necessary to assign blacks to a previously underutilized white elementary school, district officials notified white parents and invited them to transfer to other schools. All but seven white children did transfer (out of 376 who had been enrolled). The superintendent later defended his actions by saying that he wanted "to maintain some semblance of a white school system, a white population in the school system."[52]

In contrast to the high-profile resistance put up by the eleven former Confederate states, the Border region dismantled its de jure schools relatively quickly and quietly. A great many Border districts in fact desegregated immediately, including the large urban districts in Washington, DC, and Baltimore. Although white students comprised only about one-fourth of its total enrollment, Washington eliminated virtually all-black schools after two years of desegregation, an achievement that would, of course, be short-lived. Baltimore's approach was much more tentative. Its free-choice policy resulted in just 3 percent of its blacks attending schools with whites in the first year, and 7 percent in the second. Even after seven years of desegregation, more than two-thirds of its black students were still attending all-black schools. Regionwide, the response was remarkably rapid. In the first year following the decision, 156 districts, some 17 percent of all biracial districts in the region, had begun the process of desegregation. By the 1956–1957 year, 70 percent of such districts had done so; and 30 percent of all blacks in the region were attending school with whites. By the 1963–1964 school year, only 7 percent of districts that enrolled both whites and blacks were still segregated, and more than half of all the region's blacks in public schools attended schools with whites.[53] Because of the racial segregation that characterized most big cities, this new regime left many urban schools in the region with preponderant to complete representation by one race or the other, but the deed was done, and done quickly.

Outside of the South and the Border, the 1954–1964 period witnessed comparatively little change in policies affecting the interracial contact in schools. For a small number of districts, segregation was blatant enough to be challenged by the NAACP. In 1954, that organization pressed a suit to end officially sanctioned segregation in Hillsboro, Ohio. In an eight-month period in 1961 and 1962, the NAACP reported taking action to challenge segregated schools in fifty-five Northern districts, including districts in three states in the Northeast, five in the Midwest, and four in the West.[54] Many communities in the North had been able to maintain high degrees of racial segregation by combining residential segregation with certain school-related policies. New schools were routinely built in locations that made a racially mixed student body less feasible than a racially homogenous one. A tabulation of elementary schools built in sixteen suburban Northern and Western cities between 1950 and 1965 revealed that 71 percent opened with 90 percent or more white students and another 13 percent with 90 percent or more black students, leaving only 16 percent of the schools that were racially mixed.[55] Districts also expanded the enrollment of schools, where necessary using portable classrooms, to avoid racially mixed schools.[56] To complement such policies, many districts routinely adjusted (gerrymandered) school attendance zones.[57] Another widespread practice used by districts in the North and West was the same one Atlanta officials used—to grant requests by whites to transfer between schools. For example, in the attendance areas covered by predominantly nonwhite schools, districts might create "optional zones" out of which whites could transfer to other schools in the district.[58]

Revolution, 1965–1973

If the first decade had seen little change in interracial contact in the South's public schools, the next decade witnessed a great deal. Through the efforts of all three branches of the federal government, school districts in the South were forced to go beyond the token steps of the first decade. As numerous lawsuits and appeals worked their way through various federal courts in the South, Congress passed the Civil Rights Act of 1964. Although best known for its provisions regarding public accommodation, it also contained two provisions relating to schools. It authorized the attorney general to initiate class action lawsuits against recalcitrant school districts (Title IV) and the secretary of health, education, and welfare to withhold funds to any district excluding students from schools on the basis of race (Title VI).[59] Congress followed this with the Elementary and Secondary Education Act of 1965, which provided a bonanza of new federal funding for school districts, especially districts such as those in the South. As Gary Orfield shows in his study of the 1964 act, federal bureaucrats combined the stick provided by Title VI of the Civil Rights Act with the carrot of significant new funding in the 1965 legislation to motivate many Southern school districts to comply rapidly with desegregation orders.[60] Confirmation of the importance of the threat of cutting off federal funds is contained in a survey conducted by the U.S. Commission on Civil Rights that asked superintendents to name the "major source of intervention" for effecting desegregation in their districts. Of 523 districts nationwide that desegregated between 1966 and 1975, more than one-quarter named the Department of Health, Education, and Welfare as the major motivating force.[61]

Then followed a series of Supreme Court decisions that had the effect of sweeping away much of the South's lingering segregation. In the 1968 *Green v. County School Board of New Kent County* decision, the court struck down freedom-of-choice plans, established for the first time an "affirmative duty" to desegregate, and defined desegregation as the abolition of identifiably white and black schools.[62] The next year, in *Alexander v. Holmes*, it unanimously ordered that schools had to be desegregated "at once."[63] In 1971, the court applied its view of a unitary school system to a large urban area, Charlotte, North Carolina. In *Swann v. Charlotte-Mecklenburg Board of Education*, it ruled that previously segregated districts needed to balance their schools racially to the extent possible, even if that required crosstown busing to do so.[64]

The result of these developments was a breathtaking transformation of public education in many communities in the South. In the space of just a few years—principally, 1969 to 1972—levels of interracial contact in schools shot up all over the South. Whereas 78 percent of black students attended schools that were 90 percent or more minority in 1968, by 1972 that share had fallen to 25 percent.[65] These dramatic increases in interracial contact were accomplished by means of desegregation plans that reassigned thousands of students to different schools. In districts where schools had been segregated by law, a natural avenue to desegregated schools was simply to draw boundaries around schools to achieve something akin to neighborhood schools. Where neighborhoods were themselves highly segregated, a condition applying to most big cities and many other large districts, desegregation could be achieved only by re-zoning attendance areas, sometimes made possible by closing some schools, usually with an eye toward minimizing the costs of transporting students while achieving the designed racial balance among schools. One variant of this approach was to pair previously racially identifiable schools so that one school served both school's students in some grades, say 1–3, while the other school specialized in other grades, say 4–6.[66] Among the most prominent of the Southern school districts to undergo wholesale transformation of racial attendance patterns were Charlotte, whose plan was made famous by the Supreme Court's 1971 decision in *Swann*, Norfolk, Nashville, Little Rock, Tampa (Hillsborough County), and Memphis. The period between 1969 and 1972 featured numerous desegregation plans in the South, resulting in large reductions in measured segregation (see table 1.3). Similarly effective desegregation plans were visited upon urban districts in the Border states beginning shortly afterwards, with the first major orders affecting Oklahoma City and Prince George's County, Maryland, in 1972 and 1973, respectively. In both the South and the Border, the momentum generated by *Green* and *Swann* generated a flow of new federal court orders well into the 1970s.

A question that influenced the national debate over school desegregation was how *Brown* and succeeding cases would be applied to segregation in Northern districts, where de jure segregation had never been the practice. After the Office for Civil Rights had released the results of a massive survey of enrollment patterns in the nation's biggest districts, several U.S. senators from Southern states read into the Congressional Record statistics showing substantial segregation in Northern cities.[67] The question was whether de facto segregation would be attacked with the same tools used against the formerly de jure segregated systems. In a series of cases, including cases in Pontiac, Michigan, San Francisco, Pasadena, and Ft. Wayne, Indiana, federal courts ordered desegregation remedies where residential segregation had made segregation in the public schools almost inevitable. The issue came before the Supreme Court in *Keyes v. Denver School District No. 1*. In its 1973 opinion, the Court ruled that *Brown* required desegregation in that district. Although no law had mandated segregated schools in Denver, the court reasoned, the existing segregation in schools had resulted in part from actions by school authorities and other government agencies.[68] As in the case of the

TABLE 1.3
Selected School Districts with Major Desegregation Plans

	District	Year(s) of implementation	Decline in dissimilarity index
**	Charlotte-Mecklenburg, NC	1968	27
		1970	51
	Tacoma, WA	1968–1971	23
**	Volusia Co., FL (Daytona Beach)	1969	27
		1970	21
**	Lee County, FL (Ft. Myers)	1969	53
**	Polk County, FL (Lakeland)	1969	26
**	Rapides Parish, LA (Alexandria)	1969	27
		1980	22
**	Terrebonne Parish, LA (Houma)	1969	39
**	Cumberland Co., NC (Fayetteville)	1969	23
**	Pittsylvania Co., VA (Danville)	1969	66
**	Caddo Parish, LA (Shreveport)	1969–1970	28
**	Broward Co., FL (Fort Lauderdale)	1970	29
**	Greenville Co., SC (Greenville)	1970	64
	Pasadena, CA	1970	38
**	Norfolk, VA	1970	23
		1971	42
**	Palm Beach Co., FL (West Palm Beach)	1970–1971	39
**	Richland Co., SC (Columbia)	1970–1971	52
**	Roanoke, VA	1970–1971	57
	Stamford, CT	1970–1972	36
**	Hillsborough Co., FL (Tampa)	1971	44
**	Jefferson Parish, LA	1971	28
**	New Hanover Co., NC (Wilmington)	1971	46
**	Nashville, TN	1971	41
**	Muscogee Co., GA (Columbus)	1971	75
	Ft. Wayne, IN	1971	20
	Wichita, KS	1971	25
**	Little Rock, AR	1971	33
		1972–1973	26
**	Jefferson Co., AL (Birmingham)	1971–1972	33
**	Duval Co., FL (Jacksonville)	1971–1972	41
*	Fayette Co., KY (Lexington)	1972	29
*	Oklahoma City, OK	1972	40

TABLE 1.3 *Continued*

	District	Year(s) of implementation	Decline in dissimilarity index
**	Amarillo, TX	1972	22
*	Prince George's Co., MD	1973	35
**	Memphis, TN	1973	32
**	Waco, TX	1973	35
	Boston, MA	1974	20
		1975	20
*	Jefferson Co., KY (Louisville)	1975	51
	Omaha, NE	1976	30
	Dayton, OH	1976	46
	Milwaukee, WI	1976–1978	35
	Buffalo, NY	1976–1979	31
*	Kansas City, MO	1977	20
*	New Castle Co., DE (Wilmington)	1978	49
	Columbus, OH	1979	38
	Cleveland, OH	1979–1980	65
**	Dougherty Co., GA (Albany)	1980	27
**	Austin, TX	1980	20
	South Bend, IN	1981	30
**	Ector Co., TX (Odessa)	1982–1984	25

Source: Welch and Light (1987, table A3).

Notes: Table includes all districts and years for which the dissimilarity index declined by 20 points or more. The complete sample of 125 districts included all districts of 50,000 or more between 70 and 90 percent minority in 1968 plus a sample of smaller, more racially diverse districts (Welch and Light, 1987, p. 31).

*Districts in Border region

**Districts in South region

Border region, the North would continue to see desegregation orders well into the 1970s, and the aftermath of these orders in Boston and elsewhere would make it clear that white opposition to racially mixed schools was not confined to the South.

The question of how equitably school resources were distributed between schools attended by whites and blacks was such an important issue that Congress, by way of the 1964 Civil Rights Act, ordered the Office of Education to commission a national survey of schools. Headed by sociologist James Coleman, the resulting 1965 survey and 1966 report, *Equality of Educational Opportunity,* became an authoritative force that would influence education policy for years afterward. Its intended purpose was to document measurable differences between schools attended by blacks and whites, and its sponsors believed the report would uncover large gaps.[69] Much to everyone's surprise, Coleman and his collaborators discovered surprisingly few differences in the objective characteristics of the physical facilities or teaching staffs of schools attended by blacks and whites. If any consistent pattern of disparity did emerge in the report, it was regional: students in the South, of both races, tended to have fewer resources than those in the rest of the country. Among either nonmetropolitan or metropolitan areas, a comparison of the schools attended by whites in the South generally fared poorly relative to those to those attended by whites in the North. A similar regional comparison of schools attended by blacks reveals much the same thing.[70] In addition to this non-finding regarding racial disparities in measurable school resources, the report concluded that such resources were not statistically important in explaining differences in academic achievement. In contrast, the report said, a student's achievement did appear to be influenced by the social and economic background of his or her fellow students, a finding suggesting that desegregation might lead to higher academic achievement of low-income minority students.

RETRENCHMENT, 1974–

The year 1974 was surely a turning point in the federal government's stance on the policy of school desegregation, because in that year the Supreme Court issued the first of a series of decisions that would effectively put the brakes on government efforts to desegregate schools. To understand this turn of events, it is instructive to recall how the court's composition had changed. Since taking office in 1969, President Nixon had appointed three new justices and one chief justice, Warren Burger. How his appointments might affect the court's position on school desegregation was one of Nixon's considerations in choosing appointees, as indicated by this Oval Office conversation with attorney general John Mitchell in 1971 about a replacement for retiring Hugo Black, a liberal Alabamian.

> NIXON: As to where we stand, with Black out. We now do have to have a southerner. I really think it would be a slap to the South not to try for a southerner. So I'd say that our first requirement is have a southerner. The second requirement, he must be a conservative southerner.

MITCHELL: Yes.

NIXON: I don't care if he's a Democrat or a Republican. Third, within the definition of conservative, he must be against busing, and against forced housing integration. Beyond that, he can do what he pleases.[71]

The eventual nominee would be Lewis Powell, a conservative jurist from Virginia.

The case that came before the Supreme Court in 1974 concerned the increasingly racially isolated city school system of Detroit, the question being whether a federal court could order students to be assigned to schools across district lines for the purpose of desegregation. In *Milliken v. Bradley*, by a 5–4 vote, the court said no, with Nixon appointees Burger, Blackmun, Powell, and Rehnquist all voting in the majority. Unless it could be shown that the actions of school districts had created the very obvious interdistrict disparities that existed, the court said, no desegregation remedy could be extended beyond a single school district. With very few exceptions, this decision would prevent any desegregation on a metropolitan basis.[72] Owing to the relentless suburbanization of the middle class in American metropolitan areas and the accompanying decline of the white population in many central cities, this decision meant that interdistrict racial disparities would be exempt from any direct remedy by federal courts. Beyond the specific legal significance of the *Milliken* decision, it also represents a watershed in the court's attitude toward desegregation itself. In light of its subsequent decisions, it seems clear that *Milliken* marked the beginning of a retreat from the proactive pursuit of racial balance as a judicial objective.

To be sure, the momentum of past decisions meant that lower courts continued, for a while at least, to issue desegregation decisions. Orders that had been handed down, appealed, revised, and reaffirmed in the 1960s and early 1970s continued to be enforced using the same tools employed in earlier cases. Major desegregation plans were ordered for Border districts such as Louisville, Kansas City, Missouri, and New Castle County, Delaware. And in the North, major orders affected Dayton, Buffalo, Milwaukee, and Cleveland. Of the desegregation plans listed in table 1.3, all involved rezoning, pairing of schools, or both, and all were instigated through decisions in federal courts. Other techniques were used in some plans, including magnet schools and other voluntary transfers. And some desegregation plans were instituted through state, rather than federal, actions. For example, Hartford was ordered by state courts to institute several policies, including programs allowing students to transfer to schools in neighboring school districts.[73] But for the most part, significant changes in interracial contact were brought about through federal courts using radically modified school assignments within existing school districts.

Less radical methods were also used to raise interracial contact, sometimes at the initiation of school districts themselves rather than outside enforcement agencies. These usually involved separating school assignments from geographical attendance boundaries. One such technique was so-called open enrollment, which was equivalent to the freedom-of-choice technique used and abused by many Southern districts; another was majority-to-minority transfers, a policy allowing any student attending a school where she was in the majority to transfer to a school where she would be in the minority, automatically boosting the degree of interracial contact. Another was magnet schools, which usually meant putting special programs in older school buildings in downtown locations in hopes of attracting students from suburban locations, and at the same time producing racially mixed downtown schools. The North Carolina district of Wake County, which includes Raleigh, was one district that employed magnet schools as part of a larger, sustained effort to maintain racial balance across its schools. In 1982 it designated twenty-eight schools as magnets, most of them underutilized schools in older neighborhoods close to downtown, putting in them programs designed to attract new students. The magnets were successful on this score, making it unnecessary to close any of the downtown schools. The program was also credited with stimulating demand for housing in downtown neighborhoods.[74]

During this period the Supreme Court addressed whether the desegregation process would have an ending point. The issue had been raised earlier by the apparent need to continually adjust attendance zones to maintain racial balance in the school district in the face of continuing losses of whites.[75] In *Board of Education of Oklahoma v. Dowell* (1991), the Supreme Court ruled that, by virtue of being declared "unitary," the school district was freed of any obligation to maintain racially balanced schools, and in *Freeman v. Pitts* (1992) it reiterated that the district was not responsible for undoing the effects of de facto segregation that resulted from changes in residential patterns following the initial desegregation of schools.[76]

The next logical question was what obligations, if any, a school district would have regarding interracial contact in its schools once it was declared by federal courts to be unitary. In a decision applying to Charlotte in 2001, the Fourth Circuit Federal Court of Appeals ruled that the district's responsibility was to ensure that racial discrimination would not affect school assignments. Moreover, it forbade the district from using race in filling its magnet schools or making any student assignments, thereby cutting off the possibility of continuing the district's practice of racially balancing its schools.[77] As will be seen in chapter 2, measured segregation in Charlotte-Mecklenburg increased following this decision. Although at least one similar district (Wake County, North Carolina) attempted to modify its method of balancing schools in order to comply with this court order, it was not clear how that modification would affect racial balance.[78]

LONG-TERM TRENDS

In the decades marked by court orders and profound changes in America's schools, several trends operated in the background, behind the newspaper headlines. To varying degrees, they circumscribed the changes in interracial contact that would occur over the first half-century following the *Brown* decision.

Racial Composition

The trend with the clearest influence on interracial contact was the profound transformation in the nation's racial composition. Spurred above all by a surge in immigration, much of it from Asian and Spanish-speaking countries to the south, the resident population that was neither white nor black experienced very rapid growth. Because the U.S. Census has changed the categories it uses over the years, it is impossible to give a precise accounting of racial change over this period, but by combining various sources the changing distribution can be estimated, as in figure 1.1. At the time of *Brown*, the United States had two major racial groups. Non-Hispanic European Americans, or whites, were numerically dominant, representing some 88 percent of the total population. African Americans, or blacks, made up about 10 percent. In 1950 the Hispanic or Latino population, consisting at that time primarily of Puerto Ricans and Mexican Americans, comprised only about 1.5 percent of the total. Over the five decades covered by the figure, this distribution changed markedly, owing to successive waves of immigration. Most striking was the growing share of Hispanics. While total population over the period

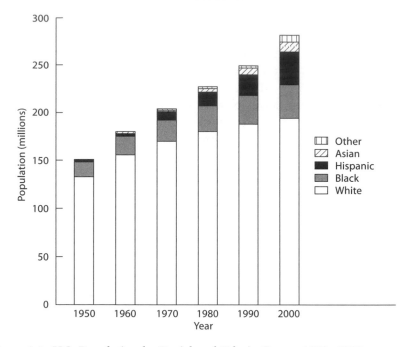

Figure 1.1. U.S. Population by Racial and Ethnic Group, 1950–2000

Sources: U.S. Bureau of the Census, *Census of Population: 1950, Characteristics of the Population, U.S. Summary*, table 36, p. 88 (Washington, DC: Government Printing Office, 1953); U.S. Bureau of the Census, *Census of Population: 1960, Characteristics of the Population, U.S. Summary*, table 44, p. 145 (Washington, DC: Government Printing Office, 1964); U.S. Bureau of the Census, *Census of Population: 1970, Characteristics of the Population, U.S. Summary*, table 48, p. 262 (Washington, DC: Government Printing Office, 1973); U.S. Bureau of the Census, *Census of Population: 1970, General Social and Economic Characteristics of the Population, U.S. Summary*, table 85, p. 380 (Washington, DC: Government Printing Office, 1973); U.S. Bureau of the Census, *We . . . the Mexican Americans, the Puerto Ricans, the Cubans, and the Hispanos from Other Countries in the Caribbean, Central and South America, and from Spain . . .* , p. 4 (Washington, DC: Government Printing Office, 1981); U.S. Bureau of the Census, *Census of Population: 1980, Characteristics of the Population, General Population Characteristics, U.S. Summary*, table 39, p. 21 (Washington, DC: Government Printing Office, 1983); U.S. Bureau of the Census, *Census of Population: 1990, General Population Characteristics, U.S. Summary*, table 3, p. 3 (Washington, DC: Government Printing Office, 1992); U.S. Bureau of the Census, *We the American . . . Hispanics*, figure 1, p. 2 (Washington, DC: Government Printing Office, 1993); U.S. Bureau of the Census, *Census 2000 Brief: Overview of Race and Hispanic Origin*, by Elizabeth M. Grieco and Rachel C. Cassidy (Washington, DC: Government Printing Office, 2001).

grew at an average annual rate of 1.2 percent, the Hispanic population increased at a rate of 5.5 percent a year. Asian Americans also increased disproportionately, growing at an even faster 7.3 percent annual rate, though from a smaller starting point.

By 2000 non-Hispanic whites comprised only 69 percent of the total population. Hispanics had become the nation's largest minority group, with 12.5 percent, followed by non-Hispanic blacks at 12.1 percent. Asian Americans had grown to 3.6 percent. To be sure, none of these classifications could be defined with absolute certainty. Not only were they dependent upon self-identification, they had, until the 2000 census, finessed the question of multiple membership. That census for the first time allowed respondents to check more than one racial category, thus assuring a growing, if justified, ambiguity regarding racial designations.[79]

Not only did nonwhites grow more rapidly than whites, but their geographical distribution shifted as well. Thus a second important demographic trend covering the period of study were the movements that changed the geographical distribution of the population, and particularly the distribution of blacks and other nonwhites. The most significant migration of the twentieth century was the movement of blacks out of the South and into the large metropolitan areas of the Northeast and Midwest. The first great wave of black migration followed World War I, and the second, smaller one followed World War II. In 1920, 74 percent of blacks in the country lived in one of the eleven Southern states; in 1950, only 60 percent did. By 2000, the percentage had fallen to 48 percent.[80] On the receiving end of this migration were metropolitan areas such as Chicago, Philadelphia, Cleveland, and Detroit. Between 1920 and 1950 the black population of metropolitan Detroit increased fourteen-fold, from 24,000 to 352,000.[81] As these blacks moved into the central cities of large metropolitan areas, whites were moving to suburban neighborhoods, many of which were in separate school districts.

The growth of the Hispanic and Asian American populations, fueled

---

Notes to Figure 1.1:
1. White, black, Asian, and other are non-Hispanic. In 2000 other includes non-Hispanics of two or more races. Asian is Asian or Pacific Islander.
2. Where a complete breakdown of non-Hispanic population was not available (the years 1950–1970), estimates of white and black non-Hispanic population were derived by apportioning the Hispanic population between whites and blacks according to the proportions of each in the overall population.

by heavy immigration during the 1990s, has been concentrated in a few states, led by California and New York. In 1990, 22 percent of California's population was foreign-born, and one-third of the country's foreign-born lived there. New York, which had been the leading destination for immigrants in 1960, had 14 percent of all immigrants in 1990. Florida and Texas were also affected by this immigration, each accounting for about 8 percent of the foreign-born in 1990.[82]

Changes such as these obviously must be borne in mind in a study of interracial contact and segregation in schools. Any comparisons involving racial composition will, for example, be affected by differences and changes in the underlying population of school-age children, whose composition is reflected, imperfectly, in that of the overall population. Precisely because of these demographic shifts, it will be useful throughout this study to distinguish segregation (measuring unevenness in whatever demographic context) from exposure, which is determined by both racial composition and segregation. In addition to this issue of measurement, a question inevitably raised by these trends is the relative importance of African Americans in any consideration of school desegregation. Fifty years after *Brown*, blacks had become just the second-largest minority group in America. These changes also served further to move the focus for the study of interracial contact away from exclusive attention to the South. By 2000, the South not only contained less than half of the country's black population, but also only 36 percent of its nonwhite population.[83] Yet, by virtue of their unique history of slavery and subjugation under Jim Crow, blacks were clearly the minority group whose plight inspired *Brown* as well as much of the civil rights era legislation and litigation. Despite their diminished numerical importance, therefore, they continue, rightly, to be a primary focus of analysis concerning school segregation.

Income Distribution

Beginning some twenty years after the *Brown* decision, the nation's income distribution began to grow more unequal. After moving gradually in the direction of increased equality for the first two decades after the decision, the nation's income distribution reversed course in the mid-1970s, becoming steadily but decidedly less equal. Families in the bottom fifth of the income distribution, who had received a collective 4.8 percent of aggregate income in 1955, saw their share rise to 5.4 percent in 1975, only to fall again, to 4.3 percent by 2000. Those in the highest one-fifth, whose share had remained almost steady between 1955 and 1975 (41.3 to 41.1 percent), enjoyed a bountiful increase in fortunes after 1975, their share rising to 47.4 percent by 2000.[84] One manifestation of this growing inequality was an increase in the number of families who could afford either to send their children to private schools or to establish residence in one of the growing number of affluent suburban neighborhoods and school districts in the nation's metropolitan areas. But another manifestation of the altered income distribution showed up exclusively in central cities: a growing number of neighborhoods marked by dilapidated housing, deteriorating infrastructure, and high crime rates became areas of intensely concentrated poverty, from which the middle class, both white and black, would seek to escape.[85]

Income changes had their regional dimension as well. One development with significance for interracial contact was the growing affluence of the South. Once the poor relation to her neighboring regions to the north and west, the South saw rapid increases in income. Whereas the South's per-capita personal income in 1960 was just 72 percent of the national average, by 2000 it was 91 percent.[86] A region that once struggled to fund its public schools increasingly became a region with an affluent, largely white, middle class, many of whom would be able to afford to send their sons and daughters to private schools.

Suburban Growth

As soon as the troops had come home from Europe and the Pacific following World War II, pent-up demand for housing joined with federally subsidized home loans and widespread automobile ownership to power a mighty move to the suburbs. Add to these an interstate highway system and a new decentralization of jobs partly spawned by those highways, and the result was a boom in suburban development that would continue unabated for decades. Not only did this movement begin to swell the suburban school districts surrounding the central cities of most metropolitan areas, in combination with the changing income distribution it served to widen the economic gap between city and suburbanized districts, an economic gap that tended to march in step with a racial gap. In 1950 the percentage of the population in metropolitan areas that was nonwhite was 13 percent inside central cities, compared to 8 percent in suburbs. By 1970 this 8 percentage-point gap had grown to 17 points, with central cities having a 23 percent nonwhite share, compared to just 6 percent in suburbs.[87]

37

Narrowing Racial Gaps

The decades after *Brown* also witnessed a convergence in two important black-white gaps. One was educational attainment. In 1950, the percentage of nonwhites with four or more years of college was 2.1 percent, one-third that of whites, at 6.3 percent. By 2000, although the gap was larger in percentage points, the proportional gap between blacks and whites had shrunk dramatically, 16.5 percent versus 26.1 percent.[88] This convergence is pertinent to the story of interracial contact because it speaks to the degree to which race represented educationally relevant social differences. If more educated parents sought to distance their children from those of less educated parents, for example, that behavior would become over time less likely to appear racially directed. This convergence in educational attainment could also affect interracial contact to the extent that it tended to equalize enrollment rates by race. This is particularly evident in examining college enrollment. As shown in figure 6.1, the college enrollment rates of blacks and Hispanics tended to converge with those of whites, thus raising the share of college students who were nonwhite. By itself this convergence would tend to raise interracial exposure rates.

Reflecting both the convergence of educational attainment and an apparent reduction in labor market discrimination, the racial gap in incomes also narrowed. In 1954 the median family income among nonwhites (which largely reflected income of blacks) was 56 percent that of whites. By fits and starts, the relative income status of blacks increased over time. By 2000 the ratio of black to white median family income was 64 percent.[89]

Growing Racial Tolerance

Although such things are not easy to measure, there can be little doubt that the racial prejudice of whites declined markedly in the fifty years following the *Brown* decision. One ready indicator is the response of white adults in national surveys to standard questions of racial attitudes. One such question especially pertinent to school desegregation was: "Do you think white students and (Negro/black) students should go to the same schools or to separate schools?" The percentage of whites endorsing "same schools" rose from one-third in 1942, to half in 1956, to three-quarters in 1970, to 90 percent in 1982. In 1995, the last year this question was asked, more than 95 percent of whites favored integrated schools.[90] This is not to say that prejudice disappeared, that it was confined to whites, or that policies to desegregate schools were widely accepted. As to the last of these points, other surveys showed that, while support for integrated schools rose steadily over time, support for government intervention to achieve it did not.[91]

FULL CIRCLE?

Over the first fifty years following the *Brown* decision, government policies regarding interracial contact in schools have traveled a road with more than a few twists and turns. What began as a repudiation of legally mandated apartheid in public schools became, for a while, an energetic pursuit of racial balance. But that energy appeared to dissipate quickly in the face of widespread white reluctance to accept very much interracial contact. An increasingly conservative federal judiciary appeared increasingly willing to make nondiscrimination, rather than racial balance, the guiding principle for desegregation policy. Over this same period, long-term trends served to transform the nation's racial composition as well as the geographical distribution of minority students, each with its own impact on the racial mix of schools. Other trends affected the demand for various schooling options, all of which would influence patterns of interracial contact. In the next chapter, empirical measures are used to document what happened to interracial contact over this period.

The world of 2004 is undoubtedly quite a bit different from that of 1954. The school resources available to students of different races in 2004, especially within districts, are certainly more equal. And disparities between districts have been reduced as well, owing to funding equalization measures adopted by many states.[92] At the same time, some measurable differences in teacher characteristics by race do remain.[93] Plainly, interracial contact remains an important aspect of American schools. In part it remains important because of such differences in resources and staffing. But more important than these considerations are the direct consequences of contact, and the lack thereof. To the extent that contact has peer effects on achievement, influences self-esteem and racial attitudes, and affects young people's further educational attainment and access to social and employment networks, interracial contact remains an important aspect of American schools.

Appendix to Chapter 1

Comparison of Electricity and Magnetism Equipment, Durham and Hillside
High Schools, Durham, North Carolina, 1950

Equipment	Durham High School (White)	Hillside High School (Black)
Transformer, 10,000V step up	1	0
Transformers	2	0
Electric chimes, 5 bell sets	1	0
Batteries, 6V	2	0
Batteries, 22½ V	3	0
Edison cells, primary renewal type	2	0
Photronic relay, Weston DC	1	0
Photoelectric relay, 100V AC, DC	1	0
Ammeters	9	0
Volmeters	16	1
Resistance boxes	3	2
Electroscopes	4	0
Voltmeters, AC	7	0
Voltmeters, DC	5	0
Crow electrical sets	1	0
Generators	2	0
Battery testers	4	0
Galvonometers, wood case	9	0
Galvanoscopes	0	2
Electromagnet	1	1
Convection current box	0	1
Electroplating outfit	0	1
Bar magnet	0	7
Pith ball electroscope	0	1
Motors	13	1
Electrolysis apparatus	0	1
Glass rods	16	0
Dry cell	0	1

TABLE A1.1 *Continued*

Equipment	Durham High School (White)	Hillside High School (Black)
Magnetic needle	0	1
Cell injectors	0	1
Rubber rods	18	0
Compasses	15	0

Source: Picott, Wright, and Knox (1950).

Table A1.2

Secondary School Facilities and Staff in 1965, from the Coleman Report (Percentage of students by race, region, and location having schools or teachers with these characteristics)

	Age of building less than 20 years	School with chemistry lab	School with language lab	Average library books/pupil	Percentage of teachers who majored in academic subjects	Average pupils per teacher
Mexican American	48	96	57	8.1	37	23
Puerto Rican	40	94	45	6.2	40	22
Native American	49	99	58	6.4	39	23
Asian American	41	99	75	5.7	40	24
Black	60	94	49	4.6	38	26
White	53	98	56	5.8	40	22
Metropolitan						
Northeast Black	18	99	47	3.8	40	24
White	64	99	79	5.3	46	20
Midwest Black	33	100	68	3.5	35	25
White	43	100	57	4.8	41	24

South	Black	74	94	48	4.5	42	26
	White	84	100	72	5.7	41	25
Southwest	Black	76	100	69	5.6	25	25
	White	43	97	97	3.7	36	26
West	Black	53	100	95	6.5	38	23
	White	79	100	80	6.3	41	23
Nonmetropolitan							
North and West	Black	64	98	32	4.5	39	20
	White	35	97	24	6.3	36	20
South	Black	79	85	17	4.0	37	30
	White	52	91	32	6.1	35	25
Southwest	Black	76	92	38	8.1	30	20
	White	44	95	19	14.8	32	21

Source: Coleman et al. (1966, tables 2 and 6b).

Note: Regions in the Coleman Report were defined as: North and West: All states not in the South and Southwest; South: Alabama, Arkansas, Florida, Georgia, Kentucky, Louisiana, Mississippi, North Carolina, South Carolina, Tennessee, and Virginia; Southwest: Arizona, New Mexico, Oklahoma, Texas; Northeast: Connecticut, Delaware, District of Columbia, Maine, Maryland, Massachusetts, New Hampshire, New Jersey, New York, Pennsylvania, Rhode Island, Vermont; Midwest: Illinois, Indiana, Iowa, Kansas, Michigan, Minnesota, Missouri, Nebraska, North Dakota, Ohio, South Dakota, Wisconsin; West: Alaska, California, Colorado, Hawaii, Idaho, Montana, Nevada, Oregon, Utah, Washington, Wyoming.

The Legacies of *Brown* and *Milliken*

> I do not see how you can ever point your fingers at a
> southern Senator or a southern school district and tell them
> that they are discriminating against black children when you
> are unwilling to desegregate schools in your own cities.
> Let me say to my distinguished northern colleagues that the
> reason you are unwilling to do it, and let me say it frankly,
> is fear of political reprisal. The question is whether northern
> Senators have the guts to face their liberal white
> constituents who have fled to the suburbs for the sole
> purpose of avoiding having their sons and daughters go to
> school with blacks.
> *Abraham Ribicoff to Jacob Javits, on the Senate floor,*
> *April 20, 1971*[1]

THIS BOOK'S PRIMARY OBJECTIVE is to document changes in interracial contact over the five decades since the *Brown* decision. It will quickly become clear that nothing like a complete accounting is possible, owing to the lack of enrollment data covering all schools over the entire period. The best that can be done under the circumstances, then, is to describe the trends and patterns using available data. To that end, this chapter presents evidence of four kinds to document changes in interracial contact in schools. First, it summarizes information on interracial contact gleaned from two national surveys, one of black Americans and the other of public schools. Next, it presents estimates of racial isolation in public schools, by region, beginning in the period of the *Brown* decision, based on patterns of enrollment within public school districts. For the years before 1968, these estimates are based on a relatively small group of districts for which information could be obtained. Third, it examines changes in interracial contact using data that allow examination on a metropolitanwide basis rather than merely within districts and that also contain information on private schools. The period covered by this more complete view, however, is restricted to the three decades 1970–2000.

Finally, the chapter presents data on interracial contact in 1999–2000, by region, for the three largest racial and ethnic groups in U.S. schools.

To anticipate the chapter's findings, it does not seem to be excessively simplistic to use two of the most famous school segregation cases to highlight two broad themes. The first and by far the most dramatic change uncovered by this review of interracial contact is the precipitous increase that occurred after *Brown* in the regions where de jure segregation had been the rule. In the Border states this occurred rapidly. In the eleven states of the former Confederacy it occurred quite grudgingly until the combined force of all three branches of the federal government in the late 1960s pushed them to a previously unimaginable level of interracial contact. Yet the South was not the only region to change in these years; its transformation was merely the most dramatic. The second theme is given special significance by the Supreme Court's 1974 *Milliken* decision, which forbade federal courts in virtually all cases from reaching beyond existing school district lines in seeking remedies to school segregation. The possibly predictable result of this restriction was that, while segregation within districts was greatly reduced, racial disparities between districts tended to widen, as the process of urban development led to the growth of predominantly white suburban school districts. Part of what *Brown* had accomplished, therefore, was gradually eroded by a process given legal weight by *Milliken*.

Survey Evidence on Interracial Contact

Two national surveys provide information on interracial contact in the public schools before the advent of comprehensive school-level surveys undertaken by the Office for Civil Rights in the late 1960s. The first is a survey of black Americans, whose answers provide a picture of racial isolation before *Brown*. The second is the massive survey of public schools conducted in 1965 as part of the Coleman Report.

In 1979 and 1980, the National Survey of Black Americans asked respondents to characterize the racial composition of the schools they attended in their youth. When sorted by the age of the respondents, these answers provide evidence on interracial contact going back to 1954 and before. As will be seen below, information on the racial composition of public schools before 1968 is not plentiful, particularly for schools outside of the South. In their 1992 study, Michael Boozer, Alan Krueger, and Shari Wolkon used this survey to calculate the proportion of blacks in the South who attended all-black and majority-black schools, by year.[2] To their surprise, they found that the isolation of black students began to dissolve before 1968, the year of the *Green* decision. Indeed, 1964 appeared to be the "watershed" year, suggesting that the 1964 Civil Rights Act and the Elementary and Secondary Education Act of 1965, with their provisions for using federal funding to encourage desegregation, were effective in bringing about measurable changes in interracial contact.

Data from this same survey can be used to ask two somewhat different questions. First, how much interracial contact was there in the North in the years before *Brown*? Second, how did these levels of contact change by region over time? Because of the relatively small numbers of survey respondents, I used decades to delineate historical periods. By noting each respondent's birth year, it was possible to assign recollections about the racial composition of elementary, junior high, and high schools to the appropriate decade. Among blacks who attended elementary school in the 1940s, for example, nearly all those who grew up in the Border or the South reported going to all-black schools, but only about one-third of those who grew up outside those regions did so.[3] In the succeeding two decades, the percentage of blacks in the Border who attended all-black elementary schools dropped steadily, to 70 percent in the 1950s and 52 percent in the 1960s. In the South, the comparable percentages were 93 percent and 75 percent, figures that reflect that region's slowness to desegregate. Meanwhile, there was little change in the North, with about one-third of blacks there attending all-black schools.[4] Fewer blacks attended all-black junior and senior high schools, but the trends at those levels were similar.

A more nuanced picture of changes in interracial contact can be obtained from estimates of the exposure rate of blacks to blacks in school, that is, the percentage of students who are black in the typical black student's school.[5] In the 1940s and 1950s, blacks attending schools in the North had very different experiences from those who were educated in the regime of official segregation; on average, the typical black student in the North attended a school that was roughly half to 60 percent black. Given the smaller share of the Northern population that was black (5 percent of the population outside the South and the Border was black in 1950, compared to 10 percent in the Border and 25 percent in the South), however, exposure rates of this magnitude still suggest significant aggregations of black students.[6] Calculated exposure rates also show that racial isolation tended to be smaller in higher grades, largely reflecting the larger size and greater diversity in junior high and high schools, compared to elementary schools. Between the 1950s and 1960s, exposure rates declined at every schooling level in the South and at two levels in the Border. In contrast, they increased in the rest of the country, probably as a result of increases in the black share of Northern school districts. In any case, these increases do not suggest a lessening of segregation in the North.

A much larger national survey, conducted fifteen years earlier for the Coleman Report in 1965, documented for the first time the substantial segregation that existed in Northern schools, and the even greater extent of it in the South. In elementary schools in the metropolitan Northeast, for example, the typical black student attended a school that was 33 percent white, while the typical white student was in a school that was 88 percent white.[7] Blacks in the South (as defined in the report) were quite severely isolated, since the typical black there attended a school that was only 3 percent white.[8] Since few schools would have been 3 percent white, this statistic may be more usefully interpreted to imply that one in 33 blacks attended a school that was 99 percent white.[9] Blacks in the other regions were not so severely isolated, but segregation there was evident as well. At the elementary level, blacks in the metropolitan Midwest attended schools where only 23 percent of the students were white on average, while whites were in 90 percent white schools on average.[10]

These large differences between the exposure rates for blacks and whites in 1965 could have two explanations. One reason why whites attended schools with higher percentages of whites was, of course, officially imposed segregation. A second possibility was that, even within regions, many whites simply lived in predominantly white counties or metropolitan areas, causing them to have mostly white classmates whether or not schools were segregated by law. To correct for this second effect, Coleman and his coauthors calculated a weighted exposure rate. Here, the exposure rates of whites to whites calculated for districts were weighted by the number of blacks in the county or metropolitan area instead of the number of whites, yielding a measure that the authors interpret as applying to "whites in areas with blacks." This adjusted exposure rate for whites is comparable to that for blacks in the sense of applying to the same set of geographical areas. In counties or metropolitan areas with a given racial composition, then, blacks and whites would be expected to be in schools with the same white percentage if schools were racially balanced. The difference between the exposure rate

and this adjusted rate for whites can therefore be taken as a
ısure of segregation. By this metric, the schools in the South,
~~~~~ elementary and secondary levels, were the most segregated of any
region. But among elementary schools in metropolitan areas, the Midwest was not far behind.[11]

SEGREGATION IN DISTRICTS SINCE *BROWN*

As noted earlier, measures of racial isolation dropped significantly in the
South, marking the transformation of its schools from being the most to
the least segregated in the country. This dramatic shift bears witness to
the combined force of federal court decisions, particularly *Green* (1968),
Alexander (1969), and *Swann* (1971), as well as the provisions of the
1964 Civil Rights Act that provided for close federal scrutiny and enabled the federal executive branch to withhold funds from districts that
did not comply with court-ordered desegregation orders. In a series of
studies, Gary Orfield and his colleagues documented the impact of these
federal actions on interracial contact, showing that the South remained
the region with the least segregated schools, followed closely by the West,
and that segregation in the Northeast actually increased between 1968
and 1980.[12]

Missing from this chronicle of changes in segregation in the various
regions over time is a sense of what went before 1968, before the advent
of nationwide detailed surveys of racial patterns of enrollment. While it
is well known that schools throughout the Border and the South were
segregated by law in 1954 (plus a smattering of districts in several other
states), knowledge of enrollment patterns across the country has been
limited to a small number of districts. The best published source of
information on enrollment patterns before 1968 is an appendix in the
U.S. Commission on Civil Rights' 1967 study *Racial Isolation in the Public Schools.*[13] This appendix presents two measures similar to that used by
Orfield, but covering only elementary schools, for forty urban districts
for various years during the period roughly 1950–1965. Although the
study itself cites no sources, the calculations appear to have been based
on school district reports or special studies.

To extend the measurement of regional patterns of racial composition
backward from 1968, I augmented this information on individual school
districts by collecting detailed enrollment data by race and school for
more than a dozen school districts for various school years over the
same approximate period, 1950–1965.[14] Some of the collected informa-

tion in fact coincided with the districts and years included in the Civil Rights Commission study, making it possible to verify the accuracy of some of the figures included in that study. These data on individual districts provide an unparalleled vantage point for assessing the extent to which public schools outside the Jim Crow regime were in fact racially integrated at the time the *Brown* decision was handed down. Qualitative descriptions of schools outside the South and Border regions certainly suggest that de facto segregation was not uncommon, but little systematic analysis has been undertaken to assess the extent of segregation in the North.

Five Illustrative Districts

As an illustration of what may be learned about the pre-1968 period, figures 2.1 and 2.2 present for five urban school districts two measures that show the impact of school desegregation on interracial contact. Chosen because data on them could be obtained for years before 1968, these illustrative districts are Charlotte (which merged with Mecklenburg County in 1960), Louisville (which was forced to merge with Jefferson County in 1975), Fort Wayne, Wichita, and Denver.[15] Charlotte instituted token integration in 1957, which meant it granted a small number of requests from black students seeking to transfer to white schools. In 1968, the federal district court ordered it to desegregate more aggressively, by means of rezoning and liberalized transfers. Then in 1970 the court ordered a thoroughgoing racial balance plan, requiring some thirteen thousand students to be bused across town, a plan that was approved a year later by the Supreme Court in *Swann v. Charlotte-Mecklenburg* (1971).[16]

Louisville, which had begun to desegregate its schools in 1956, retained substantially segregated schools into the 1960s. The adjoining Jefferson County district, which had historically educated its few black elementary students in one-room schools and sent its black high school students to Louisville or another adjacent district, still had some all-black schools as late as 1962. Following another decade and a half of gradual change, a federal court in 1974 ordered the two districts to merge and to undertake a busing program even more ambitious than Charlotte's, requiring more than twenty-two thousand students to be bused between white and black sections of what had become a very large district. When this plan was implemented in 1975, it was met by vocal and sometimes violent protests.[17]

By contrast, no apocalyptic desegregation order was ever visited upon

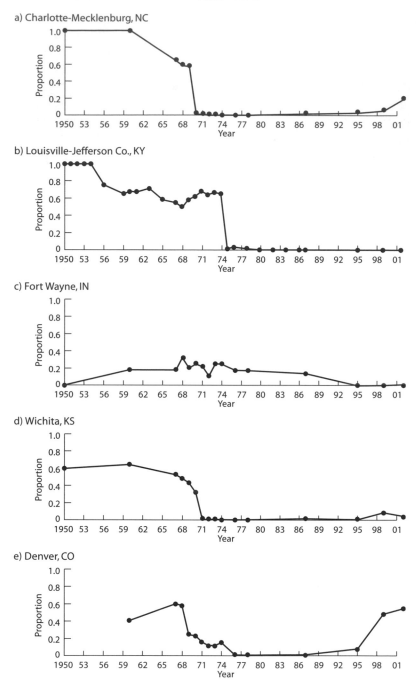

a) Charlotte-Mecklenburg, NC

b) Louisville-Jefferson Co., KY

c) Fort Wayne, IN

d) Wichita, KS

e) Denver, CO

Fort Wayne. Instead, it was the site of federal investigations, private lawsuits, a boycott, and negotiations among community groups and the school district. Like many other districts outside the region of de jure segregation, the Fort Wayne district had located new schools, gerrymandered its school attendance zones, and offered students easy transfers so as to minimize racially mixed schools. In 1971 the district agreed to a rezoning plan, and in 1977 it undertook further desegregation.[18]

Like other large districts in Kansas, Wichita had maintained officially segregated elementary schools until the early 1950s, ending the policy in 1951. The schools remained highly segregated, however, prompting federal authorities to recommend in 1968 that segregation in several elementary schools be ended. In 1969 the district offered up a limited busing plan, but an administrative judge found it wanting, ruling the district to be in violation of the 1964 Civil Rights Act and thus subject to a cutoff of federal funds. The school district thereupon responded with a comprehensive desegregation plan in 1971 calling for the busing of black and white students to achieve racial balance in all schools.[19]

In Denver, a 1969 lawsuit alleging officially sanctioned segregation in East Denver resulted in a federal court ruling in 1974 that required attendance zones to be modified and schools to be paired. The order stipulated that elementary schools have enrollments between 40 percent and 70 percent white and that secondary schools be between 50 percent and 60 percent white. The Supreme Court in its 1973 *Keyes v. School District No. 1* had ruled that such federal intervention could apply to Northern school districts if government action had contributed to segregation.[20]

Figure 2.1 traces the impact of desegregation by using a measure of racial isolation, the percentage of black students attending 90–100 percent minority schools. As noted in the methodological appendix, this

Figure 2.1. Proportion of Blacks in 90–100 percent Minority Schools, Five Districts

Sources: North Carolina Superintendent of Public Instruction, *Biennial Report for 1950–52, Part III, Statistical Report, 1951–52; Biennial Report, 1958–60, Part III, Statistical Report 1959–60*; Kentucky Department of Education (various years); Thompson (1976, pp. 336–347); U.S. Department of Health, Education and Welfare, Office for Civil Rights (1969, 1970, 1978); U.S. Department of Education, Office for Civil Rights (n.d.); U.S. Department of Education, National Center for Education Statistics (2001a); unpublished data from the Charlotte-Mecklenburg Schools, Denver Public Schools, Fort Wayne Community Schools, Jefferson County Public Schools, and Wichita Public Schools.

measure is far from perfect, in that it tends to be higher in districts with bigger shares of nonwhites. It may also be very sensitive to small changes in enrollments, since a single student can potentially cause a school to move in or out of this category. Nevertheless, it provides an easily understood metric for judging racial isolation. All calculations for school years from 1968–1969 to 1999–2000 are based on data from federally sponsored surveys such as those conducted by the Office for Civil Rights and used by Orfield and other researchers. For earlier years, calculations were made using the kind of unpublished school-level data described earlier. For each of these districts, data were collected for a representative year for each of two narrow periods: the early 1950s (roughly 1950–1954) and the early 1960s (1960–1961). Because data were obtained for different years, and in some cases for multiple years, I chose one year in each case to represent each period.[21] Data for the 2002–2003 year were obtained directly from the districts.

All five of the districts were the subject of lawsuits, judicial opinions (including more than a dozen opinions each in Charlotte and Denver), and desegregation plans. For each district, the plan or plans that effected the most racial change in school enrollments occurred between the falls of 1968 and 1978. The changes wrought by these plans show up in the sharp declines in racial isolation between these two years.

The graphs clearly indicate the radical change that occurred in the two previously segregated districts in the South and the Border. In 1954 virtually all of the black students in both Charlotte and Louisville were enrolled in all-black public schools.[22] The index of isolation fell sharply when serious school desegregation plans were implemented, which in the case of Louisville was shortly after the 1954 decision and in Charlotte not until after 1960. Even then, the isolation of black students did not end right away. In the fall of 1968 almost 60 percent of black students in Charlotte and about half in Louisville attended 90–100 percent minority schools. By 1978, however, such schools had vanished in Charlotte and were rare in Louisville. In the last years shown in the figure, this extreme form of racial isolation was absent in Louisville, but in Charlotte it returned, to affect 3 percent of black students in 1987, and 21 percent in 2002.[23]

The three Northern districts provide an interesting comparison. In the fall of 1950 Fort Wayne had no schools in the 90–100 percent nonwhite category, but by 1962 it did, when 18.5 percent of its black students attended such highly isolated schools. That portion increased to 32 percent in 1968, marking a high point of segregation in Fort Wayne among the years shown. Following the implementation of its rezoning plan in 1971, the share of blacks in these schools fell in 1978 and 1987, but in those years Fort Wayne was the most highly segregated of the five districts by this measure. By the fall of 1995, however, none of Fort Wayne's black students were in 90–100 percent minority schools. In Wichita, the legacy of officially segregated schools at the elementary level until the fall of 1952 is evident in the prevalence of racially isolated schools. In 1952–1953, 59 percent of its black students attended largely or all nonwhite schools, a remarkably high share considering that only about 8 percent of Wichita's students were nonwhite. The share remained high until after 1968, when desegregation orders in 1969 and 1971 resulted in the abolition of such highly concentrated schools. Only in the fall of 1999, when the district's overall nonwhite percentage reached 45 percent, did 90–100 percent minority schools reappear. Denver, for which no data for the 1950–1954 period are available, showed high portions of black students attending very isolated schools in the falls of both 1961 and 1968. Following desegregation plans implemented in 1974 and 1976, such schools were eliminated. However, they reappeared in the fall of 1995. As the nonwhite proportion in the district exceeded three-quarters, the share of black students attending 90–100 percent minority schools increased, exceeding one-half by the fall of 2001.

Figure 2.2 measures racial segregation in the public schools using the gap-based segregation index, the principal index used in this book. As described in detail in the methodological appendix, this index measures unevenness in the distribution of students across schools and is independent of a district's racial composition. Like the widely used dissimilarity index, it measures segregation on a 0–1 scale, where 0 represents perfect racial balance across schools and 1 represents absolute racial separation between schools for whites and schools for nonwhites.[24] A comparison between figures 2.1 and 2.2 also indicates that the segregation index corresponds closely to the 90–100 percent measure of isolation. For Charlotte and Louisville, the effectiveness of their desegregation plans is clearly evident in figure 2.2. Charlotte's initial desegregation, before the advent of crosstown busing, reduced its segregation index from its maximum 1.00 to 0.66 by 1968; the racial balancing later certified by the *Swann* decision reduced measured segregation even more, to 0.06 in 1970. Measured segregation remained low through the next two decades, then increased gradually in the years following, and stood at 0.28 in the fall of 2002. A similar story applies to Louisville, whose segregation index dropped from the near maximum before 1954 to 0.72 in the fall of

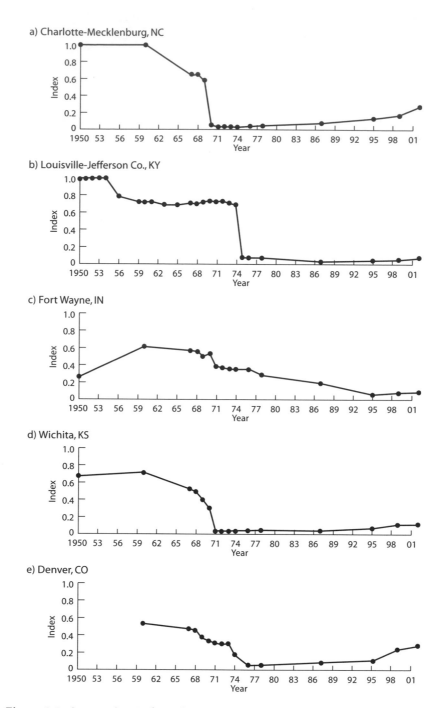

Figure 2.2. Segregation Index, Five Districts
  Sources: See figure 2.1.

1961, to 0.68 in 1974, and then to 0.08 in 1975, following the implementation of its desegregation plan in that year. After 1960–1961 the trends
in Fort Wayne and Wichita were also downward, but they differ from
Charlotte and Louisville in the 1950s by recording *increases* in segregation before 1960, Fort Wayne's being particularly steep, 0.27 to 0.61. By
2002, however, both Fort Wayne and Wichita showed relatively low levels
of school segregation. Denver's experience in the 1960s and 1970s paral-
lels those of the others, with segregation rising thereafter.

Aside from the very large declines in segregation that accompanied the
desegregation plans in Charlotte, Louisville, and Wichita, this comparison reveals two somewhat surprising things. The first is the increase in
segregation observed between fall 1987 and fall 2002 in four of the five
districts. This resegregation was largest in Charlotte (+ 0.20) and Denver
(+ 0.19). Only in Fort Wayne did segregation fall over these latter years.
The second surprise was in the degree of change in racial isolation that
occurred between the early 1960s and 1968. Measures of racial isolation
and segregation all declined during this period. Since previous studies of
segregation trends *begin* in 1968, they necessarily miss such changes earlier in the decade. Given the magnitude of these earlier changes, at least
in these five illustrative districts, it seems quite possible that much of the
desegregation that did occur after 1954 has not been fully appreciated.
Stated differently, segregation outside the previously Jim Crow states in
1960 may have been much more intense than is commonly appreciated.
It would be valuable to document, to the extent possible, these earlier
patterns of segregation.

Larger Sample of Districts

In an attempt to accomplish that, I applied the approach used in these
five districts to a larger group of districts for which school-level data or
similar measures could be obtained. By examining trends in measured
racial isolation and segregation in individual school districts over time,
these enrollment data make it possible to gain an impression of regional
patterns and trends before 1968. Using data for forty-nine districts, I
calculated or estimated values of the two measures of racial isolation
used by Orfield in his 1983 study of school desegregation.[25] Then I applied the trends observed in the sample districts to the entire region in
which they are located, allowing me to produce an expanded table showing trends in racial isolation by region.[26]

These extrapolated percentages are shown in the first two columns in table 2.1, which expands upon Orfield's table by going back and extending forward to the present. Because of the small number of districts with data for the 1950–1954 period, no extrapolations are given for the Northeast or West in the first column. For the years of de jure segregation—1950–1954 for the South and the Border and 1960–1961 for the South—the figures reflect the assumption that all schools were entirely segregated, which was virtually the case.[27] The remaining figures for the two earlier years were obtained by applying the average trend observed in the districts with unpublished early data to the regions in which they were located.

One thing that emerges from this longer time period is a better appreciation of the magnitude of the change in Southern schools. That just one-quarter of blacks in the South were in 90–100 percent minority

TABLE 2.1

Percentage of Black Students in 90–100 Percent Nonwhite and Majority Nonwhite Public Schools by Region, 1950–1954 to 2000, Fall Enrollment

Region	1950–54*	1960–61*	1968	1972	1976	1980	1989	1999	2000
Percentage in 90–100% nonwhite schools									
Northeast	—	40	42.7	46.9	51.4	48.7	49.8	50.2	51.2
Border	100	59	60.2	54.7	42.5	37.0	33.7	39.7	39.6
South	100	100	77.8	24.7	22.4	23.0	26.0	31.1	30.9
Midwest	53	56	58.0	57.4	51.1	43.6	40.1	45.0	46.3
West	—	27	50.8	42.7	36.3	33.7	26.7	29.9	29.5
U.S.			64.3	38.7	35.9	33.2	33.8	37.4	37.4
Percentage in 50–100% nonwhite schools									
Northeast	—	62	66.8	69.9	72.5	79.9	75.4	77.5	78.3
Border	100	69	71.6	67.2	60.1	59.2	58.0	64.8	67.0
South	100	100	80.9	55.3	54.9	57.1	59.3	67.3	69.0
Midwest	78	80	77.3	75.3	70.3	69.5	69.4	67.9	73.3
West	—	69	72.2	68.1	67.4	66.8	67.4	76.7	75.3
U.S.			76.6	63.6	62.4	62.9	64.9	70.1	71.6

Sources: 1950–1954 and 1960–1961: extrapolations based on unpublished and published data; 1968–1980: Orfield (1983, table 2, p. 4); 1989 and 1999: U.S. Department of Education, National Center for Education Statistics (1991, 2001a); 2000: Frankenberg, Lee, and Orfield (2003, tables 32 and 33); author's calculations.

Note: Definitions of regions are given in the methodological appendix.

*Extrapolated; see text.

schools in 1972 is all the more remarkable when laid besi
percent of blacks in such schools only about a decade befor
trast, the three regions of the North saw little change, and
was suggested generally increasing segregation.

The table also employs data from more recent national surveys to fill
out the regional trends to 1989–1990, 1999–2000, and 2000–2001. Except for the Midwest, these trends point in the direction of increasing
segregation. In the South, the percentage of black students in the most
highly concentrated schools rose from 23 percent in fall 1980 to 31 percent by fall 2001. While the South still had the lowest percentage of any
region, the convergence of the regions' measures is evident. By fall 2000
the Northeast had solidified its position as having, by these measures,
the most segregated public schools in the nation. If one compares 1960–
1961 and 2000–2001, one finds a mixed bag. Adopting as the benchmark
of isolation enrollment in the most highly concentrated schools, black
students became dramatically less isolated in the South, the Border, and
the Midwest. But in the schools of the Northeast and the West, they
became more isolated, at least from whites. Using the less extreme
benchmark based on majority nonwhite schools, a similar but less dramatic change is evident.

Segregation at the Metropolitan Area Level, 1970 and 2000

The preceding analysis, carried out at the level of the school district,
does not afford a sufficiently broad view of segregation because it does
not recognize the segregation that arises when districts within a local
area differ by racial composition. Because most metropolitan areas contain school districts with differing racial compositions, families wishing
to reduce their children's contact with students of other races or ethnic
groups can usually find a nearly homogeneous district where interracial
contact is limited. Other than the option of private schools, such residential location decisions represent the most effective way white families
can minimize the interracial contact that would arise from attending
racially mixed schools. Any complete assessment of school segregation
must therefore account for such racial differences across school districts
inside metropolitan areas.

Once the necessity of looking across school districts is granted, the question then arises, what is the proper geographical unit for measuring segregation? Segregation as it has been defined in this study arises from the unevenness of schools' racial compositions. If elementary school 1 has 10 percent nonwhite enrollment and elementary school 2, three blocks away, is 100 percent nonwhite, the unevenness in racial compositions yields a clear case of segregation. But what if those two schools were instead located at opposite sides of town, twenty minutes from one another? Or what if they were as far away as twenty miles and an hour-and-fifteen-minute ride? Or at opposite ends of the state? It seems clear that the first case indicates segregation, while the last one is something else. All bespeak disparities in the experiences of students, as indicated by differences in racial composition. But the first case, because it is obviously easier to remedy or reverse, seems relevant to public policy discussions in a way the last is not. Racially balancing the schools of a district is feasible, while balancing the schools of a state is not. So the question then becomes, what geographical area is the proper one to employ for the purpose of assessing segregation?

In this book I use the metropolitan area (or the county in nonmetropolitan areas). Metropolitan areas are creations of government statisticians, designed to be meaningful in an economic sense yet simple to construct. Simplicity is achieved by using counties as the units of aggregation (except in New England, where towns and cities are used as the building blocks, owing to the large size of counties in that region). The economic criteria employed by the census add up to the question: Does this area comprise a single housing market and labor market surrounding at least one urban core?[28] Once constructed, the resulting metropolitan areas are a disparate collection of statistical units. They differ widely in area and population. So great is the divergence that one is hard pressed to understand that they are examples of the same species. To illustrate this difference, think about a family moving to Jackson, Tennessee, and another moving to Chicago. Our first family would find in Jackson a metropolitan area with a population of 78,000, in 1990, and an area of 560 square miles, all served by a single public school district. By contrast, our second family would have confronted a vast urbanized area with 6.1 million people, spread over 1,895 square miles and three counties, and containing more than two hundred different public school districts. It is easier to accept the assumption that the Jackson metropolitan area is a single housing market than to believe the same about Chicago, and it is likewise easier to imagine a policy that racially balanced the public schools of Jackson than one that did the same in the

Chicago metropolis. For this reason, comparing the segregation of schools in these two metropolitan areas is in some sense unfair, their relative size making unevenness in racial composition a more likely phenomenon in Chicago owing simply to its vastness. While I use the metropolitan area as the basic geographic unit for measuring segregation, therefore, I do so guardedly. I also examine separately large and small metropolitan areas, to determine if there are systematic differences by size.

The principal advantage of examining segregation at the metropolitan area, rather than from the perspective of the school district, is that this approach recognizes the contribution to overall segregation made by racial disparities across districts. It turns out that many of the nation's large urban areas are checkered with dozens of separate school districts, and this balkanization is an important factor in the racial segregation of public schools.[29] To highlight the contribution of these interjurisdictional disparities to overall segregation, I separate the portion of a metropolitan area's segregation that arises because of the disparities existing within school districts from the portion associated with racial disparities between districts. In addition, I am also able to isolate the effect on overall segregation from having a portion of students attending private schools, whose racial composition as a whole typically differs from that of public schools taken together.[30] Metropolitan segregation is thus divided into components arising from racial disparities (1) within districts, (2) between districts, and (3) between public and private students in aggregate.

To illustrate how this decomposition works, table 2.2 displays information on the metropolitan area of South Bend–Mishawaka, Indiana, for 1970 and 2000.[31] In 1970 the area's 53,147 public school students attended schools in five districts, with racial compositions ranging from all-white to South Bend's 17.7 percent nonwhite. Each district's exposure rate of whites to nonwhites is also shown in the table; that these rates generally fell short of the nonwhite percentages means that schools were not balanced racially in any district. For some smaller districts in 1970 it was necessary to estimate the exposure rates, owing to the absence of school-level data; in the case of South Bend the rate for Polk-Lincoln was estimated.[32] Almost ten thousand of the area's students were enrolled in private schools in 1970, and only 3.7 percent of these students were nonwhite, creating a public/private racial disparity that contributed to overall metropolitan segregation. That segregation, divided into the three components described above, is given at the bottom of the table. Of the

TABLE 2.2

Metropolitan Area School Segregation, South Bend-Mishawaka, Indiana, 1970 and 2000

	1970			2000		
	Enrollment	Percentage nonwhite	Exposure rate[a]	Enrollment	Percentage nonwhite	Exposure rate[a]
Public districts						
Mishawaka	6,215	1.0	0.9	5,051	5.0	5.0
Penn-Harris- Madison	5,589	0.3	0.2	9,888	5.1	5.0
Polk-Lincoln (John Glenn)	1,262	0.0	0.0[b]	1,778	3.3	3.2
South Bend	34,416	17.7	10.1	20,855	46.9	43.0
Union-North	1,786	0.1	0.1	1,311	3.4	3.3
All districts	53,147	12.3	6.7	38,883	27.4	19.7
Private schools	9,774	3.7	—	7,493	9.7	—
All students	62,921	11.0	6.2	46,376	24.5	17.8
Segregation						
Within public districts			.374			.052
Between public districts			.054			.200
Public/private disparity			.010			.023
Total			.438			.274

Source: See table A2.3.

[a]Exposure rate of whites to nonwhites, or the percentage nonwhite in the average white student's school. See methodological appendix for calculation.

[b]1970 exposure rate estimated; see text.

total segregation index of 0.438, the bulk in South Bend in 1970 was due to the racial disparities within public districts. A relatively small portion, 0.054, could be attributed to racial differences across the area's five districts, and almost none of it could be attributed to the 8.6 percentage point difference in the nonwhite percentage between public and private schools.

The right side of the table gives comparable calculations for 2000. A comparison of the early and later data indicate four important changes. First, overall enrollment in the metropolitan area declined by almost one-quarter, reflecting the gradual population decline afflicting many of the urban areas of the nation's industrial Midwest. Most of that decline occurred in the central city district of South Bend, where enrollment fell by almost 40 percent. Second, nonwhite enrollment grew relative to white enrollment, its share more than doubling. Again, this change was most pronounced in the South Bend city district, where the nonwhite percentage rose from 10 percent to 43 percent. Third, segregation within the districts fell precipitously, from 0.374 to a scant 0.052, a change very much in line with those observed previously in this chapter for districts in the Midwest. The fourth change evident in the table, one that could not be reflected in the evidence from school districts alone, was the increase in segregation due to between-district disparities. As is quite evident in the listing of districts, their racial compositions diverged over the period, with the nonwhite percentage in South Bend rising much faster than in the other four. For this metropolitan area at least, this pattern of divergence had the effect of partially offsetting the significant decline in segregation brought about by the desegregation of individual districts.

To give some perspective on the patterns of metropolitan-level segregation in these two years, table 2.3 lists the country's most segregated metropolitan areas for both. In 1970, metropolitan areas in the South led the way in this dubious contest, the radically segregated past not yet having been wholly transformed in the quickening pace of desegregation orders. This result is quite in line with the comparisons shown earlier based on districts. For 2000, the list is entirely different, with three Midwest industrial centers joined by two metropolitan areas in the South. Most striking is the general decline in segregation rates. The average segregation index for these most segregated areas declined by more than 25 percent. A noteworthy feature shared by the highly segregated metropolitan areas in 2000 is the generous portion attributable to between-district racial disparities. Whereas the between-district component averaged less than 4 percent of total segregation in 1970, it explained some 84 percent in 2000.

To better discern the changes that occurred over these three decades, table 2.4 presents average segregation indices, where the metropolitan areas in the sample are all defined according to their 1990 geographical definitions. They are divided by region and by size, with those having 200,000 students or more in 2000 shown in the top part of the table, and the remaining, smaller ones shown in the bottom part. The indices are decomposed into the three components discussed above. One needs to be cautious in interpreting these components of segregation in this table, however. Although the geographical areas covered by the areas

TABLE 2.3
Most Highly Segregated Metropolitan Areas, 1970 and 2000

Metropolitan area	Components of segregation			
	Within districts	Between districts	Public/private disparity	Total
1970				
Jackson, MS	.725	.064	.061	.850
Memphis, TN-AR-MS	.732	.057	.042	.832
Jackson, TN	.808	.000	.006	.815
Shreveport, LA	.750	.030	.025	.805
Victoria, TX	.761	.007	.028	.796
2000				
Detroit, MI	.027	.599	.004	.630
Monroe, LA	.200	.326	.064	.590
Cleveland, OH	.060	.501	.024	.585
Birmingham, AL	.055	.523	.004	.582
Gary-Hammond, IN	.026	.550	.001	.577

Source: See table A2.3.

Note: Segregation indices, defined for metropolitan areas, are divided into three components: *within districts*, due to racial disparities within districts; *between districts*, due to disparities between districts, *public/private disparity*, due to disparity between public and private school enrollments. See methodological appendix for fuller explanation.

shown in the table did not change, school districts in some of them did change, mostly in the direction of consolidation. The number of districts covered by the 332 metropolitan areas in the sample declined by about 3 percent between 1970 and 2000.[33] Although the size or number of districts in a metropolitan area has no effect on total measured segregation, these factors will affect the portion of segregation attributed to within-district versus between-district disparities. Other things being equal, larger districts imply higher within-district segregation and correspondingly lower between-district segregation. Thus care must be taken in interpreting changes in the within-district and between-district components. The calculations shown in table 2.4 are based on the actual districts existing in 1970 and 2000. Because consolidation converts between-district disparities into within-district disparities, the consolidation that occurred between some districts over the period had the effect of decreasing between-district segregation. Thus the increases recorded

TABLE 2.4

Comparing Segregation by Region and Size of Metropolitan Area, 1970 and 2000

Region	No. of Metro Areas	1970 Components of segregation				2000 Components of segregation				Change 1970–2000 Components of segregation			
		Within districts	Between districts	Public/private disparity	Total	Within districts	Between districts	Public/private disparity	Total	Within districts	Between districts	Public/private disparity	Total
Large Metropolitan Areas													
Northeast	7	.226	.244	.043	.514	.080	.300	.047	.426	−.146	.056	.003	−.088
Border	4	.243	.421	.018	.681	.087	.316	.021	.423	−.156	−.105	.003	−.258
South	15	.460	.124	.012	.596	.114	.191	.027	.331	−.346	.067	.015	−.265
Midwest	8	.314	.301	.021	.636	.050	.432	.016	.498	−.266	.131	−.005	−.138
West	14	.195	.129	.001	.324	.076	.179	.021	.276	−.119	.050	.020	−.048
U.S.	48	.281	.228	.020	.528	.082	.262	.026	.370	−.198	.034	.006	−.158
Smaller Metropolitan Areas													
Northeast	60	.128	.146	.009	.283	.027	.286	.007	.320	−.101	.140	−.002	.037
Border	18	.308	.092	.009	.409	.055	.090	.017	.162	−.253	−.002	.008	−.247
South	92	.441	.065	.010	.517	.121	.123	.029	.273	−.320	.058	.019	−.244
Midwest	70	.240	.119	.005	.364	.065	.211	.008	.284	−.175	.092	.003	−.080
West	44	.129	.056	.001	.186	.070	.108	.013	.191	−.060	.052	.012	.005
U.S.	284	.254	.103	.007	.364	.075	.175	.016	.265	−.180	.072	.008	−.099

Source: See table A2.3

Notes: For definition of components of segregation, see table 2.3. Large metropolitan areas have enrollments of 200,000 or greater in 2000. Indices are weighted by 2000 metropolitan area enrollments. Definitions of regions are given in the methodological appendix. Districts in Alaska and Hawaii were excluded.

CHAPTER 2

in between-district segregation slightly understate the increases in this component that would have occurred had the 2000 district boundaries been in place over the whole period.

The overwhelming impression given by the table is one of declining segregation, though declines were not universal. Among the largest areas, average segregation did decline in every region, with the declines in the Border and the South leading the way. Among the smaller areas, large declines also occurred in those two regions, and the Midwest had a modest decline. But in the smaller metropolitan areas of the Northeast and West, segregation actually increased. Segregation within districts went down across the board, with the largest declines occurring in the South. But the declines in the Border and the Midwest are impressive; in fact, within-district segregation fell more in large metropolitan areas of the Midwest than in those of the Border states. These declines in within-district segregation were partially undone, however, by increases in disparities between districts in all regions except the Border. Surprisingly, though, metropolitan areas in the South still had the highest degree of within-district segregation in 2000, a result that contrasts with the regional averages based on all districts shown earlier in table 2.1.[34]

Segregation arising from disparities between districts was much more prevalent in the largest metropolitan areas of the Border, the Northeast, and the Midwest in 1970, and this feature in fact made the overall segregation in those areas higher than that of the fifteen largest Southern metropolitan areas. Such between-district segregation was less important in smaller metropolitan areas, because the latter simply had fewer districts and thus less opportunity for disparities to arise. The third component of segregation, associated with the tendency of private schools to have fewer nonwhites than public schools, had a comparatively minor role in explaining overall school segregation.

To see how these three components changed over the three decades, figures 2.3 and 2.4 graph them separately. The third part of figure 2.3 summarizes the thirty-year changes in metropolitan segregation, showing that a large decline in segregation brought about by desegregation within districts was partially offset by widening racial disparities between districts. The figure shows that these effects showed up in large and smaller metropolitan areas alike, with the smaller metropolitan areas showing larger increases in between-district segregation. Private school enrollment caused segregation to increase only slightly. Figure 2.4 compares changes by region, with large and smaller areas combined. These graphs reveal marked regional differences. Within-district segregation

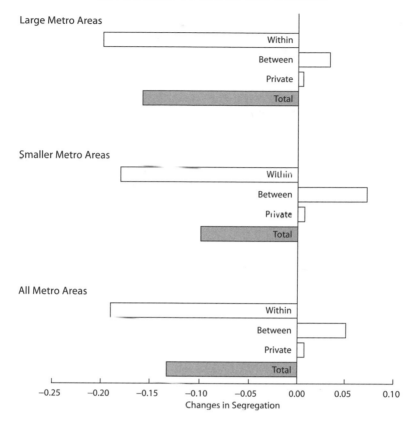

Figure 2.3. Changes in Components of Metropolitan Segregation in Large and Smaller Metropolitan Areas, 1970–2000

Source: table A2.3.

Notes: Districts with fewer than three hundred students were excluded from 1970 data and dropped from the 1999 data for comparison. For description methodology used in 1970, 2000 comparisons, see methodological appendix.

fell the most in the South, but, surprisingly, overall segregation actually fell slightly further in the Border, the only region where between-district segregation declined. In Washington, DC, for example, rising nonwhite enrollments in suburban Prince George's County had the effect of reducing between-district disparities. In all other regions, between-district disparities grew, thus increasing metropolitan segregation. The smallest declines in overall segregation occurred in the Northeast and the West, where between-district disparities offset a good portion of the within-district declines.

Thus large declines in within-district segregation were partially offset

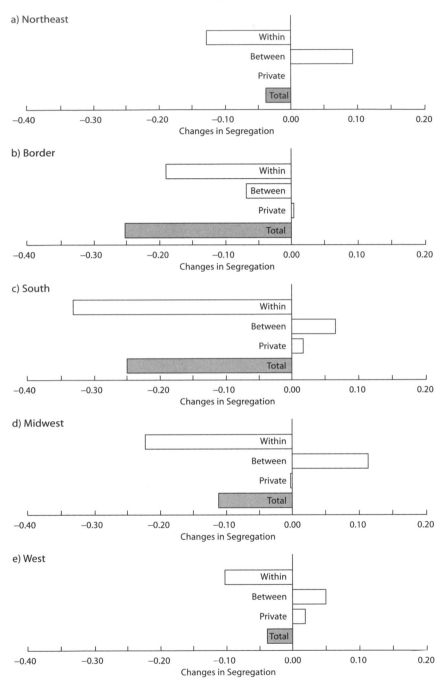

by increases in segregation between districts. These opposing and par-tially offsetting changes graphically illustrate the legacies of *Brown* and *Milliken*. By virtue of *Brown*, the succeeding Supreme Court decisions ordering the end to dual systems, and the federal government's enforce-ment efforts, segregation within districts declined markedly. But whites who wanted to cushion or avoid the effect of these actions had several means of doing so. The principal one was to seek out whiter suburban school districts. Because the *Milliken* decision virtually cut off any possi-bility that desegregation plans could cross jurisdictional lines, this resi-dential relocation had the effect of offsetting part of the increases in interracial contact brought about through the enforcement of *Brown*. Private schools had a further role in blunting *Brown*'s effect. Though in toto that effect was more than what is shown here, as is discussed in chapter 4, the role of private schools in this blunting was not a major one in most metropolitan areas.

INTERRACIAL CONTACT IN 1999–2000

Before discussing the ways in which segregation and interracial contact were affected by policy and household behavior, it may be instructive to describe the state of interracial contact in schools using somewhat more racial detail. In order to provide a brief summary of the extent of inter-racial contact in American schools, table 2.5 presents average exposure rates for non-Hispanic white, black, and Hispanic students, by region, as of the fall of 1999. Unlike virtually all of the calculated indices in pub-lished studies of school segregation, these indices include data on private schools as well as public schools. The exposure rates shown in the table divide nonwhites into three groups in order to provide more detail than is possible in the white-nonwhite division employed in most of this book. The table shows that the average white student in grades K–12 in 1999 attended a school that was 74 percent white, and thus 26 percent

---

Figure 2.4. Changes in Components of Metropolitan Segregation by Region, 1970 to 2000

Source: table A2.3.

Note: Districts with fewer than three hundred students were excluded from 1970 data and dropped from the 1999 data for comparison. For description methodology used in 1970, 2000 comparisons, see methodological appendix. Definitions of re-gions are given in the methodological appendix.

TABLE 2.5
Average Exposure Rates by Region 1999–2000

	A. Exposure of Whites to:			
Region	Whites	Blacks	Hispanics	Other nonwhites
Northeast	.804	.081	.070	.045
Border	.799	.131	.024	.039
South	.677	.178	.119	.026
Midwest	.865	.065	.040	.029
West	.648	.050	.207	.094
U.S.	.743	.104	.106	.046

	B. Exposure of Blacks to:			
Region	Whites	Blacks	Hispanics	Other nonwhites
Northeast	.481	.342	.138	.038
Border	.615	.308	.031	.043
South	.449	.397	.131	.022
Midwest	.596	.317	.050	.031
West	.445	.158	.295	.100
U.S.	.498	.309	.144	.046

	C. Exposure of Hispanics to:			
Region	Whites	Blacks	Hispanics	Other nonwhites
Northeast	.517	.182	.256	.045
Border	.681	.179	.079	.052
South	.518	.238	.215	.026
Midwest	.688	.114	.160	.034
West	.414	.066	.433	.087
U.S.	.543	.158	.249	.047

Sources: U.S. Department of Education, National Center for Education Statistics, (2001a); U.S. Department of Education, National Center for Education Statistics, (2001b); author's calculations.

Notes: Includes all schools (public and private) in metropolitan and nonmetropolitan areas. Districts in Alaska and Hawaii were excluded. Definitions of regions are given in the methodological appendix.

nonwhite. White students in the West were on average in schools with the lowest percentage of whites (65 percent), while those in the Midwest attended schools with the highest white percentage (87 percent). The average white student nationwide attended a school where Hispanic students comprised 10.6 percent of the student body, blacks comprised 10.4 percent, and other nonwhites, principally Asian Americans, comprised 4.6 percent. These exposure rates for white students varied markedly by region, with whites in the South on average attending schools with the highest percentages of black students and whites in the West attending schools with the highest percentages of Hispanics and other nonwhite students.

By contrast, black and Hispanic students tended to be in schools with smaller shares of whites. The average black student attended a school where only 50 percent of the students were white but 31 percent were black. Black students in the South were enrolled in schools with the highest black percentages in the nation, and those in the South and the West were in schools with the lowest percentages of whites. For Hispanic students, contact with white students was slightly higher, indicated by an exposure rate of 54 percent. Interestingly, Hispanic students were in schools with higher percentages of whites than were black students in every region except the West. Hispanics had higher exposure rates to blacks than did whites in all regions.

Part of these disparities in exposure rates arises naturally from the obvious fact that racial and ethnic groups are not distributed evenly across the country. The racial mix of the school-age population differed by region, state, locality, and neighborhood, as shown in table 2.6. For example, blacks were a larger share of students in the South (26 percent) than in any other region, whereas Hispanics and other nonwhites were most prevalent in the West. But the divergence in exposure rates was also driven by the tendency for students of different groups, even in local areas, to cluster in different schools. Thus, for example, although black students constituted about 19 percent of all students in Border schools, the average white student in that region was in a school that was just 13 percent black, as shown in table 2.5. The average Hispanic student in that region was in a school that was about 18 percent black, suggesting that blacks and whites were more segregated from each other than were blacks from Hispanics. Much of the attention in this book is devoted to the factors—demographic and policy-related—that determine these exposure rates and their change over time.

TABLE 2.6

School Enrollment by Race and Region, 1999–2000

	White		Black		Hispanic		Other nonwhite		Total	
Region	Number (000s)	Percent of region	Number (000s)	Percent of region	Number (000s)	Percent of region	Number (000s)	Percent of region	Number (000s)	Percent of region
Northeast	6,419	70.0	1,333	14.5	1,020	11.1	410	4.5	9,181	100.0
Border	2,790	73.6	721	18.9	108	2.9	178	4.7	3,797	100.0
South	8,609	57.1	3,892	25.8	2,207	14.6	370	2.5	15,079	100.0
Midwest	8,412	78.2	1,423	13.2	577	5.4	341	3.2	10,752	100.0
West	5,930	52.7	730	6.5	3,429	30.5	1,153	10.3	11,243	100.0
U.S.	32,161	64.3	8,099	16.2	7,341	14.7	2,452	4.8	50,052	100.0

Source: See table 2.5.

Notes: Includes all schools (public and private) in metropolitan and nonmetropolitan areas. Districts in Alaska and Hawaii were excluded. Definitions of regions are given in the methodological appendix.

Appendix to Chapter 2

TABLE A2.1
School Segregation of Blacks, 1940s, 1950s, and 1960s,
Survey of Black Americans

School Level	Region	Percentage of blacks who attended all-black schools		
		1940s	*1950s*	*1960s*
Elementary	Border	96	70	52
	South	96	93	75
	Rest of U.S.	33	30	31
Junior High	Border	91	65	51
	South	93	93	73
	Rest of U.S.	19	18	20
High School	Border	80	73	40
	South	93	89	69
	Rest of U.S.	18	11	17

School Level	Region	Estimated exposure rate of blacks to blacks		
		1940s	*1950s*	*1960s*
Elementary	Border	0.99	0.89	0.83
	South	0.99	0.98	0.88
	Rest of U.S.	0.61	0.62	0.69
Junior High	Border	0.97	0.82	0.82
	South	0.98	0.97	0.87
	Rest of U.S.	0.52	0.57	0.59
High School	Border	0.94	0.88	0.70
	South	0.97	0.96	0.83
	Rest of U.S.	0.46	0.50	0.53

Sources: Jackson and Neighbors (1997); author's calculations.
Note: Definitions of regions are given in the methodological appendix.

TABLE A2.2

Racial Isolation in 1965, from Coleman Report (Percentage white in the school of the typical black or white student)

	Elementary				Secondary			
	(1) Black	(2) White	(3) White*	(4) (3 − 1)	(5) Black	(6) White	(7) White*	(8) (7 − 5)
U.S.	16	87	76	60	24	91	83	59
Metropolitan								
Northeast	33	88	73	40	45	90	76	31
Midwest	23	90	87	64	45	91	88	43
South	3	89	80	77	3	95	91	88
Southwest	20	83	70	50	13	94	70	57
West	17	80	70	53	35	79	56	21
Nonmetropolitan North and								
West	54	89	76	22	76	94	84	8
South	10	89	77	67	11	93	91	80
Southwest	16	67	68	72	19	83	83	64

Source: Coleman et al. (1966, table 2.41.2, p. 185).

Note: Regions in the Coleman Report were defined as follows: North and West: all states not in the South and Southwest; South: Alabama, Arkansas, Florida, Georgia, Kentucky, Louisiana, Mississippi, North Carolina; Southwest: Arizona, New Mexico, Oklahoma, Texas; Northeast: Connecticut, Delaware, Maine, Massachusetts, New Hampshire, Rhode Island, Vermont; Midwest: Illinois, Indiana, Iowa, Kansas, Michigan, Minnesota, Missouri, Nebraska, North Dakota, Ohio, South Dakota, Wisconsin; West: Alaska, California, Colorado, Hawaii, Idaho, Montana, Nevada, Oregon, Utah, Washington, Wyoming.

*"Whites in areas with blacks"; weighted average of white-white exposure rate using as weights black enrollment in the metropolitan area or county. Referred to as (W(N)) in report.

TABLE A2.3
Changes in Components of Metropolitan Segregation, Large and Small Areas
by Region, 1970–2000

	Segregation			
	Within districts	Between districts	Public/private disparity	Total
Large metropolitan areas (N = 48)				
1970	.281	.228	.020	.528
2000	.082	.262	.026	.370
Change	−.198	.034	.006	−.158
Smaller metropolitan areas (N = 284)				
1970	.254	.103	.007	.364
2000	.075	.175	.016	.265
Change	−.180	.072	.008	−.099
All metropolitan areas (N = 332)				
1970	.269	.174	.015	.458
2000	.079	.225	.022	.326
Change	−.190	.051	.007	−.132
Northeast (N = 67)				
1970	.183	.201	.028	.411
2000	.055	.293	.028	.376
Change	−.127	.092	.000	−.035
Border (N = 22)				
1970	.265	.307	.015	.587
2000	.076	.239	.020	.335
Change	−.189	−.068	.005	−.252
South (N = 107)				
1970	.450	.092	.011	.553
2000	.118	.158	.028	.303
Change	−.333	.065	.017	−.250
Midwest (N = 78)				
1970	.280	.217	.014	.511
2000	.057	.328	.012	.397
Change	−.223	.112	−.002	−.114

TABLE A2.3 *Continued*

	Segregation			
	Within districts	Between districts	Public/private disparity	Total
West (N = 58)				
1970	.177	.109	.001	.287
2000	.075	.159	.019	.252
Change	−.103	.050	.018	−.035

Source: U.S. Bureau of the Census (1973); U.S. Department of Health, Education, and Welfare, Office for Civil Rights (1978); U.S. Department of Education, National Center for Education Statistics (2001a); U.S. Department of Education, National Center for Education Statistics, (2001b); author's calculations.

Note: Segregation indices, defined for metropolitan areas, are divided into three components: *within districts*, due to racial disparities within districts; *between districts*, due to disparities between districts; *public/private disparity*, due to disparity between public and private school enrollments. See methodological appendix for fuller explanation.

Sample consists of districts with 300 or more students.

Residential Segregation and "White Flight"

The extremely strong reactions of individual whites in
moving their children out of large districts engaged in rapid
desegregation suggests that in the long run the policies that
have been pursued will defeat the purpose of increasing
overall contact among races in schools.
James Coleman, 1975[1]

B Y ORDER OF a federal district court, the public schools of Louisville
and its surrounding county were merged in July 1975, and then, in September, desegregated. The desegregation plan ordered by the court called
for some eleven thousand black students to be transported from majority-black Louisville to schools in suburban Jefferson County and a like
number of whites to be sent in the opposite direction, making this one
of the nation's most extensive applications of "massive crosstown busing." Following two years of legal orders, appeals, and postponements,
the plan's eventual implementation was accompanied by protest rallies, a
boycott by whites, the burning of buses, physical violence, and the use of
tear gas by National Guard troops.[2]

When the dust of two years of turmoil finally settled and the schools
resumed routine operations, it was apparent that many white students
had left the consolidated Louisville system. Between the fall of 1973, just
before the first court order, and the fall of 1976, white enrollment in the
combined districts fell by more than twenty-three thousand, a decline of
21 percent. White enrollment in Jefferson County had actually begun to
decline in 1972, and then dropped at an accelerated rate after 1974, falling
at an average rate of 5.9 percent per year between 1974 and 1982 (see
figure 3.1).[3] Louisville was by no means unique in losing white students,
of course. Declining white enrollment was common to many large desegregating school districts during the period of large-scale desegregation
orders. Could these losses be attributed to desegregation, or did they
merely reflect the forces of urban decline and a falling birthrate? Would
these white losses ultimately undo the effort to desegregate schools by

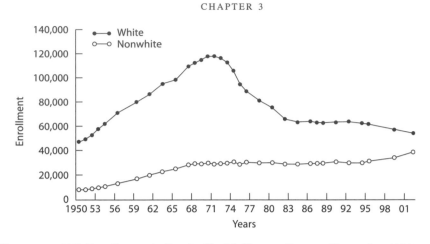

Figure 3.1. Fall Enrollment in Louisville / Jefferson County, Kentucky, 1950–2002

Sources: Kentucky Department of Education (various years); Thompson (1976, pp. 336–347); U.S. Department of Health, Education and Welfare, Office for Civil Rights (1969, 1970, 1978); U.S. Department of Education, Office for Civil Rights (n.d.); U.S. Department of Education, National Center for Education Statistics (2001a); Jefferson County Public Schools (2003); author's calculations.

Note: Unpublished data are adjusted for differences in grade coverage; see text.

resegregating urban school districts? Few questions bore more centrally on the efficacy of school desegregation as public policy than these.

A study completed in the same year as the Louisville school merger by the eminent sociologist James Coleman and two coauthors addressed these very questions, concluding that school desegregation had indeed led to significant declines in white enrollment from urban school districts.[4] There ensued a firestorm of debate over the issue of "white flight" and the efficacy of court-ordered school desegregation. Coming as it did from the author of the Coleman Report,[5] a massive federally funded study that had been used to bolster the case for racially mixed schools, and at a time when opposition to "forced busing" in cities such as Charlotte, Boston, and Pontiac, Michigan, made national headlines, the report not surprisingly touched off a lively policy debate.[6] This issue would remain the subject of intense scholarly research over the succeeding decades.

Besides the question of whether desegregation prompted whites to leave, a second, and more obvious, connection between racial patterns in schools and those in residential areas arises from the dependence of

school racial composition on residential housing patterns. Since pu
schools have traditionally been operated at the local level and have
drawn their students from within their jurisdictional boundaries, the
local population of school-age children in any district necessarily sets a
limit on the possibilities for interracial contact in that district's public
schools. Except for a few programs that permit students to transfer to
schools outside their home district and a few desegregation plans that
mandated interdistrict transfers,[7] this dependence on the district's own
population is nearly absolute, owing to the *Milliken* decision in 1974.
Thus the pattern of residential segregation takes on first-order importance in any study seeking to examine interracial contact in schools.
Even if interracial contact itself had no direct effects, the school segregation that arose from segregated residential patterns could influence the
level of resources available to various racial and ethnic groups if some
jurisdictions had more resources than others.[8]

From the outset the point must be emphasized that a host of factors
influence the location of households. That is to say, the landscapes of
American urban areas since the end of World War II have been marked
by a widespread and powerful suburban tilt. Between 1950 and 1970, the —
percentage of metropolitan area residents who lived outside central cities
increased from 42 percent to 54 percent.[9] Spurred by rising incomes,
improved highways, widespread automobile ownership, and new housing construction, thousands of middle-class families, most of them
white, headed for suburban jurisdictions. The "push" factors—taxes,
crime rates, an aging housing stock, and poverty—also had a hand in
fostering suburban growth. For interracial contact in schools, these considerations implied two things. First, schools could be no more integrated than the jurisdictions that contained them. To the extent that
these locational trends increased racial disparities among school districts
in metropolitan areas, increased segregation in the schools would be a
natural result. A second implication applied to the "white flight" question: to determine the effect of desegregation on white losses from city
school districts, it is necessary to account for the other possible reasons
why a district's white enrollment might be falling.

This chapter focuses on the connection between the racial patterns of
residential areas and those of schools. It begins by describing patterns of
racial segregation in urban areas, noting some of the forces that have
shaped these patterns. Next it turns to the "white flight" controversy and
social science research examining the effects of school desegregation.
Central to this second topic are white attitudes toward racially mixed

schools. A largely unstated hypothesis that underlies much of the relevant empirical research is what I will call the hypothesis of white avoidance—that, other things being equal, white parents prefer not to send their children to racially mixed schools and, among racially mixed schools, prefer those with the lowest proportions of nonwhite students. The chapter's second section refers to previous research and presents new evidence to test this hypothesis. Finally, the chapter considers the motivations that might underlie whites' avoidance of racially mixed public schools.

Patterns of Residential Segregation

If the history of de jure segregation of schools is the most important fact in understanding interracial contact in American schools, the second most important fact is residential segregation. America's neighborhoods are and have been highly segregated by race. Using census data showing the geographical distribution of the population across the neighborhoods of large cities, sociologists beginning in the 1940s used mathematical indices to document the extremely high degrees of segregation in the large urban areas of the country. The most prominent of these indices was the now common dissimilarity index, which measures the percentage of members of one racial group who would have to move in order for neighborhoods to be racially balanced, having a theoretical range from zero, indicating no segregation, to 1.0, indicating complete segregation.[10] A comprehensive study of residential segregation in U.S. cities illustrates the findings arising from this research. In their book *Negroes in Cities*, Karl and Alma Taeuber documented high levels of residential segregation in U.S. cities. Those in the South were the most segregated, but segregation was severe in all regions.[11] At the metropolitan level, a striking aspect of residential patterns in 1960 was the great preponderance of whites, and near absence of blacks, in the suburbs. Whereas blacks constituted 17 percent of central city residents, they were less than 5 percent of the suburban population.[12]

How this segregation arose was an instructive story that would become relevant to a host of urban policy issues. In the urban South, residential segregation had been enforced in some cities by local ordinance as well as by the customs of Jim Crow society.[13] Racial zoning was declared unconstitutional in 1917, but some cities continued to enforce it into the 1950s although the region's residential patterns often retained a "marble-cake" appearance in which relatively small but decidedly homogeneous white and black neighborhoods existed in close proximity.[14] By contrast, the metropolitan areas of the North were characterized by larger racially homogeneous districts. A great wave of black migration from the South to the large urban industrial centers of the Northeast and Midwest had occurred following World War I, and a second one had commenced following World War II. The number of blacks migrating from the South to the North increased from 197,000 between 1900 and 1910 to 525,000 and 877,000 in the following two decades.[15] Then in the 1950s the number rose to 1.5 million.[16] These migrants clustered in black ghettos in the central cities of these Northern metropolises. As blacks arrived, whites were displaced, spurring widespread white suburbanization.

Explicit discrimination helped to translate these demographic forces into segregated residential patterns. Racial discrimination by real estate agents and lenders, emboldened by the enforcement of restrictive covenants before 1948, but continuing well into the 1950s and 1960s at least, tended to enforce racially segregated residential patterns. So did outright intimidation. In 1956 the mayor of the Detroit suburb of Dearborn boasted that his city acted vigorously to keep blacks from moving in: "They can't get in here. We watch it. Every time we hear of a Negro moving in . . . we respond quicker than you do to a fire. That's generally known." By 1970 Dearborn was still nearly all-white, remaining one of fourteen Detroit suburbs, out of twenty-seven with populations of thirty-five thousand or more, that were less than 1 percent black.[17] Government policies, ranging from discriminatory lending practices of federal credit agencies to the practice in public housing authorities of avoiding racial integration, contributed to residential segregation as well.[18] When combined with the demographic pressure of growing black populations, constraints such as these led to a pattern of centralized and separated black concentrations in central cities surrounded by older white neighborhoods and newer white suburbs. Significantly, the growing black populations in some metropolitan areas soon began to fill up the central city jurisdictions, and the corresponding city school districts, the extent of the filling up depending on the relative size of these districts. By 1965, for example, the city school districts of Philadelphia, Detroit, and Cleveland had enrollments that were more than 90 percent black.[19]

In comparison to other minority groups, blacks experienced residential segregation to a most emphatic extent. The history of other immigrant groups reveals a general pattern of high initial rates of residential segregation, followed by a gradual lessening of segregation corresponding to the group's improved economic standing. For the black population, however, postwar economic advances did not bring any significant degree of residential integration. According to one study, less than 15 percent of the measured residential segregation of blacks in 1950 and 1960 could be attributed to their generally lower economic standing.[20] In contrast, improved economic status has over time tended to reduce the residential segregation of Hispanic and Asian households.[21]

The 1970 census marked a high-water mark for the residential segregation of blacks. After 1970, segregation between blacks and nonblacks began to decline, and this trend applied quite broadly by region and size of metropolitan area. This decline coincided with a brand-new phenomenon—the entrance of black residents into close-in suburbs, such as Prince George's County, outside of Washington, DC, and Inglewood, outside of Los Angeles.[22] This spilling out not only had a hand in reducing measured residential segregation, but it also led to significant increases in interracial contact in some suburban school districts. The decline also coincided with the passage of the 1968 Fair Housing Act, which outlawed racial discrimination in housing.[23] Combined with changes in federal housing policies, increasingly tolerant white attitudes, a growing black middle class, and a wave of new construction in growing areas, this new legal atmosphere allowed for a lessening of segregated residential patterns.[24] The 1970s saw residential segregation go down across the board, but levels of segregation remained high, especially in the largest and oldest metropolitan areas, and especially in the Midwest.[25]

Both trends—the suburbanization of blacks and the decline in overall segregation—continued into the 1980s. One study of 314 matched and consistently defined metropolitan areas showed that the percentage of blacks living in suburbs increased by five percentage points, from 27 percent in 1980 to 32 percent in 1990. Over the same period the share of whites in the suburbs increased by only two points, from 65 percent to 67 percent.[26] Measured segregation declined for the second decade in a row. One study found that the nation's average dissimilarity index fell by 11 percent over the decade of the 1970s and another 6 percent in the 1980s.[27] Consistent with the picture of spillover of blacks into suburbs, the continued decline in segregation was attributed to blacks moving into previously all-white or nearly all-white census tracts, not to whites moving into previously all-black tracts.[28] One study observed an interesting development in multiethnic metropolitan areas: black-white segregation tended to fall more in areas where the Asian American or Hispanic population grew rapidly, suggesting that these other minority groups might be acting as a "buffer" between blacks and whites.[29] During the 1980s the largest declines in segregation occurred in metropolitan areas that were newer, were growing most rapidly, and were in the South.[30] The 1990s saw a continuation in this decline in segregation, with the average dissimilarity index for the nation falling another 6 percent. By 2000, residential segregation was highest in the largest metropolitan areas and, by region, highest in the Midwest and lowest in the South.[31] During the 1990s segregation fell most in the South and West and in the most rapidly growing metropolitan areas.[32] Seemingly at odds with this steady decline in segregation at the level of the census tract was an increase in racial disparities among cities between 1970 and 1980 and a leveling-off between 1980 and 1990.[33]

THE EVIDENCE ON WHITE FLIGHT

To what extent did the process of desegregation itself cause white families to leave desegregating districts? This was an empirical question with considerable policy significance. "Flight" in this case did not require families to move from one district to another; it could be effectuated equally well if whites simply became less willing to move into a district.[34] Underlying the empirical work on this question was a maintained hypothesis about white preferences—the hypothesis of white avoidance. The grounds for such a preference are briefly discussed in the next section. To explore how this hypothesis manifested itself in the effect of school desegregation on residential choices of whites, researchers employed two kinds of data, one based on enrollments and the other on direct measures of residential location.

School Enrollment Data

Statistical research on the consequences of school desegregation was immeasurably aided by the collection of detailed data on the racial breakdown of school enrollments, collected for each public school in a large number of school districts. Undertaken by the Office for Civil Rights, originally in the Department of Health, Education, and Welfare, these detailed surveys covered most school years between 1968 and 1976 and for even-numbered years thereafter.[35] James Coleman, Sara Kelley, and

John Moore's 1975 study established a format that would be used as the starting point for most subsequent studies. Their model attempted to explain, statistically, the rate of change in a school district's white enrollment. Where white enrollments were declining, these changes would naturally be negative in sign. Knowing the rate of white decline left some questions unanswered, however. For one thing, the enrollment changes could not be linked exclusively to residential relocation; private school enrollment could also cause enrollment declines. In addition, demographic trends would affect white enrollment. Over the period covered by these analyses, the number of white students in the country peaked in the late 1960s and then declined by about 1 percent per year during the first half of the 1970s and 2 percent per year in the latter half.[36] In addition to these demographic trends were the forces, noted above, spurring suburbanization. Thus researchers realized that they could not equate every bit of a given enrollment decline with "flight." These considerations made it necessary to adopt an approach that would isolate those declines associated with desegregation. This was done by asking how the losses in a year of desegregation compared to the typical level of losses in other years, or to those that would have occurred in the absence of desegregation.

Coleman and his colleagues used annual enrollment data for fifty-seven large central city school districts over the period 1968–1973. To measure desegregation, they used the change in the segregation index (defined as in the present study, but using data for blacks and whites only). A desegregation order that increased the racial balance of schools would be reflected in a fall in that segregation index. If desegregation led to an unusual rate of white enrollment loss, the change in the index would have a positive coefficient in a regression, which indeed it did. Three other explanatory variables were added: the district's total enrollment, the percentage of students who were black, and a segregation index calculated between districts in the metropolitan area. The last of these was intended to reflect the availability of predominantly white suburban school districts; the existence of such white enclaves presumably would hasten white departure from a desegregating city district. By estimating a series of multiple regressions, the authors sought to determine whether desegregation itself was associated with white losses. They found that it was, with the effect being larger among the largest school districts.

Two studies were undertaken to reexamine the data used by Coleman, Kelly, and Moore. I undertook a reexamination of their study, introducing several modifications to their estimated equations.[37] One of these modifications was to replace their measure of desegregation (the change in the segregation index) with two alternatives based on the change in the exposure rate, reasoning that whites would care about the exposure rate—not the degree of racial balance—in deciding whether to leave or avoid a school district. Because the change in the exposure rate is itself a function of white losses, it could not be used as an explanatory variable without some modification.[38] I also added several explanatory variables, including a measure of the age distribution of the white population, a measure of white average income, and a measure of the geographical coverage of the central city school district. Finally, I made some changes in the sample, omitting observations affected by major annexations. Although these modifications resulted in a few differences, this reexamination generally supported the findings of Coleman et al. These new results implied, as did the original study, that desegregation was associated with losses of white students from school districts. They showed, in addition, that whites did not respond to increases in exposure in districts where the average white student would have attended (in the absence of white losses) a school that was less than about 7 percent black. This apparent nonlinearity could be part of the reason why Coleman et al. found a high rate of white response from the largest districts, where exposure rates were higher to begin with.

A more elaborate reassessment, by Reynolds Farley, Toni Richards, and Clarence Wurdock, employed a similar model but an expanded set of data and introduced an alternative method of assessing the impact of desegregation.[39] This study expanded the number of districts included to 104 and measured desegregation by the change in the dissimilarity index rather than the segregation index. This regression analysis yielded the same qualitative findings: losses accelerated when segregation declined, and then were greater out of districts with higher proportions of blacks and where white enclaves existed in the metropolitan area.[40] But this study suggested an alternative approach to assessing the effect of desegregation. This approach involved measuring deviations from a trend: how did white losses during the year of desegregation compare to those in the years before and after? By taking this approach, these researchers could distinguish the short-term effects of desegregation on white exit from the long-term effects. They concluded that desegregation's principal effect on white losses was short-term and that it had no effect on the rate of white loss in subsequent years. To be sure, these short-term effects could be significant, and they were permanent. For the average central city district undergoing desegregation, the extraordinary loss in the year of implementation was on the order of 2 to 4 percent. An important special category were countywide districts in the South, where suburban alternatives to desegregating districts were either nonexistent or not easily accessible. "Normal" white losses in these districts were quite small, although extraordinary losses in the year of desegregation averaged about 3 percent.[41]

Neither of these two studies sought to discover what aspects of desegregation whites objected to most. Instead, they measured desegregation by the change it brought about in the segregation index. It seems quite plausible that whites might care about aspects of the desegregating instrument employed—whether their children would be bused or assigned to previously minority schools, for example. As an illustration of the potential significance of such features, one study of Los Angeles revealed that parents whose children were assigned to distant schools were more likely to withdraw their children from the public schools than parents whose children were assigned to close-by desegregated schools.[42]

To discover the effects of various kinds of policies, Finis Welch and Audrey Light examined the details of desegregation plans and compared the experience of districts subject to various types of plans. To determine the effect of those plans on white enrollment losses, they compared the loss in the year of implementation to the change that had been experienced up until two years before implementation.[43] Taking this historic trend in white enrollment to reflect forces of demography and suburbanization that would have been manifested in the absence of desegregation, they assumed that deviations from this trend were the result of white withdrawals resulting specifically from desegregation. This approach can be illustrated for the case of Wichita, whose major desegregation plan was adopted in 1971, which was accompanied by a 6.0 percent decline in white enrollment. In that white enrollments had previously been falling at a rate of 3.1 percent per year between 1968 and 1969, the departure from the trend was −2.9 percent. To be sure, this approach is not without its ambiguities, one of which is that the time pattern of desegregation was not everywhere the same. Whereas some districts underwent a single court order, others experienced several of them, making the comparison between years possibly problematic.

Table 3.1 summarizes the study's major finding regarding white enrollment losses. For this table, eighty-four plans implemented after the *Swann* decision were classified into seven categories based on their use of one or more of four techniques for modifying school assignments: pairing, rezoning, magnet schools, and other voluntary features such as ma-

TABLE 3.1

Average Change in Dissimilarity Index and Average Departure from Trend in White Enrollment by Type of Desegregation Plan, 1971 or After

	Number of plans included	One-year change in dissimilarity index	Departure from trend in white enrollment,[a] implementation year
Pairing	14	−.21	−4.8
Rezone/pairing	23	−.25	−8.7
Pairing/magnets	6	−.17	−8.7
Rezone	17	−.18	−3.1
Rezone/magnets	5	−.14	−0.5
Major voluntary	13	−.11	−1.2
Other voluntary	3	−.04	−3.6

Source: Welch and Light (1987, tables 19 and 19a, pp. 55, 57).

Note: Pairing refers to "pairing and clustering." For definitions of plan types, see Welch and Light (1987, pp. 23–28).

[a]Calculated as the difference between percentage change in white enrollment in indicated year or years and average percentage change two years before and earlier.

jority-to-minority transfers. Pairing (or pairing/clustering) involved reassignments between a pair or group of schools that usually involved grade restructuring. In Little Rock, for example, predominantly white K–6 schools were paired with predominantly black K–6 schools, each pairing yielding two racially balanced schools, one serving grades 1–3 and the other serving grades 4–6, with kindergarteners attending their respective neighborhood schools.[44] Of all the techniques used in desegregation plans, pairing tended to cause the biggest disruption in students' routines. Rezoning included all other alterations of student assignments, including changes in feeder patterns and the creation of subdistricts within school districts.[45] The study also identified plans that included magnet schools and plans that relied on voluntary transfers, such as majority-to-minority transfers, wherein students were allowed to move from a school in which they were in the majority to one in which they would be in the minority.

The table's second column compares the average decline in measured segregation for plans in each category. Plans that combined pairing with rezoning brought about the largest decline in the dissimilarity index, followed by plans with pairing only. Voluntary plans resulted in the smallest declines in measured segregation. The table's third column shows the greater-than-normal one-year loss of whites observed in the year the plan was implemented. The biggest losses were associated with plans that entailed pairing plus rezoning or magnet schools; white enrollments in those districts declined by an average of almost nine percentage points more than the district's trend had indicated in the implementation year. Included in these two categories were prominent desegregation orders in Boston and Louisville in 1975 that became emblematic of "forced busing" and white opposition to it.[46] Measurable but smaller reactions to desegregation were observed in simple pairing and rezoning plans. Of all the plan types, those combining rezoning with magnets and those characterized as major voluntary had the smallest associated white declines in the implementation year.

Another comprehensive study of the white flight question, by Christine Rossell and David Armor in 1996, examined, using regression analysis for a large sample of districts, the change in white enrollment over the period 1968 to 1991.[47] Echoing the approach taken in the previous study, which used each district's historic trend to account for other forces that might affect white enrollments, these researchers added an explanatory variable measuring the "normal" percentage change in whites in districts without desegregation plans.[48] Thus the remaining estimated effects indicated deviations from preestablished trends. Their main finding was that voluntary plans entailed much smaller losses of whites than did other types of desegregation plans, the largest losses being associated with mandatory plans. That is to say, the districts least likely to lose whites over this twenty-three-year period were those whose only desegregation plan was voluntary or that never had a plan at all.

Although it is important to distinguish the effects of various types of desegregation plans on white enrollment loses, a problem exists in interpreting findings such as these. To be valid measures of the effects on white losses, tests of this sort must assume that the type of desegregation plan ordered or employed was determined independently of anticipated white losses. But it seems quite possible that this assumption may often be unfounded. That is, voluntary plans may be chosen in cases where little difficulty is anticipated in achieving desegregation goals, and mandatory plans where logistics or racial tension make voluntary plans unworkable. If reasoning of this sort is used in selecting what type of plan to use, it should not be surprising that voluntary plans are associated with smaller white losses than mandatory plans.

Evidence on Residential Choices

Because it is based on enrollment data alone, the preceding research on white losses cannot distinguish residential relocation from other possible causes of white loss, including private schools and changes in the age structure of the population. Although it would be desirable to explore the direct connection between school desegregation and the residential choices of households, the required data simply are not available. It is possible, however, to examine the effect of desegregation on white residential choice by testing what might be viewed as a corollary to the hypothesis of white avoidance. The corollary hypothesis—one that must be true if desegregation has actually been a factor in where families decide to live—is simply that racially mixed schools are a less attractive neighborhood attribute than all- or predominantly white public schools, and that this preference will influence the housing demand of white households. This preference need not apply to all whites, but only to enough households to make a difference in residential housing markets.[49] In previously published research, I have proposed two tests of this hypothesis. In the remainder of this section, I discuss the first of these tests, new research based on the second of these tests, and a new third test.

The first test of the residential implications of white avoidance is to examine the effect of school racial composition on the demand by whites for owner-occupied houses. Given a relatively fixed supply of housing in the short run, a downward shift in demand will manifest itself as a decline in price, other things being equal. Thus if whites prefer to avoid racially mixed schools, desegregation will be accompanied by a decline in housing prices in areas served by such schools. To test this simple hypothesis, I examined changes in median home values and rents in predominantly white (90 percent or more) census tracts in the Atlanta metropolitan area between 1960 and 1970, a decade in which schools attended by the white children in those tracts went from being all-white to having a variety of racial compositions. To measure desegregation I used the percentage of blacks in the relevant public high school. Other explanatory variables included the racial composition of the tract's population, a measure of accessibility to areas of employment, and several measures of the age and quality of the housing stock. The estimated effect of the desegregation variable—change in percentage of the student body that was black in the local public high school(s)—was negative and statistically significant. The average increase in black percentage in the sample's high schools (13.6 percent) implied a decrease in housing value of between 6 percent and 7 percent.[50] To summarize its implication, this statistical test supports the hypothesis that whites' housing choices are influenced by school desegregation.

A more detailed study of housing demand examined the effects of school redistricting in Shaker Heights, an affluent, racially mixed suburb of Cleveland.[51] In the fall of 1987, four of the district's nine elementary schools were closed and attendance zones redrawn, leaving the remaining schools much closer to racial balance than had previously been the case, and causing many families to lose their neighborhood schools. A detailed analysis of house prices showed that houses affected in this way declined by about 10 percent. Increases in the nonwhite percentage of assigned schools had an independent but statistically insignificant negative effect on house prices.[52] The findings of this study suggest that aspects of desegregated schools other than racial composition—including the disruption of neighborhood attendance areas and measures of school quality—are important and may explain the apparent significance of school racial composition found in other studies.

Worth noting in the context of the urban real estate market is a study that reveals one mechanism through which these preferences regarding school racial composition may be effectively channeled into housing demand. Pairs of otherwise similar metropolitan areas were identified wherein one had schools that were desegregated on a metropolitanwide basis and the other featured fragmented districts and thus more segregated neighborhood schools. For each pair of metropolitan areas, real estate advertisements were compared. Ads in areas with segregated schools were much more likely to specify the names of schools than ads where metropolitan desegregation was the rule. And the schools that were named were almost always mostly white. This finding suggests that information about the racial composition of schools was much more important for home buyers where schools differed in racial mix.[53]

A second test of the hypothesis refines the supposed white aversion to racially mixed schools by assuming that white families with school-age children will seek to avoid mixed schools more than other white households. Before whites abandon altogether neighborhoods served by racially mixed schools, a prior effect of white aversion would be a process of rearrangement, whereby white families with more children move away from areas served by racially mixed schools. To test this form of the white-avoidance hypothesis, I estimated a series of regressions, pooling together census tract data for 1950, 1960, and 1970 from nine cities whose public schools honored different desegregation policies in the three census years and whose segregation indices could be calculated using unpublished data of the sort described in chapter 2. In the Southern cities in the sample, Charlotte, Dallas, Nashville, and Richmond, school racial compositions by law bore no relation to neighborhood racial mix in 1950 and 1960; in the Border districts, Kansas City and Louisville, they bore no relation only in 1950. For the other cities, Flint, Springfield, and Denver, as well as the Southern and Border cities in later years, schools were not segregated by law, but they were in most instances incompletely integrated. The variation across districts and over time in the policy of student assignment made it possible to separate statistically the influence of tract racial composition on the residential location of whites with children.

Lacking detailed information on attendance zones for individual schools, I used several alternative measures of the exposure rate in public schools served by each census tract. These estimated exposure rates were calculated from districtwide information on segregation and census information on the racial composition of the tract. For districts whose schools were not segregated by law, I assumed that white exposure to nonwhites in public schools would be higher the higher the tract's nonwhite percentage. If the white avoidance hypothesis is correct, one would expect the white population in a tract served by racially mixed schools to have fewer children on average than the white population living in tracts served by all-white schools, indicating that white families with children (more than other whites) would avoid tracts with exposure to nonwhites in schools. For two of the three estimates of exposure, estimated regressions were consistent with this kind of rearrangement among whites, although the magnitude of the effect was small and the results were by no means definitive.[54]

A third test of the hypothesis of white avoidance of racially mixed public schools examines the metropolitanwide ramifications of school desegregation. If whites prefer to live in areas served by all- or predominantly white schools, the geographic coverage of desegregated schools should affect the location decisions of whites. In particular, the residential choices of whites, and thus the location of new housing, should depend upon the extent of disparities in the racial composition of schools. For example, a metropolitan area where the dominant school district is surrounded by many suburban districts (call this the "fragmented" metropolitan area) should experience a different pattern of white residential demand than would a metropolitan area in which the dominant district covered a large share of city and suburban residential areas (call this "near-metropolitan coverage").

Combined with the tendency of central cities to have higher nonwhite shares than the suburbs, the *Milliken* decision's virtual prohibition of desegregation extending across school district boundaries meant that desegregation's geographic coverage would necessarily be conditioned by the geographic configuration of school districts existing prior to desegregation. Other things being the same, fragmented metropolitan areas should have witnessed whites choosing to live in white suburbs rather than in central cities, assuming the hypothesis of white avoidance of racially mixed schools is correct. On the other hand, whites would not have as strong a reason to seek out white residential enclaves in metropolitan areas characterized by near-metropolitan coverage of dominant school districts. In other words, near-metropolitan districts would be less likely to create the conditions for white flight.[55]

To test this implication of the white avoidance hypothesis as it applies to residential choice, I examined changes in residential segregation between 1970 and 2000. Residential segregation was measured by the dissimilarity index, based on the residential patterns of blacks and non-blacks by census tract. Previously research has shown that measured residential segregation declined in U.S. metropolitan areas during this period.[56] The implication suggested by the white avoidance hypothesis is that segregation tended to decline the most in metropolitan areas where school districts were the least fragmented. I devised two different measures to reflect the degree to which schools in 1970 were consolidated, or approximated a metropolitanwide school district. One was a Herfindahl index of school districts (*consolidation*), whose value achieved its highest point (1.0) where a metropolitan area was served by a single school district and approached zero in metropolitan areas with many school districts. The other measure was the share of the metropolitan area's white students contained in the area's primary district (*ccshare*). By the reasoning outlined above, higher values of these measures should be associated with larger declines in residential segregation. To reflect the other aspect of jurisdictional fragmentation—the existence of racial disparities among school districts—I devised three additional measures, all of which should be associated with increases, rather than decreases, in residential segregation. Two of these measure the existence of white enclaves (defined as districts with a nonwhite percentage 10 or more points below the metropolitan area's principal district for whites). One measures the size of these districts as a percentage of all metropolitan whites (*access1*), and the other measures it as a percent of the whites in the primary school district for whites (*access2*). The last measure of inter-district disparities (*pcndif*) is the difference in the nonwhite percentage of the principal school district for whites and all other school districts in the metropolitan area.

The effect of these measures of district consolidation and disparities on residential segregation was estimated in regression equations that si-multaneously controlled for the effects of other factors, including popu-lation size, population growth rate, and region.[57] Although not definitive, these regressions provide some support for the notion that white resi-dential location responds to the geographic configuration of school dis-tricts. The estimated effects of the measures of coverage *consolidation* and *ccshare* were negative and statistically significant at the 90 percent level, suggesting that metropolitan areas where the main district had near-metropolitan coverage had larger declines in residential segregation. As for the availability of white enclaves, only one of the three measures had a statistically significant effect (at the 90 percent level)—*access1*. This result implies that metropolitan areas where markedly whiter sub-urban districts existed in 1970 were less likely than others to see declines in residential segregation.

Taken together, the evidence discussed in this section lends support for the white avoidance hypothesis. It tends to support the notion that whites prefer to avoid racially mixed schools. Not only are changes in interracial contact in schools followed by abnormally large declines in white enrollment, white residential choices are affected by school deseg-regation in ways consistent with the white avoidance hypothesis. This conclusion regarding white avoidance in the context of schools is strik-ingly consistent with the view reached by Douglas Massey and Zoltan Hajnal in their study of historical trends in residential segregation: "Thus, over the past 90 years, segregation patterns in the United States have consistently evolved to satisfy one overriding principle—the mini-mization of white-black contact."[58]

WHAT UNDERLIES WHITE AVOIDANCE?

The evidence described in the previous section has to do with how the residential choices of white households are influenced by the racial com-position of local public schools. The bulk of the evidence is consistent with the hypothesis of white avoidance—that, other things being equal, whites prefer schools and classrooms that are all-white or predominantly white. This hypothesis comes up again in the next two chapters, in the context of private school enrollment and within-school segregation. Its validity as a description of white preferences is, not surprisingly, central to the ultimate success of policies to achieve the desegregation of schools. Before proceeding any further in the analysis of white avoidance behavior, it is useful to consider briefly what might lie beneath this apparent aversion. I begin by asking whether there is evidence more direct than that discussed above to suggest that race itself is important in the preferences of whites regarding schools. Finding that there is such evidence, I then turn to two possible explanations for these preferences.

If the racial composition of schools affects their desirability from the perspective of white parents, this preference should be most apparent in situations where parents can choose a school without having to bear the costs of relocation. This is precisely the situation created by many contemporary school choice plans, wherein parents are allowed to express a preference among a set of schools, usually subject to capacity or other constraints. If, under these circumstances, white parents tend to pick schools with higher percentages of white students, other things being equal, a presumption in favor of the white avoidance hypothesis is strengthened. Directly relevant to this question is a study done by Jeffrey Henig of the choices made by parents in Montgomery County, Maryland, in 1985 among magnet schools in the district. Henig found that white parents were more likely to seek transfers to schools with low proportions of nonwhite students. Nonwhite parents, by contrast, tended to pick schools with higher nonwhite percentages.[59] In a study of several choice plans in San Diego, Lorien Rice and Julian Betts similarly found that white parents tended to choose schools with higher white percentages than their current schools.[60] But unlike the patterns identified in Montgomery County, the San Diego study found that nonwhite parents also chose whiter schools, which also tended to be schools with higher achievement levels.

Other evidence on parental preferences can be found in patterns of parental choice in a plan introduced by the Charlotte-Mecklenburg school district in 2002 whereby parents could choose to send their children to any school within one of a number of specified zones within that district. Enrollments in the most sought-after schools were allowed to exceed the schools' intended capacities through the use of temporary classrooms, resulting in utilization rates that ranged from a low of 45 percent for the least popular school to a high of 120 percent for the most popular one. Unlike the studies of Montgomery County and San Diego, however, this measure of popularity reflected the choices of both black and white parents. Comparing these utilization rates to the schools' racial composition reveals that demand tended to be greater in schools with higher percentages of whites. The correlation between a school's percentage of students who were white and its utilization rate was 0.62 for elementary schools, 0.42 for middle schools, and 0.67 for high schools.[61] While this revealed preference for schools with higher white proportions is consistent with white avoidance of racially mixed schools, it is also consistent with a general preference for schools attended by whites, as observed in the San Diego study.

To explain the apparent preference by whites for schools with higher white proportions, two alternatives present themselves: first, assessments unrelated to race, and second, racial prejudice. As to the first, David Armor notes the lack of research evidence that desegregation boosts white achievement, adding, "While persons who are racially prejudiced would undoubtedly perceive greater harms arising from desegregation, unprejudiced white persons can oppose some forms of desegregation based on a legitimate viewpoint that the costs outweigh the benefits."[62] Where desegregation plans have required white students to be transported to formerly minority schools, white parents not unreasonably may have worried that those schools would have some of the same problems that have plagued many inner-city schools.[63] If schools with predominantly minority enrollments were older, had poorer facilities, or were in neighborhoods with high actual or perceived crime rates, then school racial composition would be associated with features of schools that could well cause anxiety among white parents who want for their children what one researcher called "a safe and orderly environment."[64]

It is quite clear that more than a few desegregation plans produced school environments that were, at least in the initial weeks, anything but safe and orderly. For example, after the schools of Montgomery, Alabama, were desegregated in 1970, its Murphy High School became predominantly black and numerous racial incidents were reported. A group of white students and their parents lodged an official complaint with the federal district judge, and the faculty requested federal marshals and armed guards to be posted at the school.[65] Likewise, a detailed ethnographic study of a high school in what appears to be Pontiac, Michigan, described a school environment enveloped with anxiety in the wake of desegregation in 1971. Students, especially white students, reported being pushed and annoyed by other students in the hallways. One-third of the white students surveyed reported avoiding school restrooms to avoid being hurt or bothered, and one-quarter said they avoided halls and stairways for the same reason.[66] Classrooms in that high school were also disrupted by behavior problems and teachers' efforts to combat them.[67] Of course, white students were not the only ones to experience this kind of racial turmoil, as black students assigned to previously all-white Charlestown High in Boston found out. They soon learned never to venture into the hallways or stairways alone.[68]

Indeed, a parent of any race did not have to ascribe to deep-seated racist beliefs to have misgivings about sending a child to a distant school in an unfamiliar neighborhood, particularly if that distant school lacked accustomed facilities or academic programs.[69] Even without the complication of a long bus ride, lack of familiarity breeds anxiety. Based on his study of choices in Montgomery County, Henig concludes: "Both whites and minorities seem to direct their choices toward schools in which their children will be less likely to be racially or socioeconomically isolated. Cultural familiarity is a strong point of attraction."[70] Garth Taylor offers a similar explanation for white opposition to busing in Boston during the 1970s. Although whites did not subscribe to a belief in white supremacy, he argues, they were "fearful of minority concentration," a fear that was made worse by the prospect of desegregation.[71]

Still, there is the ever-present possibility that behavior is being driven purely and simply by racial prejudice. Surveys strongly suggest that prejudice has declined steadily, so that only a very small percentage of whites, for example, express a preference for racially segregated public schools.[72] When asked what factors are important to them in selecting a school, white parents rarely mention a desire to have a racially homogeneous student body, although it is also evident to those who ask such questions that respondents tend to be very reluctant to give socially unacceptable answers to survey questions.[73] More likely than overt racism as a motivating factor is so-called modern racism, negative feelings whites may have toward blacks and other minority groups that are not expressed in stereotypical ways but which manifest themselves, for example, in opposition to busing.[74] Although this concept has been used to explain political attitudes rather than decisions related to school enrollment, the resonance of symbols related to desegregation seems highly relevant to such personal decisions. Consider this description, as rendered by social scientists, of the symbolism related to white opposition to school desegregation:

The mythology surrounding "busing" seems to describe the forced exposure of vulnerable little white children to quite hostile and dangerous black
environments. And the way in which "busing" is conventionally presented,
in the media or in informal communication, exacerbates the problem.
What is conjured up is the picture of a very young innocent wide-eyed
(usually blue-eyed as well) child, bravely trudging a block or two to the
school in his (more usually her) neighborhood. "Busing" involves placing
that innocent child in a far distant blackboard jungle, with switchblade
knives, stealing of lunch money, assaults in restrooms, and terror, far from
the parent's benevolent protection.[75]

The authors argue that symbols such as this are instrumental in influencing political views of voters, irrespective of the voters' direct involvement in the desegregation process. For those whose children are affected,
there is every reason to believe these symbols would be more salient. By
whatever term it is called, the predilection to fear the worst seems a
likely additional factor to add to the objective aspects associated with
desegregation to create real, not just symbolic, aversion to racially mixed
schools.

The School-Residence Nexus

This chapter considers two important connections between where families live and the interracial contact that occurs in public schools. First,
patterns of residential segregation powerfully constrain racial patterns in
schools. Owing to the legal stricture embodied in the *Milliken* decision,
the public school districts in a metropolitan area can have schools no
more similar in racial composition than are the school-age populations
living in those districts. Thus the between-district racial disparities highlighted in chapter 2 as one of the major sources of segregation are the
direct result of residential segregation. Furthermore, segregated residential patterns within school districts may bring about segregation in schools
if attendance boundaries are drawn in line with neighborhoods, a practice that has been typical in this country. Thus, patterns of residential
segregation powerfully shape patterns of school segregation.

   The attitude of law and policy toward this almost ironclad correspondence depends on whether the hand of government action can be
found in these residential patterns. The Supreme Court ruled in *Milliken*
that apparent de facto segregation in schools can become subject to judi-

ition only to the extent that state action could be shown to
ental in bringing such segregation about. The court's minor-
1974 decision argued that this requirement was too stringent,
sisting that in some instances the only way to bring about real
desegregation was to combine predominantly nonwhite central city districts with mostly white suburban districts. After *Milliken*, this latter
view received little attention because the point became effectively moot.

The second connection between residential location and schools goes
the other way: to what extent has school desegregation itself affected
people's choices about where to live? Extensive research has examined
this empirical question, and most of it supports the hypothesis of white
avoidance: white families evince apparent aversion to racially mixed
schools and take measures to avoid them where possible, especially when
nonwhite percentages in schools are high. This avoidance is easiest to
observe when whites enroll in private schools, which is the subject of the
next chapter. Of greater long-run importance, though more difficult to
observe, are residential shifts. Over time, as children age out of school,
new households form, families relocate to different metropolitan areas,
and developers choose the location of new developments, urban households adjust to a continually evolving residential equilibrium. Because
whites care about the racial composition of schools—in addition to
other aspects, to be sure—the spatial character of school racial mix affects where they live. In highly fragmented metropolitan areas where
central cities are surrounded by numerous and accessible suburban
school districts, the conditions are ripe for whites to seek refuge in white
enclaves. But where school districts are geographically large, escape is
more difficult. The combination of large districts and desegregation plans
that maintain racial balance makes the search for white enclaves a difficult undertaking. Thus the spatial design of desegregation has become a
determinant of urban residential segregation and, in turn, the prospects
for continued interracial contact in schools.

Appendix to Chapter 3

TABLE A3.1

Estimated Pooled Regressions Explaining Proportion of White Population
Fourteen or Younger, Nine Cities, 1950, 1960, and 1970

	(1)	(2)	(3)
E1	−.070		
	(2.1)		
E2		−.043	
		(2.2)	
E3			.027
			(0.9)
Percent nonwhite	.090	.097	.071
	(6.6)	(6.3)	(7.0)
Percent new housing units	.116	.116	.115
	(17.5)	(17.4)	(17.3)
Percent owner occupied	.107	.107	.106
	(14.5)	(14.4)	(14.4)
Miles from central housing district	.0032	.0034	.0034
	(3.3)	(3.5)	(3.5)
Year 1960	.029	.029	.028
	(8.0)	(7.9)	(7.4)
Year 1970	.005	.005	−.001
	(1.2)	(1.3)	(0.1)
Constant	.140	.140	.139
	(17.1)	(16.9)	(16.4)
R^2	.469	.469	.469

Sources: U.S. Bureau of the Census, Census of Population and Housing, Census Tract
Reports, 1950, 1960, and 1970 (Washington, DC: Government Printing Office, 1951,
1961, 1971), tables 1–3 (1950), tables P-1, P-2, and H-1 (1960), tables P1, P2, H1, H2
(1970); author's calculations.

Note: Dependent variable is percent of white population fourteen or younger. Observations are census tracts; N = 1,911. Regressions are weighted by white tract population. Outlier observations are omitted. All regressions employ city fixed effects. Cities
included were Charlotte, Dallas, Denver, Flint, Kansas City, Louisville, Nashville, Richmond, and Springfield. Numbers in parentheses are t-statistics. Variables reflecting exposure rates for whites in public schools are:

(*Table A3.1 note, cont.*)

E1 = (1 − S)n, where S is the segregation index for the district in corresponding year and n is tract percent nonwhite.

E2 = 0 in the South in 1950 and 1960 and in the Border in 1950; otherwise equal to n.

E3 = exposure rate of whites to nonwhites in the district in the corresponding year.

TABLE A3.2

Estimated Regressions Explaining Changes in Residential Segregation, 1970–2000

Equation	1	2	3	4	5
consolidation	−.075* (.040)				
ccshare		−.070* (.037)			
access1			.074* (.039)		
access2				.001 (.004)	
pcndif					−.022 (.043)
Growth	−2.440** (.704)	−2.433** (.704)	−2.388** (.707)	−2.513** (.717)	−2.593** (.716)
ln population	−.0020 (.0081)	−.0014 (.0080)	−.0020 (.0079)	.0047 (.0077)	.0065 (.0074)
South	.004 (.022)	.004 (.022)	.006 (.023)	−.011 (.023)	−.016 (.021)
Border	−.058** (.029)	−.058** (.029)	−.056* (.029)	−.061** (.029)	−.076** (.029)
West	−.149** (.025)	−.148** (.025)	−.148** (.025)	−.155** (.026)	−.160** (.025)
Midwest	−.049** (.021)	−.046** (.021)	−.047** (.021)	−.054** (.022)	−.056** (.021)
Constant	−.089 (.098)	−.088 (.099)	−.162* (.085)	−.183** (.087)	−.195** (.086)
R^2	.295	.295	.295	.281	.282

Sources: U.S. Bureau of the Census, (1973); U.S. Department of Health Education, and Welfare, Office for Civil Rights (1978); U.S. Department of Education, National Center for Education Statistics, (2001a); U.S. Department of Education, National Center for Education Statistics, (2001b); author's calculations.

Notes:

Data exclude districts with fewer than 300 students.

(*Table A3.2 notes, cont.*)

Dependent variable is change in index of dissimilarity between blacks and nonblacks, based on census tracts, using 1970 metropolitan area definitions for 1970 and 1990 definitions for 2000. Number of observations was 187; standard errors are shown in parentheses. * indicates coefficients that are statistically significant at the 90 percent level, **, at the 95 percent level.

Where metropolitan areas are defined using the 1990 area definitions and students include all public and private K–12 students of a given designation, explanatory variables are defined as follows:

consolidation $= \Sigma P_k^2$, where P_k is the percentage of metropolitan area enrollment residing in school district k in 1970;

ccshare = number of white students in district with the largest number of whites as a percentage of all white students in the metropolitan area, 1970;

access1 = *sum* W_k/W, where *sum* W_k is the sum of white enrollments in all districts for which the percentage white exceeded the percentage white in the district enrolling the largest number of whites by more than 10 percentage points and W is the total number of white students in the metropolitan area, 1970;

access2 = *sum* W_k/W_k^*, where W_k^* is the white enrollment in the district with the largest white enrollment, 1970;

pcndif = *pcn** − *pcnother*, where *pcn** is the nonwhite percentage in the district with the largest white enrollment and *pcnother* is the nonwhite percentage in all other districts in the metropolitan area, 1970;

growth = Exponential growth rate in metropolitan area population, 1970 to 2000, using 1990 metropolitan area definitions;

ln population = natural logarithm of 1970 metropolitan area population, using 1990 metropolitan area definitions.

Regional dummy variables are defined in the methodological appendix; Northeast is the omitted category.

Outliers in the census tract data were eliminated based on several criteria. Tracts were retained only if the percentage of the population that was nonwhite was less than 95 percent. If the total black male (female) population age fourteen or younger was greater than the total male (female) population age fourteen or older, then the tracts were eliminated due to the likely measurement error in these cases. Furthermore, tracts were eliminated if the total population was less than fifty. The regressions were weighted by the total white population in the tract.

99

The Private School Option

Even schools that considered themselves liberal took
refuge in the policy of "We'll accept any qualified
candidate who applies," and then sat passively when
no qualified Negroes turned up.
Charles Merrill, 1967[1]

PRIVATE SCHOOLS in America are a heterogeneous lot, as any close examination will demonstrate. As illustration, consider just three private schools. Derby Academy, a school in the Boston suburb of Hingham that was founded in 1784, enrolls students from prekindergarten to ninth grade. It describes itself as "a structured environment and a joyful place. Classrooms are well-ordered and teachers are nurturing. Expectations are clearly articulated and age-appropriate. Values are consistently upheld." Located on a twenty-seven-acre campus on the South Shore, the school completed a $5.1 million capital campaign in 2002, funding among other things a new theater and an endowment for faculty enrichment.[2] Some 1,200 miles to the South, a much more modestly endowed private school operated in Raymond, Mississippi, just outside of the capital city of Jackson. Central Hinds Academy, established in 1970, enrolls students from kindergarten to twelfth grade. Its Web site described its mission this way: "We seek to give every student a Christian centered education that is also based on good citizenship and patriotism. The aggressive extra-curricula and co-curricula programs allow us to nurture our young people and promote the benefits of good sportsmanship and fair play."[3] A third school, located in Denver, is Our Lady of Lourdes School, one of the nation's eight thousand Catholic schools. Enrolling students from kindergarten through eighth grade, it offered, according to its Web site, "a unique opportunity for personal and spiritual growth through Catholic education. . . . It is our goal to lead our students to an awareness of the possibilities in developing their God-given talents. We wish to teach them by example, in working together with their parents, of the strength in community and common goals."[4]

As three of the roughly twenty-seven thousand private elementary and secondary schools operating at the turn of the twenty-first century,[5] these schools were part of a long and honored tradition in American education. Not only did private schools predate public ones, they have retained a small but significant share of elementary and secondary school enrollment, accounting for about one-tenth of all K–12 students in 2000. As a group, private schools are different from public schools in their smaller average size, their ability to select who will attend, the large share of them that have a religious orientation, and their tendency to be both more affluent and whiter than neighboring public school districts. It is the last of these characteristics, of course, that makes private schools especially pertinent in studying interracial contact. The three private schools described above serve to illustrate the contrast in racial compositions that so often exists in contemporary American communities. In the fall of 1999, 93 percent of Derby Academy's 274 students were white. By comparison, just 73 percent of the public school students in the Boston metropolitan area were white. The racial contrast was even sharper in the case of Mississippi's Central Hinds Academy. Of its 414 students in the fall of 1999, all but one were white; this compared to a white share of 42 percent among all of the students attending public schools in surrounding Hinds County. Denver's Our Lady of Lourdes featured considerably more racial diversity, with just 81 percent of its students white; yet this share was above that of the Denver metropolitan area (66 percent white) and the Denver city district (24 percent white). Although it is common for private schools to be whiter than surrounding public schools, this is by no means the rule, particularly among Catholic schools. The Catholic schools in Denver, for example, ranged from 0 percent to 96 percent white in the fall of 1999.[6]

For the most part, however, American private schools have historically represented islands of whiteness in comparison to neighboring public school systems. Whether or not racial motives play a significant role in private school enrollment, private schools must be part of any complete assessment of interracial contact in schools. They are important, most obviously, because their student bodies are whiter, on average, than their public school counterparts, thus creating racial and economic gaps between public and private schools. Because of these differences, their very existence necessarily alters the makeup of the public schools. In addition, if the academic achievement of students is influenced by the characteristics of other students in their classrooms, or if private schools are simply more effective in teaching students, such enrollment spillovers will have real effects on the quality of public education. If these effects on achievement are important, an increase in private enrollments could widen the much-discussed racial achievement gap.[7] More generally, private schools and their distinctive racial makeup will be important to the extent that racial separation has any significant effects on students, including effects on racial prejudice or opportunities in the labor market. To this extent, any racial disparities arising from private schools have effects similar to those arising from disparities among public schools, but with the additional complication created by the religious orientation and other unique emphases featured in most private schools. Issues such as these, in addition to racial integration, are relevant to current debates over school choice and government-funded vouchers.

To assess the empirical importance of private schools in determining interracial contact, this chapter begins with a review of trends in private enrollment and evidence on interracial contact in private schools. It then considers the demand for private schools, including evidence that demand is stimulated by interracial contact in the public schools. Special attention is paid to the growth of private schooling in the South. The chapter then presents a decomposition of segregation that takes explicit account of segregation within the private school sector as well as the overall racial disparity between the public and private sectors. The chapter concludes by posing the question of whether private schools have actually exacerbated racial segregation.

TRENDS IN PRIVATE SCHOOL ENROLLMENT

The last four decades of the twentieth century witnessed two major trends in private school enrollment: a nationwide decline in Catholic parochial schools and a rise in non-Catholic private schools, particularly in the South. As a share of all private school enrollment, Catholic enrollments fell from more than 85 percent in 1960 to less than half by 2000. This decline in Catholic schooling was most pronounced in large cities, where central city schools saw much of their population base move to the suburbs. Whereas the number of Catholic high schools in the country fell 28 percent in the twenty-five years ending in 2000, for example, those in the largest cities declined by 36 percent.[8] By 2000, Catholic schools still represented an important segment of private enrollment, but nothing like the dominant share they constituted in 1960. Because Catholics and Catholic parochial schools have been concentrated in the Northeast and Midwest, the disappearance of Catholic schools led to a sharp decline in the overall private share of school enrollment in those regions. In contrast to those in the North, private schools in the relatively impoverished South had been slow to develop in the decades before 1954, but this began to change as white parents in numerous Southern communities turned to them in the wake of school desegregation orders. Soon after the *Brown* decision, private schools became a vehicle of escape in Virginia's "massive resistance" to desegregation, in which local officials closed public schools rather than integrate them. In Prince Edward County, whites organized private schools, obtaining financial support from public funds as well as nonprofit organizations.[9] Again in the years immediately following the Supreme Court's decisions in *Green* and *Alexander* in 1968 and 1969 that finally eliminated dual school systems in the Deep South, all-white "segregation academies" sprang up in Mississippi's cotton belt. Yet the regional move to private schools was much more widespread.

The regional trends in private school enrollment are shown in figure 4.1.[10] Between 1960 and 2000, the percentage of students in grades 1–12 enrolled in private schools in the Northeast fell from 21.8 percent to 13.1 percent. The decline in the Midwest, some six percentage points, was almost as large. The Border and West regions experienced much smaller decreases in the private share during the 1960s, and by 2000 the decline in the Border's private share had nearly been reversed. But the South's experience was distinctive. With relatively few Catholic schools, it began the period with a private share of only 5.0 percent. This share increased modestly during the 1960s, and then more rapidly during the 1970s, ending at 9.1 percent by 2000. By 2000 the rates of private enrollment across all the regions had converged remarkably in comparison to where they had stood in 1960. For the nation as a whole, private enrollment fell from 13.6 percent in 1960 to 9.8 percent in 1990, after which it rose again, to 10.3 percent in 2000.[11]

Table 4.1 provides a more detailed picture of private school enrollment for the 1999–2000 year, using detailed school-level data. Among the five regions, private enrollment was most common in the Northeast and lowest in the South and West.[12] The largest metropolitan areas in each region exhibited the highest rates of private enrollment, followed by the smaller metropolitan areas, with the lowest rates in counties outside of metropolitan areas. In every region, the percentage of students attending private schools in the large metropolitan areas was more than twice that of nonmetropolitan areas. Owing to our interest in interracial contact, enrollment by whites in private schools is particularly important.

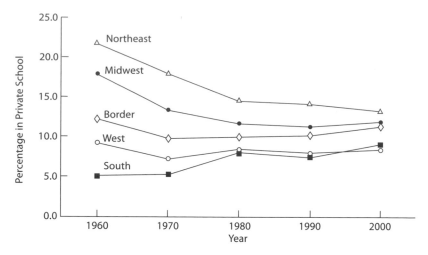

Figure 4.1. Percentage in Private School, Grades 1–12, by Region, 1960 to 2000

Source: U.S. Bureau of the Census. See table 4.1.

Note: Definitions of regions are given in the methodological appendix.

Using school-level enrollment data by race makes it possible to calculate the percentage of whites who attended private school, and this is shown by region in the last column of table 4.1. A striking aspect of this column is the similarity across regions it reveals. Except for the Northeast, whose rate of private school enrollment for whites was almost 20 percent, whites in the rest of the country enrolled at rates within a fairly narrow band around 14 percent. Thus, the rate for whites in the South was comparable to those in all regions except the Northeast.

These patterns in private enrollment have a direct bearing on interracial contact because private schools have been, and remain, whiter than public schools. In 1970, for example, 90 percent of the nation's private school students were white, compared to 80 percent in public schools. By 2000, the white percentage in private schools was 77 percent, compared to 62 percent in the public schools.[13] Such statistics are insufficient to describe interracial contact, of course: not only do the sizable regional differences in racial composition affect contact, but, more important, so does segregation between schools in regions and communities. Although they have not received as much attention as public schools in this connection, private schools have a role in these patterns of segregation. The question is, how big a role?

TABLE 4.1

Percentage of K–12 Students in Private School by Region and Metropolitan
Status, and Percentage of Whites in Private School by Region, 1999–2000

| Region | School enrollment (000s) | Percentage of students in private schools | | | | Percentage of whites in private schools |
		Large metro areas	Small metro areas	Nonmetro counties	All	
Northeast	9,169	17.4	11.7	7.9	13.8	19.9
Border	4,354	14.4	11.6	4.5	11.1	16.5
South	14,773	10.3	9.0	4.8	8.4	14.3
Midwest	10,491	14.7	11.7	6.7	11.3	13.8
West	11,265	9.7	6.7	3.9	8.1	12.5
U.S.	50,052	12.6	10.0	5.4	10.1	15.0

Sources: U.S. Department of Education, National Center for Education Statistics
(2001a); U.S. Department of Education, National Center for Education Statistics
(2001b); author's calculations.

Note: Large metropolitan areas are defined as those with K–12 enrollments of 200,000
or more in 1999–2000. Alaska and Hawaii are not included in West and U.S. totals.
Metropolitan area assigned to region on basis of largest county within area. Definitions
of regions are given in the methodological appendix.

INTERRACIAL CONTACT IN PRIVATE SCHOOLS

How much segregation is there *within* the private school sector? Has this
changed over time? Unfortunately, the kind of school-level data that
were used to measure segregation in the public schools is both rarer and
more recent for private schools, which is the reason this source of segregation could not be reflected in the comparison over time presented in
chapter 2. The best that can be done is to take two pieces of available
data to see if this form of segregation differed by region and if it increased or decreased over time. The only available sources of information on interracial contact in private schools as early as 1970 are found
in two surveys, one of Catholic schools and the other of independent
private schools. Data from these surveys were matched to similar tabulations constructed using a survey of private schools undertaken in 2000
in order to give at least a rough answer to these questions.

Table 4.2 summarizes the comparison of Catholic schools. Data on the

TABLE 4.2
Interracial Contact in Catholic Schools, 1970 and 2000

Region	Exposure of nonblacks to blacks		Percentage black		"Segregation" based on regional benchmark	
	1970	2000	1970	2000	1970	2000
	Elementary					
New England	.016	.045	2.7	6.9	0.40	0.35
Mideast	.027	.062	4.8	13.0	0.44	0.53
Great Lakes	.018	.028	4.8	8.2	0.64	0.66
Plains	.009	.017	1.9	3.0	0.53	0.43
Southeast	.040	.039	13.0	8.8	0.69	0.56
West/Far West	.035	.029	4.9	4.5	0.29	0.36
Total U.S.	.025	.038	4.9	8.4	—	—
	Secondary					
New England	.011	.038	1.2	4.4	0.04	0.13
Mideast	.030	.077	3.4	11.3	0.12	0.31
Great Lakes	.032	.057	4.2	8.1	0.24	0.30
Plains	.013	.026	1.4	3.3	0.06	0.21
Southeast	.049	.043	9.3	5.5	0.47	0.22
West/Far West	.029	.043	2.9	5.3	0.01	0.18
Total U.S.	.030	.054	3.7	7.5	—	—

Sources: National Catholic Education Association (1971); U.S. Department of Education, National Center for Education Statistics (2001b); author's calculations.

Note: Regions used in the 1970 report were defined as: New England—CT, MA, NH, RI, VT; Mideast—DE, DC, MD, NJ, NY, PA; Great Lakes—IL, IN, MI, OH, WI; Plains—IA, KS, MN, MO, NE, ND, SD; Southeast—AL, AR, FL, GA, KY, LA, MS, NC, SC, TN, VA, WV; West and Far West—AK, AZ, CA, CO, HI, ID, MT, NV, NM, OK, OR, TX, UT, WA, WY. Calculations for 2000 employed these regional definitions.

For 1970, calculations were based on black and nonblack enrollments given by five categories of racial composition.

racial composition of Catholic schools were collected in a survey conducted in the fall of 1970, where blacks were the only identified minority group. Schools were placed into one of five categories, by racial composition, making it possible to approximate the exact exposure rate of nonblack students (most of whom were white in 1970) to blacks in Catholic schools, by region.[14] The table shows that the average nonblack student in an elementary-level Catholic school in the United States in 1970 attended a school that was 2.5 percent black; in high schools the comparable figure was 3.0 percent. These exposure rates differed by region, being the lowest in the Plains and New England and highest in the Southeast.[15]

That these exposure rates were lower than the corresponding ones for public schools reflects, of course, the lower percentage of blacks attending Catholic schools. The new information that this 1970 survey reveals is the degree to which racial disparities existed among Catholic schools. Although one would like to know about disparities among Catholic schools in the same local areas, this information cannot be gleaned from the 1970 survey since its finest geographical detail was the region. It is possible to determine only, for example, that 13.0 percent of elementary Catholic school students in the Southeast were black, but the average nonblack attended a school in which only 4.0 percent of its students were black. This difference indicates that the racial compositions of schools differed within the region. Calculating the percentage gap between these two percentages gives a ratio similar to the segregation index introduced in previous chapters, but since it uses as its benchmark racial composition that of all schools in the region, that ratio is not the same as the segregation indices calculated for local areas, such as those presented in chapter 2. That said, the ratios shown in the last pair of columns indicates that racial disparities *among Catholic schools within regions* were greatest in the Southeast (a regional definition very close to the South region used in the present study).[16] Close behind for elementary schools, and a more distant second for secondary schools, was the Great Lakes region.[17] The smallest disparities were in the West and Far West region.

Between 1970 and 2000, within-region racial disparities in Catholic schools fell in the Southeast and increased in the Mideast, Great Lakes, and the West and Far West. By 2000, Catholic elementary schools remained far from being racially balanced within any of the regions. At the high school level, they were closer to being racially balanced. The calculations suggest, in summary, that some segregation existed by virtue of racial disparities among Catholic schools. To determine how much this source of segregation matters at the local level, calculations are presented below for 2000 using school-level data.

For non-Catholic schools, only rough nationwide tabulations are available to suggest how racial compositions changed over time. The National Association of Independent Schools, an association comprising about eight hundred of the country's oldest and best-endowed private schools, surveyed its members in 1969 to determine their racial mix. A matching tabulation for 2000 was made using information from the National Center for Education Statistics' Private School Universe, to see how much these private schools had changed over the three intervening decades. The percentage of schools with no blacks at all declined, from 13 to 5 percent, and the percentage where blacks attended but were 5 percent or less of all students also declined, from 67 to 52 percent.[18] These figures suggest that white students in these well-established private schools were experiencing low but rising levels of exposure to blacks over this period. Over the three decades, therefore, interracial contact was expanding, if modestly, in both Catholic and independent private schools. To determine the degree of contact in all private schools, it will be necessary to examine data for a single year, as is done below.

Demand for Private Schools and "White Flight"

In exploring the link between private schools and interracial contact, it is natural to ask whether race enters into households' enrollment decisions. Like many other goods and services purchased by households, private school education may be studied using economic models of demand. Chief among the standard variables used in such models are, of course, price and income. The services of private schools are seen as a "normal good," one whose demand rises with income, and empirical work strongly supports this notion.[19] Whether this income effect reflects the demand for more "units" of education or the wish to separate one's children in schools from those from lower income brackets is not a question the economics research can easily determine. Because similar motivations might also underlie a family's decision to move to a suburban school system, some of the published research on the subject seeks to model the demand for private schools as an alternative to "voting with feet," whereby households choose to live in the jurisdiction whose public schools and other public services best suit their preferences.[20] Building on this model, some research has shown that households are more likely to turn to private schools in metropolitan areas offering less choice, that is, with fewer school districts. The fewer public alternatives that exist, the reasoning goes, the more likely a household will not find the right level or variety of schools in the public sector and thus be motivated to choose a private school.[21]

Religious and other values-related considerations also appear to be important influences on the demand for private schools, although their effect is difficult to model. This much is suggested by the explanatory power of variables measuring the percentage of Catholics in a community and by a survey finding higher rates of private enrollment among families that are active participants in religious congregations.[22] The importance that religion and values in general have for demand is also suggested by the fact that more than three-quarters of private schools have some stated religious orientation.[23] As the continuing controversy surrounding prayer in school demonstrates, a large number of families—many from conservative religious traditions and many in the South—are unhappy with the absence of religious practice in public schools. It would be shortsighted to ignore the force of this dissatisfaction in explaining the continuing demand for private schools, especially in the South, where fundamentalist Christians are most prevalent.

The Race Factor

Still, one aspect of private school demand that is inseparable from the issue of interracial contact is the degree to which private enrollments may be motivated by the desire to avoid racially mixed public schools. Like residential moves to escape the effects of desegregation, this form of "white flight" tends to reduce interracial contact by moving white students from schools with higher to schools with lower nonwhite concentrations. As the examples of Virginia's "massive resistance" and Mississippi's "segregation academics" amply illustrate, some instances of private school growth were quite obviously a direct consequence of school desegregation. In Mississippi, private enrollments in the state nearly tripled in the wake of desegregation, rising from 23,181 in 1968, immediately before the *Green* decision, to 63,242 in 1970, immediately after *Alexander*. To be sure, some of the schools that sprang up in those years were short-lived, but most of the increase in private enrollment became permanent. By 1980, the state's private enrollment stood at 50,116.[24]

Another example of apparent "white flight" to private schools was that of Louisville, whose schools were desegregated in 1975 by means of extensive busing between the city and surrounding Jefferson County. The court order, announced in 1974, caused enrollments in Catholic schools to rebound from a seven-year decline, waiting lists at the city's two established independent private school to balloon, and a crop of new private schools to open their doors. Besides being almost exclusively all-white, most of these new schools shared three characteristics: with one exception, they taught fundamentalist Christian precepts;[25] they followed conservative, no-frills educational philosophies that eschewed the "new math" as well as evolution; and they offered only the most rudimentary physical facilities, most lacking both cafeterias and science labs.[26] When asked about the reasons for sending their children to one of these new private schools, most parents who were interviewed for one study cited desegregation and their concerns about its attendant effects on safety, discipline, and academic programs.[27]

Few of the published statistical studies of private school enrollment delve into the specific reasons that parents cite for choosing private schools, but a number of them do relate schooling choice to the racial composition of the public schools. For example, two empirical studies found racial mix in public schools to be statistically significant in explaining private school enrollment in Mississippi, a state whose public schools featured some of the highest nonwhite shares in the nation.[28] Another study examined private enrollment in Florida following desegregation in the early 1970s. Like Mississippi, Florida featured geographically large school districts, which made private schools a much more feasible means of avoiding the effects of desegregation than moving to another district. This study showed that whites were more likely to move their children to private schools the greater the increase in the black percentage in the public school to which their children were assigned. Economic wherewithal was also important, in that private enrollment rates rose with income. Prejudice, both racial and social, played a role as well, but was more potent in predicting whether a parent would *consider* the private school option than actually exercise it.[29]

Recent studies as well have found that the choice of private schools was significantly associated with the racial composition of public schools.[30] One such study examined enrollment changes associated with immigration, which usually involves students who are members of minority groups. In secondary schools (but not in elementary schools) the study found strong evidence of flight by native whites out of public schools in response to immigration: one white native student enrolled in private school for every four new immigrants entering the public schools.[31]

Tipping Points

A phenomenon first associated with rapid turnover in racially changing neighborhoods is the notion of a "tipping point," some racial threshold beyond which whites would rapidly exit the neighborhood. If the decisions of individual white families to stay in the neighborhood depended on its racial composition—each family having its own maximum acceptable nonwhite percentage—even a small change in racial mix could cause a chain reaction, if the nonwhite percentage exceeded the critical values of individual families, each of whose decision to leave would raise the nonwhite percentage, thus affecting the decisions of other white families. The racial composition at which this process of exodus begins is the tipping point.[32] In a study of the private school boom in Mississippi following desegregation, I found patterns of demand that corresponded to this characterization, with the white sensitivity to racial composition showing much greater intensity in counties with black percentages greater than about 55 percent. This white hypersensitivity in predominantly black counties in the state led to the virtual abandonment of the public schools by whites in some counties.

In light of these rather dramatic effects, it is more than a little interesting to know if behavior such as this, observed in the early 1970s, continued, and whether it applies to other states as well. These questions are addressed in figure 4.2 using data for nonmetropolitan counties in 1999–2000 for the state of Mississippi and the South region. Metropolitan counties are omitted because in them residential relocation may provide an alternative means of avoiding desegregated schools and thus do not provide as clear a test of the effect of racial composition on private enrollment.[33] Each panel in the figure plots the proportion of white students enrolled in private school against the proportion nonwhite among all the county's students.[34] Superimposed over each scatter diagram is an estimated regression line best fitting the data, each having a "kink" to reflect the nonlinearity of white behavior.[35] The racial compositions where these kinks occur can be interpreted as tipping points, beyond which whites react with heightened sensitivity to potential increases in racial composition in schools.

The first of the panels in the figure, for Mississippi, puts to rest any doubt about whether the patterns of white avoidance observed in the first years following desegregation might be temporary. They were not. A kink in private enrollment was evident at 0.48, or 48 percent, nonwhite, beyond which rates of white exit accelerated rapidly. Below that kink point, the proportion of whites in private schools tended to increase by a little less than 3 percentage points for every 10 percentage point increase in the county's nonwhite proportion. Above that point, however, the rate of increase jumped to 17.5 percentage points per 10-point rise in the nonwhite percentage. For a county where half of all students were nonwhite, about 17 percent of whites would be expected to enroll in private

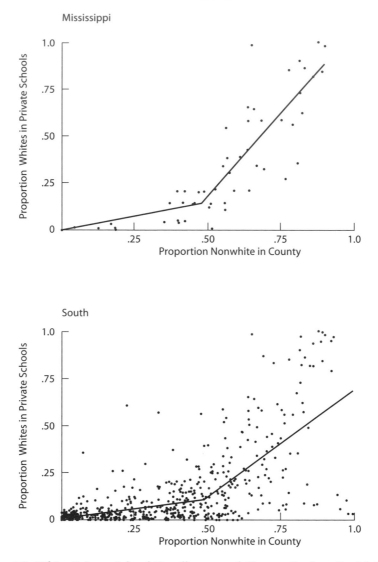

Figure 4.2. White Private School Enrollment and County Student Racial Composition, Nonmetropolitan Counties, 1999–2000

Source: U.S. Department of Education, National Center for Education Statistics (2001a); U.S. Department of Education, National Center for Education Statistics (2001b); author's calculations. See methodological appendix.

schools, but for one in which four-fifths were nonwhite, some 61 percent of whites would be expected to choose private schools. The other panel in the figure reveals that the white response to the share of nonwhites in school population over the whole nonmetropolitan South was very similar to that of Mississippi alone, showing a kink in the response at 49 percent nonwhite. In fact the pattern of white enrollment response in all nonmetropolitan areas in the country, not shown in the figure, could also be described by such a nonlinear reaction function, with a kink point at 51 percent nonwhite.[36] In nonmetropolitan counties, therefore, whites enrolled in private schools at rather modest rates in counties with white majorities. But in those counties where blacks and other nonwhites constituted large shares of the school-age population—and these were principally in the South—these private enrollment rates increased rapidly. It is worth adding that income also affected private school demand, with higher private enrollment rates in counties with larger shares of whites with high incomes.[37]

Especially striking were the counties where whites virtually abandoned the public schools altogether. In 1999–2000, private schools enrolled more than half of all white students in forty-one nonmetropolitan counties, twenty-nine of which are in Mississippi, Alabama, or Georgia. Many of them lie in the South's black belt counties that once used slave labor to cultivate cotton, and many were among the counties with the largest disparities in funding between schools for whites and blacks in the days of de jure segregation.[38] They were also the counties where social divisions in the Jim Crow era were most rigid and severely enforced. Sunflower County, Mississippi, the location of John Dollard's 1937 classic *Caste and Class in a Southern Town*, in 1999–2000 continued to operate largely separate schools for whites and blacks, wherein 73 percent of all whites attended private schools. A similar story applies to nearby Washington County, where 58 percent of the whites were in private schools in 1999–2000. That county's major town, Leland, was still largely segregated twenty years after the advent of school desegregation.[39] The most extreme examples of racial separation effected through private schools were ten counties in Alabama and Mississippi, where private schools claimed more than 90 percent of all white students.[40] In these and other Deep South counties with high proportions of blacks, where relations between the races historically were marked by separation and inequality, private schools became—and continue to be—the primary means of maintaining segregation in schools.

It is not unusual for patterns such as these to be characterized as "white flight," a term implying that private enrollment is fueled primarily by the desire of whites to escape or avoid racially mixed public schools. Though nowhere precisely defined, it seems fair to say that the term usually carries with it the suggestion that racial or racist motives constitute the primary motivation for the behavior in question—in this case enrolling in a private school. Is the term justified in this case? On the one hand, empirical analysis such as that shown here has demonstrated a statistical association between the racial composition of public schools rates of private enrollment, specifically the rates among whites. This relationship is not confined to the South or to nonmetropolitan areas. The fact is that whites are more likely to choose private schools where the public school alternatives have significant proportions of non-whites.[41] This said, the evidence is not inconsistent with alternative explanations, based for example on whites' antipathy for low-income students, for schools with poor resources, or for schools in high-crime neighborhoods, each of which is likely to be correlated to racial composition. In fact, one study of white private enrollment in Mississippi sought particularly to distinguish the effects of race and low income, finding that such enrollment was sensitive to the presence of low-income blacks in the public schools, but not to the presence of low-income whites or blacks in general.[42]

Casting further doubt on a simplistic racial motive for private school enrollment are the clear indications that parents seek and private schools provide other distinctive attributes not offered in public schools. Perhaps the most salient of these attributes is religious content and practice. Not only are the vast majority of private schools affiliated with religious organizations, a large number of them, especially outside the metropolitan areas of the North, satisfy a demand for religious orientation that was once, but is not longer, available in public schools. The continuing debate over prayer in the public schools testifies to the depth of feeling on this issue. On February 6, 2000, some fifteen thousand people gathered in the football stadium of the West Monroe High School Rebels in Monroe, Louisiana, for a "prayer rally" to protest efforts by the American Civil Liberties Union to challenge the tradition of public prayers before football games.[43] By their nature, private schools are in a position to offer such religious practices. That component of demand should not be ignored in assessing the extent to which racial motivations underlie the demand for private schools.

The South's Contrary Trend in Private Schooling

Both in and outside of its metropolitan areas, whites in the South turned to private schools in the wake of school desegregation, boosting private enrollments in that region over the same period the comparable share was falling in the North and West. Four main factors explain this divergent regional trend. First and most obvious was the dramatic change in the racial composition of public schools in the South. As documented in chapter 2, the schools in the South underwent a bigger transformation than those in any other region. A second and related factor was the large size of public school districts throughout most of the South. In contrast to the metropolitan areas of the North and Midwest, those in the South have far fewer districts. It may even be the case that the existence of de jure segregation in public schools decades ago encouraged Southern states to use counties, rather than towns and cities, as the basic organizing unit for public school administration, since whites needed no separate districts to achieve racially separate schools. For whatever reason, the large size of the districts in the South meant that, when desegregation came, whites seeking to avoid its effects typically did not have the option so widely available in the North and West, to move to a nearby predominantly white enclave. Thus private schools became the readiest avenue for exit. And in most districts outside metropolitan areas, private schools were the only alternative. The clearest indication of the link between desegregation and private enrollment in these nonmetropolitan areas is the finding that the rate at which whites enrolled in private schools tended to rise with the nonwhite percentage in the county, increasing markedly in counties with percentages of nonwhite students higher than 50 percent.

The third factor contributing to the South's divergent trend in private enrollment was the region's low proportion of Catholics. For reasons wholly unrelated to school desegregation, Catholic parochial school enrollment in the country has been declining since about 1960,[44] so that in regions of the country where those schools were the predominant form of private schools, private enrollments faced a declining trend to start with, a trend that affected the South to a much lesser extent.

A final reason for the South's increase in private enrollment was its economic integration into the national economy, bringing with it rising personal income and an influx of migrants from other regions. Whereas the region's per capita personal income was 72 percent of the national average in 1960, by 2000 it had risen to 91 percent.[45] These changes in turn led to an increase in demand for schooling and, specifically, private schooling. The South, in short, became more like the rest of the country. Middle-class whites, like their counterparts in other regions, demanded good schools and they often ascribed school quality to those schools having comparatively small shares of nonwhites.

Accounting for Private Schools in Measuring Segregation

Chapter 2 presents a method of decomposing school segregation into three parts. Missing from that decomposition, however, was a fourth component of segregation, attributable to racial disparities among private schools. To the extent that private schools of an area differ from one another in racial composition, the exposure of whites to nonwhites (the proportion nonwhite in the average white student's private school) will be less than it would have been if all private schools had identical racial composition. This gap, between the actual and maximum exposure rate in private schools, is the basis for the fourth component of segregation. Because school-level data for private schools were not available for 1970, only the overall public-private racial gap could be reflected in the indices used in comparing 1970 and 2000 segregation. In the present section, I employ 1999–2000 data on the racial composition of individual private schools to add that fourth component.[46] Thus school segregation for each metropolitan area is split up into four parts: (1) the portion due to racial disparities among the schools within public school districts; (2) the portion due to racial disparities between public school districts; (3) the portion due to racial disparities among individual private schools; and (4) the portion due to the difference between the racial composition of the public and private school populations. As in chapter 2, school districts are grouped by metropolitan area, using the same 1990 definitions for both years of data, and calculations based on metropolitan areas with total school enrollments of 200,000 or more are shown separately from smaller areas.[47] In addition, nonmetropolitan counties are analyzed in a parallel fashion, taking the county rather than the metropolitan area to be the relevant local area for analyzing segregation.

Segregation indices, divided into the four components, were calculated for 332 metropolitan areas.[48] The decomposition can easily be illustrated using the case of St. Louis. In 1999–2000, the exposure rate of whites to nonwhites in all schools in the St. Louis metropolitan area was

13.2 percent, whereas the percent nonwhite in the school population was 27.6 percent, yielding a relatively high segregation index of 0.522.[49] If, hypothetically, every public school district had balanced its schools so that all the schools in a district had the same racial composition, the exposure rate would have been higher, 14.3 percent. The difference between that rate and the actual 13.2 percent rate is due to disparities within districts. Imagining a second hypothetical step—to a situation in which the public schools in all districts were racially balanced at a single metropolitanwide percentage—yields a considerably higher calculated exposure rate of 25.6 percent. The difference between this rate and the first hypothetical rate of 14.3 percent is attributable to the fact that the various public school districts in the St. Louis area had different racial compositions, and no amount of racial balancing within those district boundaries could eliminate the segregation arising from those disparities between districts. A final hypothetical calculation assumes a situation not only of racial balance across all public schools, but also across all private schools, with each private school having a nonwhite share equal to that for all private schools taken together. This change increases the exposure rate a little, to 26.7 percent, and the difference is attributable to racial disparities among private schools. The fourth and final component of metropolitan segregation, the difference between that exposure rate and the nonwhite percentage among public and private students in the metropolitan area (27.6 percent) is the portion due to the gap between the public and private nonwhite percentages. These four components, each expressed as a ratio to the nonwhite percentage, yield the four components of segregation. The overall segregation index of .522 is split into the portion due to imbalance within districts (.040), that due to disparities between districts (.411), that due to racial disparities among private schools (.038), and that due to the overall racial disparity between public and private schools (.034).[50] Typical of the nation's biggest metropolitan areas, the largest part of St. Louis's segregation in 1999–2000 can be attributed to the differences in racial composition among public school districts—in St. Louis's case, between the largely black St. Louis City and East St. Louis districts and a host of predominantly white districts—while the contributions of the other three factors are each much smaller in magnitude.

Similar calculations were made for nonmetropolitan counties as well, where measured segregation is based on gaps within each county rather than within each metropolitan area. The calculations for nonmetropolitan counties were then aggregated to the state and regional levels by taking averages weighted by enrollment.[51] Because the notion of segregation itself is rooted in the existence of racial disparities among individual schools, the diversity, and therefore usually the size, of the geographical unit of observation will influence the degree of measured segregation. Thus large, diverse metropolitan areas will tend to have more segregation than smaller, more homogeneous ones. By the same token, less segregation is apt to be measured in individual counties than in metropolitan areas, which are usually composed of more than one county. But counties are the best and most natural unit for assessing segregation outside metropolitan areas; the next logical unit, the state, is clearly too large, since racial balance at the state level is an unrealistic and rather unappealing standard of comparison.[52] Because counties thus tend to cover smaller and less diverse geographical areas than metropolitan areas, one expects that between-district disparities will be less important in the nonmetropolitan counties.

To give a sense of the levels and decomposition of segregation, table 4.3 presents findings for eight selected metropolitan areas. Among the largest metropolitan areas shown, the most segregated one was Detroit. As was typical of the nation's most segregated metropolitan areas, the bulk of segregation in Detroit could be attributed to racial disparities between school districts, of which there were 109. Such interdistrict disparities accounted for 0.599 of the total 0.684 segregation index.[53] As can be seen by examining the third and fourth components of overall segregation, private schools contributed to segregation in all these cases, but their importance tended to be rather modest. Among the four large metropolitan areas shown in the table, private schools contributed the most to segregation in Washington (0.046 + 0.017), which also had the highest rate of private school enrollment among whites.

Segregation differed among the smaller metropolitan areas shown in the table as well, with Tuscaloosa, Alabama, having the highest index of the group and Chico, California, the lowest. Not surprisingly, these metropolitan areas had fewer districts on average, meaning that the contribution of disparities among districts was smaller than for the larger metropolitan areas. The district with the largest interdistrict component was Tuscaloosa. Although it had only two districts, those districts differed sharply in racial makeup: the county district was 24.8 percent nonwhite while the city district was 72.4 percent. The contribution of private schools to overall segregation ranged from 0.009 in Chico to 0.046 in Louisville.

To obtain an overall assessment of segregation patterns and partic-

TABLE 4.3

Illustrative Calculations for Eight Metropolitan Areas, 1999–2000

	Number of districts	Enrollment	Percent nonwhite	Percentage in private schools		Components of segregation				
				White	Nonwhite	Within districts	Between districts	Among private schools	Public/private disparity	Total
Large metropolitan areas										
Washington, DC	15	787,368	50.3	17.1	8.4	.088	.242	.046	.017	.393
Charlotte, NC	11	261,700	33.6	14.0	3.6	.132	.085	.018	.026	.261
Detroit, MI	109	837,347	31.5	12.3	8.0	.027	.599	.054	.004	.684
Denver, CO	18	361,744	34.1	9.8	5.4	.075	.255	.021	.006	.356
Smaller metropolitan areas										
Fort Wayne, IN	9	74,277	19.0	17.1	7.1	.129	.103	.025	.012	.269
Louisville, KY	12	182,831	21.3	24.1	3.8	.048	.107	.003	.043	.202
Wichita, KS	24	116,656	28.2	18.4	22.4	.059	.141	.132	.002	.334
Jackson, MS	12	96,555	50.8	41.5	5.1	.065	.305	.057	.188	.615

Sources: U.S. Department of Education, National Center for Education Statistics (2001a); U.S. Department of Education, National Center for Education Statistics, (2001b); author's calculations.

Notes: Components of segregation are: *within districts*, due to racial disparities within districts; *between districts*, due to racial disparities between districts; *among private schools*, due to segregation among private schools; *public/private disparity*, due to public-private racial disparity. See methodological appendix for fuller explanation.

Large metropolitan areas are defined as those with K–12 enrollments of 200,000 or more in 1999–2000.

TABLE 4.4

Components of Segregation by Region, Metropolitan and Nonmetropolitan Areas, 1999–2000

	Metropolitan areas Components of segregation					Nonmetropolitan counties Components of segregation				
	Within districts	Between districts	Among private schools	Public/ private disparity	Total	Within districts	Between districts	Among private schools	Public/ private disparity	Total
Northeast	.055	.294	.057	.028	.434	.011	.041	.019	.009	.081
Border	.076	.240	.031	.020	.366	.022	.023	.004	.009	.058
South	.117	.158	.025	.028	.328	.051	.029	.004	.053	.135
Midwest	.057	.329	.039	.012	.436	.014	.035	.006	.003	.058
West	.074	.159	.028	.019	.280	.025	.075	.005	.006	.111
U.S.	.079	.226	.036	.022	.362	.030	.038	.006	.023	.096

Sources: U.S. Department of Education, National Center for Education Statistics (2001a); U.S. Department of Education, National Center for Education Statistics, (2001b); author's calculations.

Note: For definition of components of segregation, see table 4.3. Definitions of regions are given in the methodological appendix.

ularly the contribution of private schools, table 4.4 summarizes school segregation for the nation by region and metropolitan status. For all metropolitan areas, the average gap-based segregation index was 0.362, of which 0.226, or 62 percent of the total, can be attributed to disparities among public school districts. Disparities between schools within districts was second in importance, accounting for 0.079, or 22 percent of the total. Contributing somewhat less was private enrollment: taken together, the disparity in average racial composition of public and private schools and differences among private schools accounted for 0.058, or about 16 percent of total segregation. Metropolitan areas in the Northeast showed the highest average level of segregation attributable to private schools, and the Northeast and Midwest showed the highest overall levels.

The table's right panel gives comparable figures for the nation's nonmetropolitan counties. The average segregation indices are considerably smaller than those for metro areas. It must be remembered that, in calculating segregation indices for nonmetropolitan areas, the racial composition of individual schools are compared to that of the county, whereas they are compared to that of the metropolitan area in calculating the metropolitan indices. Since nonmetropolitan counties are virtually always smaller and less racially diverse, it is not surprising that their calculated segregation indices tend to be smaller. Still, it is worth remarking on the low level of segregation within nonmetropolitan districts; for the nation, its average of 0.030 is less than half the already low 0.079 for metropolitan areas. Private schools accounted for about onefourth of nonmetropolitan segregation overall, but more than 40 percent in the South. These comparisons help to put in context the findings discussed earlier about private schools as a vehicle for white avoidance. In those relatively few counties in the South where blacks made up a very large share of the school population, private schools were used as the principal means by which whites avoided schools where their children might otherwise have been in the minority. Together with the generally large geographic size of districts in the South, which precluded in most places the alternative of nearby predominantly white districts, these factors made private schools a comparatively important part of school desegregation in the nonmetropolitan South.

To conclude this discussion of segregation and its decomposition, it is worth emphasizing that the segregation indices calculated in this chapter differ in two significant respects from conventional calculations based on segregation within districts: they include private schools, and they examine disparities within metropolitan areas or nonmetropolitan counties rather than just within school districts.

Do Private Schools Exacerbate Segregation?

Because private schools enroll whites at higher rates than nonwhites and students from high-income families at higher rates than those from less affluent families, it might appear to follow that the existence of private schools must necessarily increase the overall degree of racial and economic segregation in schools. As James Coleman, Thomas Hoffer, and Sally Kilgore point out in their study of private schools, however, disparities such as these are only one of two factors determining the effect of private schools on overall segregation.[54] The other depends on the extent of segregation *within* the private sector. It would be possible for the existence of private schools to decrease overall racial segregation, for instance, if private schools were less segregated than public schools and if this difference were large enough to offset the racial disparity in enrollment rates. Using data from the High School and Beyond survey, the authors in fact conclude that private schools had little impact on overall racial segregation in schools.[55]

To answer the question of how private schools affect school segregation, I use the reasoning of Coleman, Hoffer, and Kilgore but apply it slightly differently, and I use local areas for calculations since segregation is most appropriately calculated using local racial composition as the point of comparison. The slight modification is in the benchmark segregation index to be employed for comparison, used in place of the segregation index calculated for public schools. This benchmark segregation index was calculated for the enrollment pattern that would result if all private schools were closed and their white and nonwhite students were reassigned to public schools in proportion to the actual enrollments of whites and nonwhites, respectively, in those public schools. If the actual segregation in 1999–2000 exceeded this hypothetical level, then private schools can be said to have increased the overall level of segregation. Table 4.5 gives the results of this calculation. The table's second column presents enrollment-weighted averages for this hypothetical segregation rate. For each region, this benchmark segregation is below the actual segregation rate, demonstrating that segregation in schools would have been less severe if private schools had not existed. In contrast to the conclusion enunciated by Coleman, Hoffer, and Kilgore,

TABLE 4.5

Overall and Benchmark Segregation in K–12 Schools by Region, 1999–2000

Region	Segregation index	
	Overall	Benchmark
Northeast	0.309	0.283
Border	0.177	0.150
South	0.224	0.192
Midwest	0.250	0.240
West	0.240	0.229
U.S.	0.245	0.224

Sources: U.S. Department of Education, National Center for Education Statistics (2001a); U.S. Department of Education, National Center for Education Statistics, (2001b); author's calculations.

Notes: Benchmark segregation in public schools is a segregation index calculated for the hypothetical distribution in public schools if private school students were returned to public schools in proportion to each public school's enrollment. Enrollment totals for each region are those listed in table 4.1.

For definition of segregation index, see text and methodological appendix.

Definitions of regions are given in the methodological appendix.

therefore, private schools do appear to have contributed to racial segregation in K–12 schools, though their contribution is significantly less than that attributable to racial disparities among public school districts.

It should be remembered that such comparisons remain speculative to the extent that they depend on indices comparing actual enrollment patterns with hypothetical patterns. To the extent that those hypothetical patterns are unrealistic, the comparisons are unreliable. In the hypothetical closing of private schools, whites and nonwhites are assumed to return to public schools in proportion to the actual public enrollments by race. If, perhaps because of their greater average affluence, private school students were disproportionately likely to enroll in public schools with lower minority percentages, the benchmark segregation would understate the segregation that would obtain under the realistic counterfactual, thus making it less likely that private schools actually increase overall segregation.

Appendix to Chapter 4

TABLE A4.1

Percentage of Students in Private School, Grades 1–12, by Region, 1960–2000

	1960	1970	1980	1990	2000
Northeast	21.8	17.9	14.6	14.1	13.1
Border	12.1	9.7	9.9	10.1	11.3
South	5.0	5.2	7.8	7.5	9.1
Midwest	17.9	13.3	11.6	11.1	11.7
West	9.1	7.1	8.2	7.8	8.3
U.S.	13.6	11.0	10.5	9.8	10.3

Sources: 1960: U.S. Census Bureau, *Characteristics of the Population, United States Summary, Tables 105, 114 and 275* (Washington, DC: Government Printing Office, 1964); 1970: U.S. Census Bureau, *Characteristics of the Population, United States Summary, Table 154* (Washington, DC: Government Printing Office, 1973); 1980: U.S. Census Bureau, *Characteristics of the Population, United States Summary, Table 239* (Washington, DC: Government Printing Office, 1983); 1990: U.S. Census Bureau, *Characteristics of the Population, United States Summary, Table 147* (Washington, DC: Government Printing Office, 1993); 2000: U.S. Census Bureau, American Fact Finder, http://factfinder.census.gov/servlet/BasicFactsServlet, downloaded July 18, 2003.

Note: Definitions of regions are given in the methodological appendix.

TABLE A4.2

Estimated Regression Equations Explaining Proportion of White K–12
Students Enrolled in Private Schools, Nonmetropolitan Counties

Equation	1	2	3
Sample	Mississippi	South	U.S.
n	.29*	.20*	.15*
	(3.2)	(8.0)	(10.3)
n − Θ	1.46*	.94*	.83*
	(7.1)	(13.1)	(16.7)
Θ	.48	.49	.51
Pc50	.119	.315*	.268*
	(0.3)	(3.6)	(6.9)
Constant	−.016	−.032	−.004
	(0.3)	(2.6)	(0.8)
R^2	.822	.546	.390
N	74	849	2,381

Sources: U.S. Department of Education, National Center for Education Statistics
(2001a); U.S. Department of Education, National Center for Education Statistics
(2001b); author's calculations.

Note: Variables are defined as follows:

n = proportion nonwhite of all K–12 students in county

Θ = nonwhite proportion inflection point yielding best fit

n − Θ = 0 if n ≤ Θ; n − Θ if n > 0

Pc50 = proportion of white families with income $50,000 or more in 1989

Asterisks denote coefficients that are significant at the 95 percent level.

Inside Schools: Classrooms and School Activities

Even in the lunchroom you'll see it. You'll have a table of
African-American students over here and a table of white
students over there. It's not something you do to them;
it's something they do to themselves.
Georgia middle school teacher, c. 1990[1]

Even a cursory observation of most public schools will make clear
that a school's overall racial composition does not necessarily determine
the racial composition of the students in an individual classroom, a table
in the cafeteria, or a sports team. Consider the case of a middle school in
Winston-Salem, North Carolina. In the fall of 2000, 80 percent of the
students in this school's seventh-grade English classes were white, but its
individual seventh-grade English classes varied in racial composition
from 63 percent to 100 percent white. In another middle school in the
same district, where whites comprised only 41 percent of the seventh-
grade students, the English classes varied even more widely, with several
classes having no whites in them but one class being all-white. A third
school in another North Carolina district, a high school, was 27 percent
black in 2001. While blacks were overrepresented in advanced placement
(AP) calculus, with 40 percent of that class being black, they were underrepresented in AP biology (17 percent black), AP English (12 percent),
and AP history (10 percent).[2] Although such variation is not necessarily
typical of North Carolina or the nation, these three examples illustrate
the effect of classroom assignments that can create racial disparities
within schools.

Even greater disparities may exist outside of class. In many schools the
lunch period is the most segregated half-hour of the school day, with
racially mixed tables the rare exception. For example, one study of
a middle school in the Northeast included careful documentation of
lunchroom seating patterns over a two-year period in the mid-1970s.
Out of the 250 students usually in the cafeteria, on a typical day fewer
than fifteen sat next to a student of another race.[3] Even more pronounced patterns of segregation were observed in two newly desegre-

gated Florida high schools about the same time, extending to almost complete racial division between the two serving lines at one school.[4] And segregated cafeterias were also the rule in integrated suburban high schools in St. Louis during the 1990s.[5] Likewise, racial cleavages are often apparent in school-sponsored sports teams and clubs. Consider one Massachusetts high school. In the 1997–1998 school year 37 percent of its students were nonwhite. Yet it had two all-white sports teams (field hockey and indoor cross-country), four other all-white organizations (yearbook, Girls State, Interact Club, and drama club), and three organizations with no whites at all (Latin club, Latino-American Club, and Asian-American Club).[6]

In most schools, particularly middle and high schools, considerable latitude exists for racial disparities to exist across the smaller groups through which students pass each day. Because contact at this more personal level is crucial to many of the potential effects of integrated schools, it is important to consider interracial contact at the level of the classroom, the lunchroom, and the playing field. While some of this contact results from the decisions of students themselves, much of it is subject to the direct or indirect control of schools. Among the devices under the control of schools are academic tracking and ability grouping, policies that divide students in some academic subjects into separate classes offering instruction at different levels. If students in racial groups are disproportionately assigned to different tracks, interracial contact will necessarily be less than it would have been had assignments been random. The racial disparities that result from such assignments have in fact been one argument against tracking as a practice in schools.[7] Schools can also influence patterns of interracial contact through disciplinary practices, which affect who will be in school at all, and through the selections made in tryouts for athletic teams and performing arts groups. Extracurricular activities play a significant role in the high school experience, as illustrated by the fact that more than half of all high school students participate in athletic teams alone.[8]

The importance of segregation inside schools arises from two quite separate concerns. The first is its possible effect on academic achievement. For many of the same reasons why education experts have worried about the detrimental effects of segregated schools, a movement has arisen within education policy circles to reduce the role of ability tracking in schools. According to its opponents, tracking is bad policy because homogeneous grouping lacks educational merit, tracking assignments are often not made fairly, and those assignments are too inflexible. These opponents argue that any benefits to high-achieving students from homogeneous grouping are more than offset by harm to those students condemned to the lower ranks of the tracking hierarchy. Students assigned to lower tracks not only lose contact with high-achieving students, they are also more likely to be taught by teachers with little or no training in the subjects they are teaching.[9] Tracking is doubly distasteful when administrators make assignments in a discriminatory manner, a point to which I return below. And because in practice track assignments become tantamount to permanent placements, critics assert, students who start off in a low track are effectively condemned to slower classes, less stimulating peers, and more constrained opportunities beyond graduation.[10] But tracking also has its proponents, who argue that it has value as an educational policy and is not merely one way to discriminate by race or class.[11]

These were the issues at stake in a legal challenge brought against the Rockford, Illinois, school district in the 1990s. In this decision, a federal court ruled that the district had used academic tracking to segregate its students by race. Not only had the district used racially biased methods in assigning students to tracks, it had among other things also devised a pull-out program for minority students so that they attended "separate classes for significant portions of the day."[12]

A second reason for the importance attached to segregation within schools is its potential damage to racial attitudes and acceptance. A question of long-standing interest has been the extent to which interracial contact may lead to more tolerant racial attitudes. The classic presentation of contact theory, and the conditions under which contact can lead to reduced prejudice, is given by Gordon Allport in his 1954 book, *The Nature of Prejudice.*[13] According to this theory, contact between racial groups can lead to reduced prejudice if the contact is prolonged, if it is between equals who are pursuing a common goal, and if it is sanctioned by authorities. Because it reduces interracial contact, segregation within schools can short-circuit this process by removing one of its preconditions. Yet it seems equally clear that contact is not a sufficient condition in this process of prejudice reduction. The way instruction is structured, for example, may also be a crucial factor. One study of middle schools reports more interracial friendship where schools used an instructional organization based on teams, as opposed to traditional structures based on individual performance.[14]

Interracial contact outside the classroom has as much or more potential to influence attitudes and induce cross-race friendships. The conditions established for the contact theory to work would appear to be met by active school-sponsored organizations, especially school teams. Those who have examined the role of extracurricular organizations in the personal development of adolescents appear to agree on the importance of interracial contact, though views diverge on exactly which social mechanisms are most important. From one perspective, extracurricular activities are valuable to the extent that they form a bridge to interracial friendships.[15] A contrasting perspective on the importance of contact in extracurricular organizations holds that the "weak ties" built in such groups are more important to interracial relations because of their role as a bridge between the largely homogeneous social circles of school. Not only are cross-race friendships relatively rare, their presence may jeopardize same-race friendships. Mere acquaintances have the virtue of linking otherwise separate groups.[16]

PATTERNS OF CLASSROOM SEGREGATION

That racial segregation has existed within many schools is hardly novel. Numerous studies have uncovered it, ranging from blatant racial separation to otherwise nondiscriminatory class assignment policies that produce racial disparities across classrooms. An example of blatant separation was schools in south Texas, which, in the years immediately before *Brown*, commonly placed Mexican American children in separate classrooms.[17] In 1963 Milwaukee was found to be doing the same thing to its black students, by placing them in entirely separate classrooms within otherwise predominantly white schools. Rapid growth in black enrollment had caused overcrowding in the district's black schools, leading school authorities to take this step.[18] Similar practices were employed by some Southern districts in the immediate aftermath of thoroughgoing desegregation in the late 1960s. In the fall of 1970 a group of six nonprofit organizations sent monitors to more than four hundred districts in the South to assess local school policies regarding interracial contact. Some districts in predominantly black counties, in an attempt to keep whites from being vastly outnumbered in any class, established minimum numbers or percentages of whites in assigning students to classrooms. In at least a few districts schools established classes that were completely segregated by race. Where classrooms contained both whites and blacks, they found some instances of strict segregation within those classrooms. In a few of these an actual physical barrier—a row of empty seats or movable chalkboards—enforced the separation; elsewhere it was imposed or self-imposed.[19]

But blatant tactics such as these were neither widespread nor long-lasting. In the South, the combination of desegregation and tracking produced immediate racial differentiation across classrooms. When track assignments were based on standardized tests, tracks ranging from college preparatory to vocational quickly became racially distinctive, with the lower tracks being completely or predominantly black, often with black teachers assigned to them.[20] An example of this phenomenon is Louisiana's Washington Parish, a district that began using standardized tests to group its white elementary students in 1953 but included blacks in this testing only after the black and white schools were combined in 1969. In the resulting assignments, whites predominated in the upper tracks, leaving the bottom tracks nearly all-black.[21] To be sure, not all districts practiced tracking. One urban district in the South, for example, explicitly discouraged tracking and forbade racially unrepresentative classrooms for periods of seventy-five minutes per day. This was, however, a majority-black district led by a majority-black school board.[22]

Tracking was by no means confined to the South. One study of tracking reports that its use increased in the urban North during the late 1950s, in the wake of Sputnik and the influx of blacks from the South and Hispanics from Puerto Rico and Mexico.[23] Another study, based on interviews with a sample of school officials, found that the use of tracking increased after court-ordered desegregation.[24] Other research found that tracking was used heavily in the Southwest in districts where Hispanics were numerous.[25] The example of Rockford, Illinois, noted above, is a particularly well documented case, since the federal court's findings of fact are part of the judicial record. In an attempt to comply with state desegregation mandates during the 1970s, that district "desegregated" some of its schools with high nonwhite percentages by establishing predominantly white gifted programs within them. One of these programs was established at Wilson Middle School in the fall of 1975. Whereas nonwhites had comprised 48 percent of enrolled students in the previous school year, they made up only 8 percent of the new gifted program in 1975.[26] Because the program used entirely separate classes, the federal court concluded that the district had effectively created "a school within a school" for white students.[27] About the same time, the U.S. Office for Civil Rights (OCR) undertook a detailed investigation of the New York City public schools, looking in part for evidence of within-school segregation. The resulting report found segregation in classroom assignments in about one-fifth of the thousand schools in the system.[28]

Indeed, routine policies of academic tracking tend to segregate students within schools by producing classrooms with different racial compositions. These differences arise not only because the percentage of students eligible by objective placement criteria may differ among racial groups, but also because of the effect of discriminatory placements and parental pressure. In its study of New York City cited above, the OCR reported that it could find no rationale for classroom assignments in one-quarter of the approximately two hundred New York City schools cited for segregated classroom assignments. In the remainder, the report said, "criteria to place minority students in low-ability groups are often both vague and subjective."[29] Another study of placements into ninth-grade honors English classes revealed that, holding constant achievement test scores and previous placements, students in higher socioeconomic groups were more likely to be placed in honors classes. As evidence of racial bias, black and Hispanic students were less likely to be so placed, controlling for these other factors.[30] One force acting on classroom and track assignments was parental pressure: schools might yield to pressure exerted by middle class parents to give their children favorable placement.[31] Even where students of different abilities shared the same classrooms, interracial contact could be affected by ability grouping within classrooms. A detailed study of teaching methods and classroom dynamics in one desegregated middle school showed, for example, that the use of homogeneous ability grouping as a classroom instructional method reduced opportunities for interracial contact.[32]

What do these patterns of classroom segregation imply for overall rates of interracial contact? The first study to measure the extent of classroom-level segregation in many schools was an analysis of enrollment patterns in 1976 by P. R. Morgan and James McPartland. Using information collected by means of questions added to the regular federal survey of public schools, they analyzed assignments in some forty-four thousand public schools. Each surveyed school provided information on the student enrollment in eighteen representative classrooms. The authors employed a gap-based segregation index very similar to that used in this book, where an index of 0 indicates that all classrooms in a school were racially balanced and an index of 1 indicates complete racial segregation within a school.[33] For the United States as a whole, they found a small degree of intraschool segregation in elementary schools, more in middle school grades, and the most in high schools. Average index values were 0.056 for elementary; 0.074 for middle schools, and 0.112 for high schools.[34]

Even for high schools, the patterns existing beneath this relatively low average index nevertheless included some rather noticeable disparities.

For example, the authors remark on the existence of predominantly black classrooms "even in schools where such classrooms are most improbable."[35] Among high schools that were 70–89 percent white, for example, more than 5 percent of the sampled classrooms had enrollments that were less than 10 percent white. This number of predominantly black classrooms is greater than what would be expected had students simply been distributed randomly.[36]

Two additional features of this study are worth noting. First, the authors found that schools in the combined South and Border region had the highest rates of within-school segregation, and the West had the lowest. The indices for the combined South and Border region were 0.068 for elementary, 0.094 for middle school, and 0.134 for high school, all of which are at least 20 percent higher than the national average. A second, and not unrelated, pattern uncovered in the study was that between segregation and the racial composition of schools. They found that classroom segregation rose with percent black in the school to a maximum and then fell in the schools with the highest black percentages, forming an inverted-U shape. The schools showing the highest rates of segregation were those between 30 and 60 percent black.[37]

In a more recent analysis of segregation within schools, Helen Ladd, Jacob Vigdor, and I used detailed administrative data on the racial composition of individual classrooms in North Carolina public schools.[38] Utilizing these classroom-level data, we calculated exposure rates of the kind used in previous chapters for students in grades 1, 4, 7, and 10.[39] Other than data and geographical coverage, the approach we used in this study differed in three ways from the study described above. Instead of using a sample of eighteen classrooms per school, we sampled every student's main classroom in grades 1 and 4, and every student's English class in grades 7 and 10. Second, we calculated segregation by comparing each classroom's interracial contact to the racial composition of the district, rather than to each school. This more comprehensive measure of segregation was then divided into two parts: the portion due to racial disparities within schools and the portion due to racial disparities between schools. Third, we divided students between white and nonwhite rather than black and white.

Figure 5.1 summarizes our main findings concerning average rates of segregation across all of North Carolina's 117 districts in 1994–1995 and 2000–2001. The length of each bar in the graph corresponds to the average rate of segregation for a grade in one of the two years. These bars reveal that segregation was generally low in the state, averaging 0.20

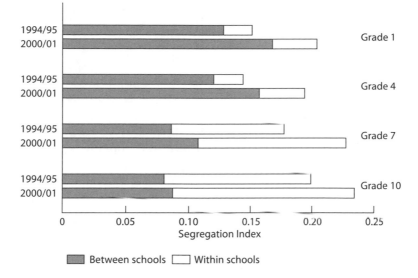

Figure 5.1. Segregation between Schools and within Schools in Four Grades, North Carolina Public Schools, 1994–1995 and 2000–2001
Sources: North Carolina Department of Public Instruction, North Carolina Education Research Data Center; Clotfelter, Ladd, and Vigdor (2003a).

in grades 1 and 4 in 2000–2001 and 0.23 in grades 7 and 10. The graphs also show that segregation rose in the state between 1994–1995 and 2000–2001 at every grade level, reflecting the trends noted in chapter 2 toward increased segregation during the 1990s. To show the relative importance of the two components of segregation, each bar shows the between- and within-school portions separately. In grades 1 and 4, within-school segregation was very low, indicating that the classrooms within schools tended to be almost completely balanced racially. In fact, the small degree of observed imbalance in the elementary grades was no more than what one would expect, had students in each school been *randomly* assigned to classrooms.[40] But in the upper grades within-school segregation was much higher: 0.12 in grade 7 and 0.15 in grade 10. Consistent with the findings based on the 1976 survey, this higher within-school segregation reflects the tendency for academic classes such as English to be split up by academic track and for those tracks to have different racial compositions.

Segregation between schools showed an opposite pattern—highest in elementary grades and lowest in tenth grade. This pattern reflects the greater racial disparities between elementary schools, caused by the larger number of elementary schools and their tendency to reflect racially seg-regated residential patterns. High schools, usually larger and serving larger geographic areas than elementary schools, tend to be more uni-form in racial composition within each district. To sum up, most seg-regation in elementary grades was due to disparities between schools, whereas most segregation in grades 7 and 10 was attributable to segrega-tion within schools.[41]

How important is within-school segregation compared to the between-district disparities found to be so important in examining segregation at the metropolitan level? Recall that, as demonstrated in the analysis pre-sented in chapter 2, disparities between districts generally contributed more to metropolitan segregation than did disparities between schools within districts. If North Carolina was typical of most states in this re-spect, within-school disparities were likely to be a significant factor in metropolitan segregation only at the middle and high school levels. To address this question directly for North Carolina, table 5.1 presents cal-culations for the public schools in all of the state's metropolitan areas in 2000–2001 and three of them separately. For these metropolitan areas, between-district disparities contributed relatively little to metropolitan segregation. In grades 7 and 10, in fact, such between-district disparities were on average less important than within-school disparities. The insig-nificance of between-district racial disparities in North Carolina arose from the generally small number of districts in most metropolitan areas. In fact, four of the state's eleven metropolitan areas in 2000–2001 were served by a single district.[42] The effect of having multiple districts is suggested by the heightened importance of the between-district compo-nent in Greensboro-Winston-Salem-High Point, the metropolitan area in the state with the largest number of school districts. To be sure, the seventeen districts in that metropolitan area was a far cry from the scores of districts in the large metropolises of the Northeast and Midwest. It will suffice to observe that, in North Carolina at least, within-school segregation played a minor role in elementary grades, but was relatively important in school segregation in upper grades.

How did classroom segregation in North Carolina in 2000—2001 compare to that uncovered in the national study based on 1976 patterns? To answer this question, I present calculations of segregation for North Carolina designed to be comparable to the earlier national study. Like the earlier study, these segregation indices were calculated separately for each school, by grade level, and students were grouped by white and black rather than white and nonwhite.[43] As shown in figure 5.2, both

TABLE 5.1

Public School Segregation in Metropolitan Areas of North Carolina, 2000–2001

	Grade			
	1	4	7	10
All metropolitan areas				
Within schools	.03	.04	.12	.14
Between schools	.18	.17	.13	.10
Between districts	.08	.08	.08	.06
Total	.29	.29	.33	.31
Charlotte-Gastonia (7 districts)				
Within schools	.03	.03	.12	.14
Between schools	.22	.20	.17	.13
Between districts	.09	.10	.10	.08
Total	.33	.33	.39	.35
Greensboro-Winston-Salem-High Point (11)				
Within schools	.02	.04	.11	.13
Between schools	.23	.22	.17	.15
Between districts	.16	.15	.14	.11
Total	.41	.41	.42	.39
Raleigh-Durham-Chapel Hill (7)				
Within schools	.03	.04	.15	.17
Between schools	.13	.12	.07	.06
Between districts	.07	.06	.08	.05
Total	.23	.23	.30	.29

Sources: Clotfelter, Ladd, and Vigdor (2003a, table 5, pp. 1496–1497).

studies show that segregation within schools tended to be highest in schools with larger percentages of black students, but only up to a point. In schools with few whites, segregation was lowest, corresponding to the findings discussed above. Both studies also indicate that within-school segregation tended to be higher in middle schools and high schools than elementary schools. Comparing the degree of segregation within schools, these findings suggest that North Carolina districts in 2000–2001 were more segregated than the national average in 1976–1977 in middle schools and high schools, but that segregation in elementary schools was low in both samples.

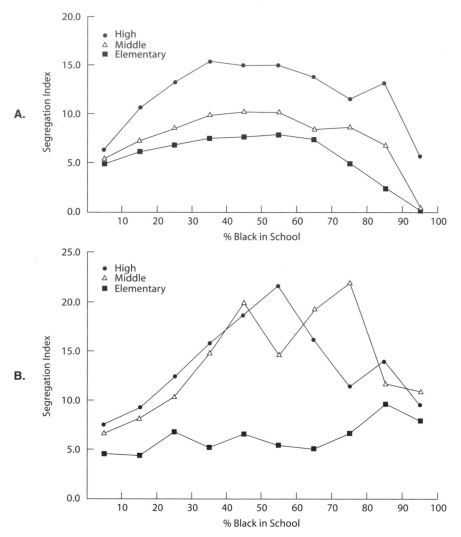

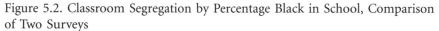

Figure 5.2. Classroom Segregation by Percentage Black in School, Comparison of Two Surveys

A. 1976–1977: Morgan and McPartland, U.S.

B. 2000–2001: North Carolina

Sources: Clotfelter, Ladd, and Vigdor (2003a); A: Morgan and McPartland (1981, table 4); B: North Carolina Department of Public Instruction, North Carolina Education Research Data Center; School Activity Report Data, 2000–2001; authors' calculations.

Note: Segregation index based on school-level data. See text.

Explaining Classroom Segregation

The foregoing makes clear that racial balance among the classrooms in public schools was by no means the rule, though many elementary schools came very close to it. In racially diverse public high schools, and to a lesser extent middle schools, classes typically differed in racial composition. Black students were generally less likely to be assigned to advanced or honors classes and more likely to be assigned to special education tracks for the mentally retarded than white students.[44] It is useful to consider why this is so. One possibility is that disparities such as these arose from the scrupulous adherence to a policy of ability grouping. However, the evidence does not support this hypothesis. Instead, it suggests that disparities arose from an imperfect, racially biased adherence to achievement criteria.

Evidence of racial discrimination in track assignments appears in various social science studies. I will cite three. In 1992 Adam Gamoran analyzed the placement of ninth graders into honors English classes in five Midwestern communities. He found that, holding both achievement scores and social class constant, minority students were less likely than whites to be assigned to the honors classes.[45] In a 1993 study, Jeannie Oakes showed that, controlling for achievement test scores, whites were more likely than Hispanics to be placed in an accelerated course. She obtained similar results for placement of students in a college preparatory course in ninth grade.[46] And, in a 2001 study of English placements in three Charlotte high schools, Roslyn Mickelson identified a pattern of preferences toward whites in advanced placement, International Baccalaureate, and academically gifted twelfth-grade English classes. Black students were consistently more likely to be placed in regular English classes, holding constant scores on a standardized language test.[47] These practices can result in starkly segregated classrooms. One middle school teacher in Johnson County, Georgia, described tracking in her school this way: "We track throughout. The upper social classes are found in the upper group. We have two influential black families, and both of their kids are in the upper group. You might have thirty kids and two will be black in the top group, and at the bottom you might have twenty-five kids and two of them white."[48]

To explain such assignment practices, one might naturally think of racial prejudice on the part of teachers and school administrators as a driving force. Indeed, there is some indirect evidence to support this view. One study of fifth-grade teachers in ninety-four schools across the country showed that ability grouping within classes was more often used in the South, by teachers who had negative views of the educational benefits of integration, and in classrooms with more blacks. However, ability grouping was also used more often by black teachers, controlling for other variables, making it impossible to make easy inferences about racial prejudice.[49] And such patterns are commonly observed outside the South, as a 1993 federal court decision regarding Yonkers, New York, illustrates.[50]

Another likely explanation for biased classroom and track assignments arises in interactions between parents and principals. Parents who want their children to be in advanced classes contact the school and lobby for their children to be so placed. Consistent with the middle school teacher's statement quoted above, sociological studies reveal that middle-class parents are more likely than parents with lower incomes not only to make such requests but to be successful in obtaining the desired placements.[51] Since many districts do not restrict their advanced classes on the basis of scores alone, such requests can often be granted without breaking any rules; yet the resulting assignment pattern can show the kind of bias revealed in the studies referred to above. The reasons that motivate parents to make such requests may be purely academic, or may have to do with keeping a child with her friends. Whatever the proximate reasons in the particular cases, however, the aggregate effect is to give higher socioeconomic-status parents—usually white or Asian American—disproportionate influence in determining assignments to tracks.[52] For their part, school administrators may see advantages in accommodating the wishes of high-status parents, since doing so enhances the chance of keeping them in the district, or, at the very least, reduces complaints and solidifies political support.[53] An illustration of this reason for tracking is the south Georgia school district of Calhoun County, which had a 70 percent black enrollment in 1995, but whose high school academic tracks were racially distinct. A federal investigation sought to determine whether discrimination contributed to this racial difference, causing several dozen white families to withdraw their children. One school board member remarked, "They're just abandoning the school. Before it's all over, we're probably going to lose some more. When you lose white kids, when you lose their families' support, it's going to hurt the school system."[54] Similarly, tracking in suburban high schools in St. Louis was found to minimize the potential opposition from white parents and students to a desegregation program that buses black students from the central city.[55] One study critical of academic tracking summarizes the calculus of school administrators this way: "School districts have been willing to trade off black access to equal education opportunities for continued white enrollments in the school system."[56]

CONTACT IN EXTRACURRICULAR ACTIVITIES

Schools provide many opportunities outside of classrooms for interracial contact—or segregation. Some of these, such as friendships and social cliques, are largely outside the ambit of school control. But schools typically do have some influence over extracurricular organizations and sports teams. In light of the importance that some psychologists have attached to participation in such school activities, it is important to examine the patterns of interracial contact in them. The racial significance of this dimension of school life is indicated by the frequent references to extracurricular activities in localized descriptions of school desegregation. A description of racial integration in the schools of Cincinnati right after World War II reported that one high school, where blacks made up about half of the students, had discontinued most social events altogether.[57] Similar stories emerged from the observation of newly desegregated Southern districts in the fall of 1970, with many of the observed schools sampled canceling school dances. Some attempted to accommodate both racial groups, for example, by racially balancing their student government bodies and their cheerleading squads.[58] Indeed, the phenomenon of racially separate school proms and homecoming courts was reported to be a widespread practice in some Georgia districts into the 1990s.[59]

But the authority of the school extends only so far, leaving the extent of interracial contact in extracurricular activities largely in the hands of students themselves.[60] One conspicuous manifestation of individual choices is the extent of racial segregation in the stands at school athletic events. A study of one desegregated high school in the Midwest in the mid-1970s reported that the stands at football games were racially segregated.[61] Another study of a Memphis high school about the same time reported that whites simply stopped attending football games following desegregation, as the school's football team became predominantly black.[62] The phenomenon of segregated stands remained in some places, including the football games in one Georgia community into the 1990s.[63]

Less visible, but more universal, school clubs and sports teams reveal the combined influence of official sanction, personal preference, and group cleavage. Case studies of desegregated schools, both North and South, reveal identifiable racial patterns, with blacks dominating such teams as basketball and football; whites, swimming and golf; and Hispanics, soccer and baseball.[64] To be sure, each school had its own history and peculiarities. In the Memphis high school that was the subject of one in-depth study, whites retained control of the student government and many clubs despite their dwindling proportion in the school, aided by the practice of holding meetings at night or away from school, which blacks could not easily attend. But there were exceptions. Although the yearbook staff and ROTC in this school remained all-white, for example, the chorus became a black activity and the band emerged as one of the only racially mixed extracurricular activities.[65] Interestingly, the study of a desegregated Midwestern school also found the school band to be, unlike other organizations, racially mixed.[66] Special-interest clubs hold potential for racial and ethnic differentiation. One study of a New York City high school found that most social clubs were explicitly oriented to particular racial and ethnic groups, the exception being student government and drama.[67]

To provide a more contemporary assessment of interracial contact in school activities, I examined school yearbooks for 193 high schools for the 1997–1998 school year, obtained from a publisher of yearbooks.[68] Table 5.2 presents a summary of the data collected for these high schools, divided by region and type of school. Not surprisingly, the public schools on average had larger average enrollments, but the average number of organizations did not clearly differ by size of school. Among the public high schools, those in the South had much higher percentages of black students than those elsewhere, although other nonwhites were more common outside the South, differences that were very much in line with aggregate enrollment statistics for the nation. These differences were reversed among the sampled private schools, although the relatively small number of private schools included in the sample may not be representative of private schools as a whole. Below the racial composition for schools is displayed the composition of school organizations. These data reveal that, on average, nonwhites participated proportionately less (based on numbers of members by race) than their white compatriots. For all the schools in the sample, the weighted average percentage nonwhite in organizations was 20.7 percent, somewhat less than the 24.9 percent share of nonwhites in total enrollment.[69]

The degree of interracial contact in school organizations depends on

TABLE 5.2
Means of Selected Variables by Region and Type of School

| | Non-South | | South | | |
	Private	Public	Private	Public	All
Number of schools	20	89	6	78	193
Means[a]					
School enrollment	704	1,419	825	1,275	973
Number of organizations	43	57	64	49	53
School racial composition (%)					
Black	10.3	6.4	3.4	31.8	17.5
Other nonwhite	8.0	8.8	8.0	5.8	7.4
Total nonwhite	18.3	15.2	11.4	37.6	24.9
Organizations' racial composition (%)					
Black	8.6	5.5	2.9	27.4	15.1
Other nonwhite	8.3	6.7	4.2	4.0	5.6
Total nonwhite	16.9	12.2	7.1	31.4	20.7
Underrepresentation of nonwhites in organizations[b]	−1.4	−3.0	−4.3	−6.2	−4.2

Source: Clotfelter (2002, table 1).
Notes:
[a]Means are weighted by school enrollment.
[b]Difference between nonwhite percentage in organizations and the nonwhite percentage in school.

three factors. First, the racial composition of a school's extracurricular organizations necessarily depends on the racial mix of the school. A school with no nonwhites can have no nonwhites in its teams and clubs, so there obviously can be no interracial contact. Second, interracial contact depends on the degree to which students of different racial and ethnic groups participate in extracurricular activities. If students of any group join organizations at a lower than average rate, the potential for interracial contact is necessarily lessened.[70] For the sample of 193 schools, nonwhites comprised a smaller share of the membership of organizations than they did of school enrollment (see table 5.2), confirming that, for this sample at least, the average rate of memberships per student was higher for white students than nonwhite students.

A third factor affecting interracial contact is the evenness with which students of the various groups are distributed across organizations. If a significant number of clubs or teams are composed entirely of students of one racial group, the potential for interracial contact obviously will be lessened. Indeed, an inspection of the yearbooks for these schools reveals that such homogeneous groups were by no means uncommon. Out of the entire sample of 8,849 organizations in 193 schools, 3,114 (or 35.1 percent) were exclusively white and 253 (or 2.9 percent) were exclusively nonwhite. Even if one looks only at high schools with nonwhite enrollments between 10 and 90 percent (covering 101 schools), fully 19.0 percent of the organizations were all-white, and another 3.6 percent were exclusively nonwhite.

In order to look more closely at aspects of interracial contact in school organizations, table 5.3 groups the 193 schools by racial composition. To examine the relative rates of membership between white and nonwhite students, column D shows the gap between the percentage of nonwhites enrolled and the percentage of nonwhites in school organizations. Whereas nonwhites were slightly overrepresented in organizations in the eighty-four most preponderantly white schools (those in the first two rows), they were underrepresented in schools with 10 percent or more nonwhites. Measured by the percentage point difference, this gap tended to rise with the percent nonwhite in the school; measured by the proportional difference between the two rates, however, the degree of underrepresentation neither increased nor decreased systematically.

Also of interest is the calculated exposure rate in organizations, shown in column E. This rate is calculated as in the previous chapter and is interpreted as the percentage nonwhite in the average white student's school organization. Two schools with the same overall racial mix in school organizations, for example, would have different exposure rates if all the organizations in one school had the same racial makeup while organizations in the other school differed in racial composition. In the extreme, a school whose organizations were entirely segregated by race would have an exposure rate of zero, meaning that the average white student was in an organization with no nonwhites and the average nonwhite student was in an organization with no whites. If school groups in each school all had the same racial composition, this exposure rate would equal the percentage nonwhite in all organizations (shown in column C). For all the organizations in the sample, the average exposure rate was 0.153, meaning that the average white member was in an organization that was 15.3 percent nonwhite. Of course, this exposure rate

TABLE 5.3
Interracial Contact in School Organizations by School Racial Composition

	A	B	C	D	E	F	G	H	I	J
		Percentage nonwhite					Average number		Percentage in organizations where they are in 25% or less minority	
Percentage nonwhite in school	Number of schools	School	All organizations	Under-representation of nonwhites[a]	Exposure rate to nonwhites	Membership segregation index[b]	Nonwhites exposed to whites	Whites exposed to nonwhites	Whites	Nonwhites
Less than 5%	55	3.0	3.7	0.7	.034	.081	1	28	0.0	92.7
5–10%	29	7.0	7.4	0.4	.063	.149	2	27	0.0	81.7
10–15%	19	11.6	9.9	−1.7	.080	.192	3	24	0.1	67.7
15–20%	11	17.4	14.8	−2.6	.114	.230	3	20	0.2	49.9
20–25%	14	21.9	15.3	−6.6	.124	.190	4	21	0.2	51.3
25–30%	9	27.1	23.3	−3.8	.174	.253	5	17	0.4	26.6
30–40%	14	34.7	24.5	−10.2	.188	.233	6	17	0.5	28.1
40–50%	15	45.0	36.6	−8.4	.259	.292	10	18	1.8	15.6
50–60%	13	56.1	43.4	−12.7	.293	.325	9	11	2.6	8.8
60% and more	14	80.9	69.6	−11.3	.510	.267	17	7	26.5	2.1
All	193	24.9	20.7	−4.2	.153	.261	5	21	2.7	53.5

Source: Clotfelter (2002, table 3).

Note: Means are weighted by school enrollment.

[a]Difference between the nonwhite percentage in organizations and the nonwhite percentage in school. A negative number indicates under-representation of nonwhites.

[b]100*(percent nonwhite − exposure rate)/percent nonwhite. See Clotfelter (2002).

differs across schools, tending to rise with the percentage nonwhite in the school

To summarize the gap between the exposure rate and the overall nonwhite percentage in organizations, a segregation index was calculated analogous to those used in previous chapters.[71] This measure ranges from zero, signifying racially balanced organizations, to 1, signifying that the school's organizations are completely segregated by race. Note that this is a measure of racial balance across a school's organizations, and is independent of the degree of over- or underrepresentation of nonwhites in organizations. A striking finding, shown in column F of the table, is the tendency for membership segregation to be higher in schools with higher percentages of nonwhites. For the whole sample, the actual degree of interracial exposure (15.3 percent nonwhite in the average white student's organization) is some 26 percent less than it would be if all school organizations within each school had the same racial composition (20.7 percent nonwhite). Combining the effect of this membership segregation with the lower rate of participation in organizations among minority students reveals an even larger gap between the degree of actual interracial contact in organizations and the rate that would exist if participation rates were equal *and* all organizations were racially balanced— about 39 percent ($100(0.249 - 0.153)/0.249)$).

Instead of looking at percentages, one might instead like to know the *number* of students from another racial group any student member is typically exposed to in school organizations. Columns G and H of table 5.3 give these averages. Based on the sample of yearbooks, white students who were members of school groups could expect on average to be in an organization with five nonwhites. By contrast, the average nonwhite member was in an organization with twenty-one whites. Not unexpectedly, the number of nonwhites for the average white increased with the school's overall nonwhite percentage, while the number of whites for the average nonwhite fell.

One other question of interest is whether students are in organizations in which they are significantly outnumbered by other racial groups. This situation would be uncommon if school organizations were characterized by "tipping points," thresholds beyond which members of one group will tend to abandon an organization.[72] In his study of a desegregating high school in Memphis during the 1970s, Thomas Collins reported that, except when they were starters, whites stopped participating on school teams when they were no longer in the majority on the team.[73] To see whether a phenomenon like this might be at work inside high schools, columns I and J of the table give the percentage of white and nonwhite members, respectively, who belong to an organization in which a student's own racial group is 25 percent or less of the total membership. Column I shows quite clearly that this situation almost never occurs for white high school students. Only about 3 percent of the white members were in organizations where whites were one-quarter or less of the group. For nonwhites, the experience was quite different: more than half of the nonwhite members were in groups where they were outnumbered by whites by at least three-to-one. Although these data do not prove there is a tipping point for whites in school organizations, they are consistent with the existence of one somewhere below 75 percent.

Half-Full or Half-Empty?

Over the course of a student's school day, interracial contact has more to do with conversations and encounters in hallways, classrooms, and after-school activities than it does with the school's overall racial composition. To be sure, the racial mix of the student body necessarily sets the bounds for what interracial contact is possible, but the details of contact within the school must be considered in any comprehensive assessment. This chapter investigates contact of two kinds—in classrooms and in extra-curricular activities. It omits extended reference to research on friendships, which is referred to below in chapter 7. Suffice it to say that empirical studies of racially diverse schools suggest that interracial friendships, especially close friendships, are relatively rare. For example, studies indicate that students are six to ten times more likely to name friends of the same race as friends of another race.[74]

In assessing what desegregation has meant for actual interracial contact, it must be acknowledged that school authorities have permitted a degree of segregation to arise across classrooms in most schools. This segregation is most pronounced in high schools and least so in elementary schools. Where it exists, it appears almost always to be associated with some form of academic tracking, by which classes of the same subject are differentiated by academic level. But research indicates that assignments to tracks tend to be racially biased, making classrooms more segregated than they would have been had assignments been made strictly on "objective" criteria. The evidence suggests that this bias results at least in part from the efforts by administrators to accommodate the wishes of middle-class parents to assign their children to more advanced classes. By isolating these children in what may be viewed as a "school within a school," officials may be hoping to keep these children and their parents from leaving their public schools. But these decisions come at a cost. Not only do these assignment practices reduce interracial contact in classrooms, they also tend to put minority students in classrooms with less experienced and less adequately trained teachers.[75]

Although they are much less under the control of school officials, extracurricular activities may also cushion the effect of desegregation on white students and their parents. By providing opportunities for student social interaction with relatively lower rates of interracial contact, sports and other extracurricular activities tend to complement the reduced interracial contact offered in classrooms. At the same time, they offer to nonwhite students meaningful opportunities for participation not subject to the dominance that may characterize some formal academic aspects of school. In these respects extracurricular activities are complementary with classroom assignments in reducing interracial contact below the levels that would exist if the school environment were racially balanced in its entirety.

Over against this actual and well-documented tendency for classrooms and activities to offer diminished interracial contact, it is important to consider an alternative benchmark. If, instead of racial balance within each school, the standard for comparisons were the level of interracial contact that exists for school-age children outside of school entirely, the judgment is quite different. Considering how rare friendships or neighborhood associations are across racial lines, the levels of interracial contact observed in classrooms, school clubs, and sports teams are impressively high.

Appendix to Chapter 5

TABLE A5.1
Between-School and Within-School Segregation in North Carolina,
2000–2001, Four Grades, Alternative Racial Groupings

	Grade			
	1	4	7	10
White-Nonwhite				
Between Schools	.17	.16	.11	.09
Within schools	.04	.04	.12	.15
Total	.20	.20	.23	.23
White-Black				
Between Schools	.19	.17	.12	.09
Within schools	.04	.05	.12	.13
Total	.22	.22	.24	.23
White-Hispanic				
Between Schools	.14	.10	.07	.05
Within schools	.06	.06	.18	.29
Total	.20	.16	.25	.33
Black-Hispanic				
Between Schools	.14	.10	.08	.05
Within schools	.09	.10	.21	.28
Total	.23	.20	.29	.32

Sources: Clotfelter, Ladd, and Vigdor (2002, table 4).

Higher Learning and the Color Line

A Negro university . . . does not advocate segregation by
race, it simply accepts the bald fact that we are segregated,
apart, hammered into a separate unity by spiritual
intolerance and legal sanction.
W.E.B. DuBois, 1933[1]

*B*ROWN V. BOARD OF EDUCATION addressed the racial segregation of
grade schools and high schools in places like Topeka, Kansas, and Sum-
merton, South Carolina. Except for references to legal precedents, that
decision contained no mention of colleges, and certainly not colleges in
places like Ann Arbor, Michigan, or Cambridge, Massachusetts, where
legal segregation was not practiced. Yet the logic of the *Brown* decision,
together with other powerful social forces, would bring about a transformation of college student bodies that in some ways was even more per-
vasive than that experienced by the nation's public elementary and secondary schools.

This transformation is well illustrated by considering how the racial
composition changed in the freshman class of that most emblematic of
American institutions, Harvard College, an institution that had broken
the color barrier well before the turn of the twentieth century. The college's annual "face book" of 1954 contained the pictures of 1,167 entering freshmen. Of these, ten (0.9 percent) were African Americans, and
another eight (0.7 percent) were Asian Americans. Counting foreign
nonwhites, just 2.4 percent of the entering class in 1954 was nonwhite.
Ten years later, in 1964, these percentages had increased only slightly: 1.9
percent African American, 0.9 percent Asian American, and 3.5 percent
all nonwhite, including foreign students.[2] Compare these freshman classes
to the entering Harvard College class of first-year students—now including women—in 2002. This entering class was 6.8 percent African American, 17.4 percent Asian American, 7.2 percent Hispanic, and 1.4 percent
other minorities. An additional 11.6 percent of the class were from foreign countries.[3] Apart from foreign students, then, the overall nonwhite
percentage had increased from 1.6 percent in 1954 to 32.8 percent in

2002. This astounding change in racial composition was no doubt shaped in part by Harvard's transformation from a mostly regional college dominated by privileged prep school graduates to a national institution marked by meritocratic admission standards.[4] Yet from one perspective even Harvard's change in racial composition has been less radical than those at institutions that had previously enrolled only whites—institutions such as Duke or the University of Virginia.[5] The fact remains that racial diversity increased dramatically in colleges and universities in all regions of the country, both public and private.

The significance of changes such as these arises out of the role of higher education as keeper of the keys to affluence and influence in American society. As college attainment has spread to increasing shares of the population, the economic importance of a college education has grown along with the earnings gap between high school and college graduates.[6] At the same time, the perceived value of attending the most selective colleges and universities has resulted in a growing concentration of top students in a relatively small number of elite institutions. In light of these developments, it is little wonder that the issue of affirmative action should have generated such fierce debate.[7] As *Bakke* gave way to *Hopwood* and California's Proposition 209 and then to the 2003 Supreme Court rulings in the University of Michigan cases, the issue of diversity in college enrollment assumed a prominent place in policy debate.[8] The importance of affirmative action cannot be appreciated without understanding the changing racial patterns in college enrollment and interracial contact. This chapter therefore begins by describing the enrollment patterns existing at the time of the *Brown* decision and notes several aspects of higher education that distinguish it from education at lower levels in ways that affect interracial contact. It then uses several sources of data to trace changes over time and comparisons across regions and types of institutions. Finally, it notes the importance for interracial contact of current policy issues in higher education.

INTERRACIAL CONTACT IN COLLEGES, 1954

At the time of the *Brown* decision, the nation's colleges and universities were highly segregated by race. Black students were rare at most institutions, and altogether absent in others. In the South and Border regions, virtually no whites were enrolled with blacks in undergraduate colleges, and only a handful of black students attended graduate and professional schools. Indeed, the vast majority of the nation's sixty-three thousand black collegiate students were concentrated in one of the roughly one hundred historically black colleges and universities (HBCUs). Although the *Brown* decision did not deal directly with colleges and universities, several of the most important early challenges to segregated education brought by the NAACP concerned graduate education in universities. Prominent among the cases resulting from these challenges were a pair decided in 1949: *Sweatt v. Painter*, on behalf of a black applicant to the University of Texas law school, and *McLaurin v. Oklahoma State Regents for Higher Education*, on behalf of a black applicant to the University of Oklahoma's school of education.[9] The Supreme Court ruled in both cases that the states had failed to provide equal education to blacks. The plaintiff in the first case never matriculated, but McLaurin did, albeit under the condition that he sit in a hallway outside the classroom containing the white students. These rulings had no impact on undergraduate education, however, since all of the states with de jure segregated public school systems also operated segregated public colleges.

The nearly complete segregation in the South and Border states was made possible by the existence of a wholly separate set of institutions for blacks. Established through the mostly good intentions of religious denominations and Northern philanthropists, the devotion of state governments to the principle of racial separation, and the federal government's provision in the 1890 Morrill Act for separate land-grant colleges, these institutions trained black teachers and farmers and produced the bulk of the black bourgeoisie during the decades of de jure segregation.[10] Unlike the all-black elementary and secondary schools, whose doom had been sealed by *Brown*, these relics of the Jim Crow era lived on well past "desegregation." These HBCUs would become the most prominent institutional feature distinguishing the desegregation that occurred in higher education from that at the elementary and secondary levels. In 1954 segregation between blacks and whites in the South was absolute at the undergraduate level and virtually so at the graduate level. By that year, four Southern states—Texas, Louisiana, Virginia, and Tennessee—had admitted blacks into graduate programs in their state universities. In the Border states, the color line had been broken at the graduate level in Maryland, West Virginia, Missouri, Oklahoma, and Kentucky, although public undergraduate education there, too, was still segregated until 1954, when Kentucky began integration at the undergraduate level.[11] The rule of segregation in these regions applied as well to virtually all private undergraduate education before 1954.[12]

Outside the South and Border regions, many predominantly white colleges and universities enrolled black students in 1954, but interracial contact remained quite low. The NAACP's official publication, *The Crisis*, regularly listed enrollment statistics for predominantly white colleges that enrolled blacks. Listed in table 6.1 are the prominent institutions that were listed for the fall of 1954. Although this surely does not constitute a complete list of racially mixed institutions, it is suggestive of patterns in institutions presumably thought to be most accommodating to black students. The colleges and universities shown in table 6.1 had generally very low percentages of black students. Of the colleges, only Berea and Oberlin, both with long traditions of racial openness, had black shares as high as 1 percent.[13] Among the universities listed, the proportions ranged from zero to 3 percent. What explained these low shares? For one thing, blacks made up a relatively small percentage of the popu-

TABLE 6.1
Blacks as a Percentage of Undergraduates, Selected Colleges and
Universities, Fall 1954

Institution	Black percentage
Colleges	
Barnard	1.0
Bates	0.5
Berea	1.3
Bowdoin	0.3
Dartmouth	0.6
Mount Holyoke	0.5
Oberlin	2.2
Smith	0.2
Tufts	0.3
Universities	
Ohio State University	3.0
University of Illinois	0.3
University of Kansas	1.6
University of Nebraska	0.0

Sources: National Association for the Advancement of Colored People (1955); Irwin (1956); Cobb (1998, p. 28); "400 at Columbia View Civil Rights," *New York Times*, March 28, 1954, p. 72; author's calculations.

Note: Figure for Ohio State based on fall 1953 enrollment; figure for University of Illinois based on graduate and undergraduate enrollment.

lation in the North. Whereas blacks made up one-quarter of the population of the South in 1950 and one-tenth in the Border states, they were only 5 percent of the population in the remainder of the country.[14] Another reason for the low interracial contact in the North was that two states in the North maintained HBCUs of their own: Ohio had Central State University and Wilberforce University, and Pennsylvania had Cheyney State College and Lincoln University.[15] A final reason for the low rate of interracial contact in Northern colleges and universities was simply the paucity of blacks attending college at all. As shown in figure 6.1, blacks enrolled in college at only half the rate of whites in 1961. Combined with the geographic concentration of the black population, these low rates of college enrollment left relatively few black students in Northern colleges. By one estimate, only about four thousand blacks entered college in the North in 1954, compared to about twenty-thousand who entered HBCUs, most of which were located in the South.[16]

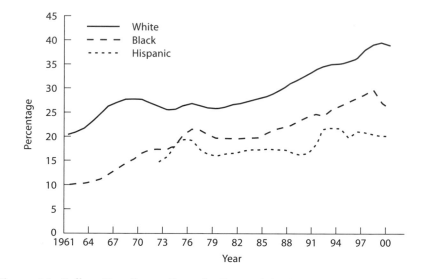

Figure 6.1. College Enrollment Rates by Race, 1961–2000
Sources: 1961–1966: U.S. Bureau of the Census, Current Population Reports, series P-20, table 3.5; 1967–1988: U.S. Bureau of the Census, Current Population Reports; Clotfelter, Ehrenberg, Getz, and Siegfried (1991, table 2.7); 1988–2000: U.S. Bureau of the Census, Current Population Reports, series P-20, table 1.
Note: Figures are three-year moving averages of college enrollments as percent of eighteen- to twenty-four-year-olds.

Distinctive Aspects of Higher Education
and Its Desegregation

As is documented below, the patterns of segregation so evident in 1954 did break down beginning in the 1960s, but for reasons that appear somewhat unrelated to the forces working at the elementary and secondary level. Five aspects stand out in distinguishing the changes in interracial contact in American higher education from those in grades K–12.

Historically Black Institutions

The most prominent of these aspects is the one noted earlier, the existence of a set of identifiably black institutions that had been established during the Jim Crow era. These HBCUs and the issues they raise have virtually no parallel in elementary and secondary schools. The closest analogy is the role of historically black public high schools, many of which represented tradition, outlets for black leadership, and sources of community pride. Because of the consensus that HBCUs should be preserved, their continued existence and the predominance of blacks in their student bodies necessarily insured that some minimum degree of segregation would remain in higher education.

The role that HBCUs have played in segregation in higher education can be appreciated by looking at the long-term trend in enrollments by race since 1954. Table 6.2 presents estimates of full-time undergraduate enrollment in selected years. It is worth emphasizing that more precise measures are unavailable, owing to the lack of administrative records detailing enrollments by race. The table is compiled from published estimates, official statistics, and survey findings from four years. As can be seen clearly, the proportion of college students who were black increased steadily over this period, rising from 3.9 percent in 1954 to 10.7 percent in 1998. (By comparison, the black percentage in the U.S. population in these years was about 10.5 percent and 12.3 percent, respectively.)[17] Although the number of blacks attending college grew over this entire period, HBCUs more or less stopped growing after 1967. Part of the explanation of why the HBCUs failed to garner a share of the growth in black enrollment was geographic: black population grew much faster outside the South than in it. Whereas 70 percent of the black population lived in one of the eleven states of the South in 1950, only 47 percent did

153

TABLE 6.2

College Enrollment of Black Students: Numbers and Percentages of Total
Enrollment, and Percentage of Black Students Enrolled in Historically Black
Colleges and Universities, 1954–1998

Year	Full-time undergraduate enrollment (000s) Total	Full-time undergraduate enrollment (000s) Blacks	Percentage black	Blacks in HBCUs (000s)	Blacks not in HBCUs (000s)	Percentage of blacks in HBCUs
1954	1,627.4[a]	63.2[b]	3.9	52.7[b]	10.5	83
1967[c]	4,764.8	245.4	5.2	150.0	95	61
1976	6,030[d]	588.9[e]	9.8	147.0[e]	441.9	25
1998	7,556.3[f]	810.4[e]	10.7	159.5[e]	650.9	20

Sources:

[a]Estimated from U.S. Department of Education, National Center for Education Statistics (2001c, table 173, p. 202). Total enrollment for 1954 × ratio of full-time to total enrollment for 1959 = 2,446,693 × (2,421,016/3,639,847) = 1,627,399.

[b]Plaut (1954, p. 310) estimates in 1954 that 4,000 blacks entered Northern colleges and fewer than 20,000 entered predominantly black colleges. To obtain the ratio of full-time enrollment to entering students: estimated 1955 full-time enrollment as above, as 2,653,034 × (2,421,016/3,639,847) = 1,764,645 (from U.S. Department of Education National Center for Education Statistics, table 173). Total freshman in 1955 were 670,000 (table 182), so ratio of full-time enrollment to freshman was 2.634. Applying that ratio to Plaut's estimates yields estimates of 10,536 in Northern colleges and no more than 52,680 in HBCUs.

[c]Egerton (1969, p. 6).

[d]U.S. Department of Education, National Center for Education Statistics (2001c, table 188, p. 217).

[e]Author's calculations. Based on Higher Education General Information Survey (HEGIS), 1976; Integrated Postsecondary Education Data System (IPEDS), 1998.

[f]U.S. Department of Education, National Center for Education Statistics (2001c, table 181, p. 211).

in 2000.[17] Add to this an apparent decline in the allure of all-black colleges for many African Americans, which may have resulted from changing attitudes, increasing opportunities to attend predominantly white institutions, and states' comparatively low levels of support for public HBCUs. Whatever the reason, the single most important fact about segregation in higher education lies in the declining importance of these historically black institutions. In 1954 higher education in the United States was highly segregated, and this was because roughly five-sixths of all blacks attended all-black colleges and universities. Although those institutions remained predominantly black over the succeeding decades, their importance waned, and increasing numbers of blacks entered predominantly white institutions. Therein lies much of the decline in segregation in higher education.

Attendance and Cost

A second distinctive aspect affecting racial patterns in higher education is its characteristics related to attendance and financing. Unlike public elementary and secondary education, which is subject to compulsory attendance laws and free provision, college is quite voluntary, and college attendance typically requires out-of-pocket payments to cover tuition, fees, room, and board. To be sure, some institutions accept virtually all applicants, and college costs are heavily subsidized, so that some students pay nothing out of pocket. But together these features of voluntary attendance and cost significantly reduce the proportion of individuals of all races who attend college. These features also have the effect of stratifying college attendance by academic achievement and social class, leaving prominent four-year institutions with more affluent student bodies than comprehensive and community colleges.[19] Because of the real financial burden imposed by college costs, federal programs, including the G.I. Bill, Pell Grants (formerly Basic Education Opportunity Grants), and subsidized loans have an effect on college attendance rates.[20] Since 1954 these rates have risen across the board, as shown in figure 6.1. As a percentage of eighteen- to twenty-four-year-olds, the college enrollment rate for blacks more than doubled between 1961 and 2000, rising from about 10 percent to 30 percent, before falling to 26 percent. Over the same period, the rate for whites also increased, from about 20 percent to slightly less than 40 percent. Rates for Hispanics have lagged, standing at about 20 percent in 2000. These changes in college enrollment rates have obviously affected the racial makeup of the college-going population, and thus the demographic foundation for interracial contact.

Civil Rights Law

The third distinctive characteristic affecting interracial contact in higher education is the body of civil rights law that applies specifically to colleges and universities. Most important were federal laws and court decisions applying to state systems of higher education, which in the South and Border had been segregated through the use of public HBCUs. The

Supreme Court's decisions in the challenges to the separate-but-equal principle in education in the years leading up to *Brown* meant that states were hard put to justify excluding blacks from many graduate programs. As noted earlier, however, those segregation decisions had little force regarding undergraduate enrollments, since substantially equal facilities were available for both blacks and whites and in any case did not cause states in the South to desegregate their state systems of colleges and universities. Title VI of the 1964 Civil Rights Act, which forbade racial discrimination in any state education system receiving federal assistance, added force to federal enforcement efforts. But not until the 1970s, when the NAACP initiated suits that resulted in a series of decisions under the name of *Adams*, did public undergraduate enrollments in the South experience much desegregation. These cases required the federal authorities to devise guidelines for desegregating state colleges and universities, placing most states in the South and Border under the supervision of the federal government.[21] In 1992 the Supreme Court went further in a case concerning Mississippi's virtually segregated public system of colleges and universities. It ruled that the state needed to take steps beyond mere race-neutrality in desegregating that system, without specifying what those steps should be.[22] Like *Adams*, this decision highlighted a central question facing those who would desegregate formerly dual state systems of higher education: was desegregation worth sacrificing the public HBCUs? Given the strong support for these institutions, states and courts have been loath to institute policies that would mortally wound HBCUs. Nonetheless, federal efforts had the effect of pressuring states in the South and Border to take steps to desegregate their state systems of higher education. As the data presented in this chapter will show, the states of the South showed uneven but measurable progress toward this objective after 1972.

Another civil rights issue touched directly on the admissions function—affirmative action. The constitutional propriety of admission policies designed to increase the share of underrepresented minorities was tested in the landmark *Bakke* case in 1978. In that decision, the Supreme Court ruled that colleges and universities could, under certain circumstances, give preferential treatment to minority applicants. Such treatment could be justified only if there were a strong governmental justification for increasing racial diversity and if the policies adopted were necessary to achieve it. Simple racial quotas were ruled out altogether.[23] A federal appeals court decision in March 1996 threw into limbo the status of affirmative action in college admissions,[24] spurring the state of

Texas to adopt a substitute policy. Its Ten Percent Plan guaranteed to the top 10 percent of every high school admission to the University of Texas, thus exploiting the racial segregation of the state's public schools to insure that minority applicants would gain admission without affirmative action. In a pair of cases involving admissions at the University of Michigan, the Supreme Court in 2003 affirmed the constitutionality of racial considerations in the pursuit of racial diversity, but only when they could be applied in a detailed review of applications, as opposed to a formula.[25]

Large Private Sector

The fourth aspect of higher education that makes its desegregation experience distinctive is the importance of private institutions. In 1954, 45 percent of college students attended private colleges and universities.[26] Although that share has declined over time, the private share has remained significant (it was 23 percent in 1998).[27] Furthermore, these private institutions included some of the most prominent, prestigious, and influential institutions in the country. Although they did not face the pressure exerted by *Adams,* they were nevertheless sensitive to the racial diversity of their student populations.[28] Not only did some of these institutions tout diversity as a desideratum, owing to its presumed educational benefits, their allegiance to the principles of meritocratic admissions and equality of access caused them to become quite sensitive on the issue of racial diversity.[29] As will become clear, the racial composition of selective colleges and universities changed dramatically in the two decades following the *Brown* decision.

Campus Size

The fifth distinctive aspect of higher education to be kept in mind in assessing changes in enrollment patterns is perhaps the most obvious: the large enrollment of many individual institutions. Whereas the typical high school seldom enrolls more than 2,500 students, some colleges and universities have enrollments many times as large. With even more force than in the case of high schools, then, racial composition cannot be assumed to equate to interracial "contact" in the literal sense. Sheer size opens possibilities for self-segregation of many forms, such as housing, course selection, and extracurricular activities, including fraternities and sororities.[30] For the purposes of measurement, however, interracial contact in colleges and universities is measured here using the same types of campus-level measures applied to elementary and secondary schools in previous chapters. It is sufficient to keep in mind that such measures have a different significance on a campus of 20,000 students than in a high school or college enrolling only 1,500. Another aspect of size is the wider attendance areas of colleges and universities, as compared to most K–12 schools. While the latter must take its students from a local area whose racial composition may be quite distinctive, due to residential segregation, colleges and universities typically draw students from large areas. Not only does this fact give colleges at least the theoretical ability to diversify their student bodies, it also affects the kind of benchmark for comparison that one might want to employ in assessing how "segregated" such institutions are.

How Interracial Contact Changed in Higher Education

Trends in Twenty-Eight Institutions

As in the case of elementary and secondary schools, the federal government began collecting data on the racial composition of colleges and universities in the late 1960s, but there exists little information for earlier years to gauge the racial composition of individual institutions, apart from the fact of near universal segregation of undergraduate enrollments in the eleven Southern states before about 1960. What appears to be the best source of data on college racial compositions before the late 1960s is the College and Beyond survey, which contacted adults who had attended one of a handful of mostly private colleges and universities as freshmen in the fall of 1951. As can be seen from the list of institutions covered by the sample (see table 6.3), a majority of the private universities, all of the colleges, and three of the four public universities are outside of the South. Although these data may be subject to differences in mortality and response rates, and despite the unrepresentative nature of the sample of institutions, these data provide the best snapshot available of racial composition for that period. When combined with data from subsequent federal surveys, this survey provides an unparalleled time series stretching over five decades, at least for the institutions included in the College and Beyond sample.

Using these data, table 6.3 shows average racial composition, calculated for each of four types of institutions. Perhaps the most striking fact revealed in the table is the very low percentage of blacks and other non-

TABLE 6.3

Average Racial Composition of Full-Time Undergraduates in Twenty-Eight Selective
Colleges and Universities, 1951–1998

	1951	1967	1970	1976[a]	1976[b]	1986	1998
11 private universities							
Percent white	99.1	96.9	93.6	88.2	87.6	82.6	67.9
Percent black	0.3	1.8	4.0	5.6	5.6	5.3	7.0
Percent other nonwhite	0.7	1.4	2.4	6.2	6.8	12.1	25.2
Total	100.0	100.0	100.0	100.0	100.0	100.0	100.0
10 liberal arts colleges and women's colleges							
Percent white	98.1	95.8	92.5	90.0	89.7	84.6	73.5
Percent black	1.0	2.8	5.7	6.4	6.0	5.1	6.1
Percent other nonwhite	0.9	1.4	1.9	3.7	4.4	10.3	20.3
Total	100.0	100.0	100.0	100.0	100.0	100.0	100.0
4 public universities							
Percent white	98.4	97.7	95.5	86.8	93.7	90.6	81.9
Percent black	1.0	1.4	2.8	8.9	3.9	4.8	6.6
Percent other nonwhite	0.6	0.9	1.7	4.3	2.3	4.7	11.5
Total	100.0	100.0	100.0	100.0	100.0	100.0	100.0
3 HBCUs							
Percent white	0.0	1.3	1.8	0.4	2.3	5.4	0.6
Percent black	99.9	98.5	97.7	99.4	95.9	92.5	97.3
Percent other nonwhite	0.1	0.3	0.5	0.2	1.9	2.1	2.1
Total	100.0	100.0	100.0	100.0	100.0	100.0	100.0

Sources: 1951 and 1976a: College and Beyond Survey, unpublished data; 1967: *Chronicle of Higher Education* (1968); 1970: U.S. Department of Health, Education, and Welfare, Office for Civil Rights (1972); 1976b: U.S. Department of Health, Education, and Welfare, National Center for Education Statistics, *Higher Education General Information Survey*, fall 1976; 1986 and 1998: U.S. Department of Education, National Center for Education Statistics, *Integrated Postsecondary Education Data System*.

Notes: Colleges and universities listed are a subset of those covered in the College and Beyond survey, described in Bowen and Bok (1998, appendix A). For 1951 and 1976a, calculations are based on survey participants whose race was recorded in the College and Beyond survey. Institutions providing no racial breakdown for 1951 or 1976 were excluded from the sample where other sources of racial breakdown were not available.

The institutions included were: private universities: Columbia, Duke, Emory, Northwestern, Princeton, Rice, Tufts, Tulane, University of Pennsylvania, Vanderbilt, and Yale; private colleges: Bryn Mawr, Denison, Hamilton, Kenyon, Oberlin, Smith, Swarthmore, Wellesley, Wesleyan, and Williams; public universities: Miami of Ohio, Michigan, Pennsylvania State, and the University of North Carolina; historically black colleges and universities: Morehouse, Spelman, and Xavier.

Averages for each category are weighted by 1976 enrollments.

whites enrolled in the sampled institutions in 1951, other than the HBCUs. The black percentage in the eleven private universities was only 0.3 percent and just 1.0 percent in the private colleges. In the three public universities, likewise, 1.0 percent of the former undergraduates were black. Adding other nonwhites increased the nonwhite percentages to 1.0, 1.9, and 1.6 percent, respectively. In light of the preponderance of Northern institutions in the sample, these findings suggest that the strict segregation that ruled in Southern and Border colleges and universities in 1951 was nearly matched by institutions in other regions, at least among the sampled institutions. The next year for which comparable data are available is sixteen years later, and the changes revealed in the table are either dramatic or modest, depending on one's viewpoint. In that year of 1967 the black percentage in the sampled private universities had increased by 1.5 percentage points and by 1.8 points in the colleges. For the public universities the increase was even smaller. Although these were surely large proportional increases, the share of blacks in these institutions remained small.

After 1967, however, the percentages of blacks and other nonwhites increased more rapidly in these colleges over the next nine years. By 1976 the percentages of blacks had increased to about the level at which they would remain for the next twenty years.[31] Among other nonwhites, however, the increases continued without interruption throughout the period. Thus the eleven private universities, where blacks averaged 1.8 percent and nonwhites 3.2 percent of all undergraduates in 1967, had student bodies by 1998 that were 7.0 percent black and almost one-third nonwhite. The increases among selective colleges and public universities was not as steep, but sizable nonetheless. By contrast, the racial composition in the three HBCUs changed only marginally over the forty-seven-year period, remaining largely black and almost entirely nonwhite. The striking fact illustrated by table 6.3 is that these predominantly white colleges and universities were virtually all-white in 1951 and remained, as a group, more than 90 percent white until after 1970.

Public Higher Education in the South and Border

In order to document trends for a much wider set of colleges and universities, it is necessary to go to a shorter period, owing to the scarcity of data on racial composition for the 1950s. Thanks to compilations done by the Southern Education Reporting Service, it is possible to document in some detail the desegregation in public colleges and universities in the Border and South from the early 1960s. The public institutions in these regions were, of course, central to the changes in interracial contact after 1960, not only because of their adherence to de jure segregation but also because of the large share of the nation's black college students they enrolled and the growth they would experience in the 1960s and 1970s. Figure 6.2 presents the median state segregation indices for four-year public institutions in the six Border and eleven Southern states, beginning, for most them, with the fall of 1961.[32]

As shown in the figure, integration was already under way in the Border states by 1961; that process continued virtually without interruption in each of the six states until 1986. By contrast, the desegregation of the four-year public institutions in the South was accomplished much more grudgingly. In 1961 Southern colleges and universities were almost completely segregated. Almost no whites attended predominantly black state colleges and universities, and very few blacks attended predominantly white ones. Those who did cross the color line in these early days were mostly graduate students. By 1970 the South's public institutions were still highly segregated, but tremendous change had occurred in that first decade of desegregation, the median segregation index having fallen to 0.782.[33] In that year, the states with the most segregated systems of four-year colleges were Mississippi and North Carolina. Tennessee had the region's lowest level of segregation. Between 1970 and 1986, segregation declined in all eleven states of the region; Mississippi remained the most segregated. But 1986 was the end of the universal decline in segregation. After 1986 segregation in the public four-year institutions increased in four Border states, causing the region's median index to increase. Segregation increased in two states of the South, although that region's median continued to fall.[34]

Community colleges provide an interesting contrast to the four-year institutions. Most of them did not even come into being until after the *Brown* decision, and therein lies the reason why their history is so different from that of the four-year institutions. Nationwide, enrollment in two-year public colleges exploded between the mid-1960s and the mid-1970s. In the three decades beginning in the fall of 1956, total community college enrollment grew by 0.5 million, 2.6 million, and 0.8 million, respectively.[35] Among the states investing most heavily in community colleges were two in the South—Florida and Texas.[36] Started in 1933, Florida's public two-year colleges had been strictly segregated from the

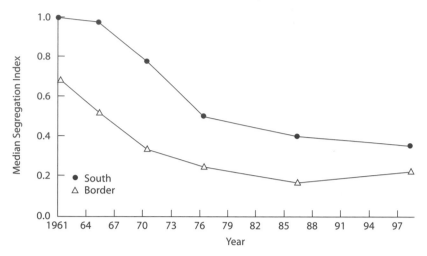

Figure 6.2. Median Segregation Rates, Four-Year Public Colleges and Universities, Border and Southern States
   Source: table A6.1.

start. Freestanding community colleges were founded as all-white institutions, and black community colleges were placed in existing all-black high schools under the direction of the high school principals.[37] But in 1966 the state closed these black community colleges and integrated the others. In 1961 Texas had some all-white, but only one all-black community college. All of the states of the South integrated their community colleges in short order and with a minimum of fuss. Because they were designed to serve entire counties or other similar large areas, because there existed few historically black public junior colleges, and because their growth began after the *Brown* decision, it was perhaps natural for this sector of higher education to accommodate most easily the dictates of desegregation, and so it did.

Trends since 1967 in 175 Institutions

Data limitations make it harder to document the desegregation of colleges outside the Border and South. The best source is occasional tabulations on enrollments by race that are available beginning in the late 1960s nationwide. However, none are in electronic form for years before 1976–1977. To gain a sense of trends and changes in racial makeup before that year, and how they differed by region, I collected enrollment data for a sample of 175 large institutions nationwide and traced the changes beginning as early as the fall of 1967.[38]

Figure 6.3 summarizes these data by showing the exposure rate of whites to nonwhites in these 175 institutions. As used in previous chapters, the exposure rate is simply a weighted average of the nonwhite percentage of the institutions in each category, where white enrollments are the weights. The exposure rates can be interpreted, therefore, as the percentage nonwhite in the typical white college student's college or university. Because only a portion of all institutions are covered in the table, no effort is made to calculate how "segregated" colleges were using these data, only how the racial composition of predominantly white institutions changed. For 1967, only calculations for private institutions could be made, because the data source combined enrollments for multicampus state systems and could therefore not be used to measure exposure rates on public college campuses.

The figure suggests that racial composition in predominantly white colleges and universities changed markedly after 1970, both in and outside of the South. Despite the South's higher percentage of nonwhites in 1970, its predominantly white four-year public institutions enrolled lower percentages of nonwhites. This gap remained small but positive in this sample throughout the period, as the rise of Hispanic and Asian American enrollments pushed up exposure rates in succeeding decades.[39] For the two-year colleges, exposure rates started out higher than in four-year institutions in 1970 and remained higher for the entire period shown. Interestingly, exposure rates in the two-year colleges outside of the South increased more rapidly than the comparable ones for the South.

For the private four-year institutions, the thirty-one-year span documented in figure 6.3 reveals an impressive increase in exposure rates in all regions. In the South, these private colleges and universities, which had been segregated entirely until the early 1960s, had enrollments that were only 3.4 percent nonwhite in 1967. Those in the North were not much different; there the typical white student was in a student body that was 4.0 percent nonwhite. Exposure rates increased in both regions for the next nine years, with the Southern institutions remaining behind. They continued to increase in both regions into the 1980s and 1990s. Although the Northern private institutions followed in figure 6.3 show high exposure rates, the full sample shows that exposure rates in the South in private four-year institutions were almost the same as for the rest of the country in the last two periods.

163

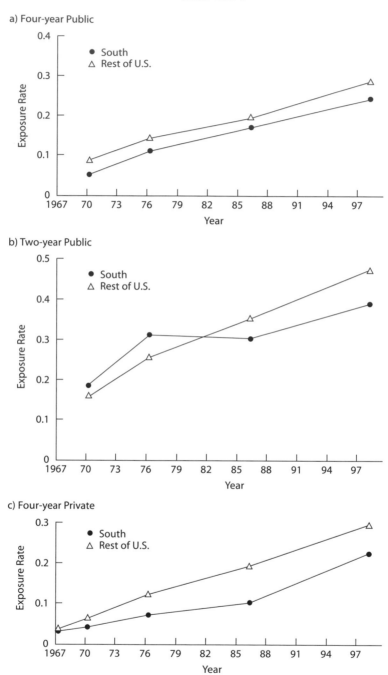

a) Four-year Public

b) Two-year Public

c) Four-year Private

Trends by Region for All Undergraduates, 1976–1998

To obtain a full view of segregation at the college level, it is necessary to cover all institutions, but as already discussed this means restricting the years of analysis, owing to the lack of electronic data covering years before the fall of 1976. Using the more recent universal data, table 6.4 presents average exposure rates by region based on full-time fall enrollment of undergraduates for 1976, 1986, and 1998. The first set of exposure rates, shown on the left side of the table, are comparable to those shown in figure 6.3, and give the percentage nonwhite in the average white college student's institution. For the United States, the average white student attending a four-year state college or university in 1976 was part of an undergraduate student body that was 13.2 percent nonwhite. By 1998, that typical white student attended a state school that was 22.6 percent nonwhite.

Among four-year public institutions, the most dramatic changes were in the South and West, with exposure rates roughly doubling in both regions. The explanations for the increases in exposure in these two regions are different, however. In the South, there were two reasons. The first was the deliberate policy of desegregation pursued in public systems, especially those under federal scrutiny following the *Adams* rulings. The second reason in the South was the failure of HBCUs to expand their enrollments. As a consequence, the increases in nonwhite enrollments in the South poured into new or formerly white institutions, thereby increasing exposure rates. In the West, the primary reason for the increase in white exposure to nonwhites was the dramatic demographic changes wrought by immigration. Between 1976 and 1998, the percentage of four-year public undergraduates in the West who were Hispanic increased from 5.5 to 13.1 percent. The percentage who were Asian Americans increased from 6.4 to 16.5 percent.[40]

Nationwide, whites attending community colleges also saw an increase in the percentage of nonwhites, from an average of 19.7 percent in 1976 to 30.0 percent in 1998. Here again demographics played a large role, with rates in the West and Northeast increasing by more than 10 percentage points each.

Figure 6.3. Exposure Rates of Whites to Nonwhites in 175 Large Colleges and Universities, Three Types of Institutions, Various Years
Source: table A6.2.

TABLE 6.4
Exposure Rates by Institution, Type, and Region, Fall 1976, 1986, and 1998

Type and Region	Exposure rates[a] Whites to nonwhites			Exposure rates[b] Blacks to nonblacks		
	1976	1986	1998	1976	1986	1998
Four-year public						
Northeast	.134	.161	.196	.749	.729	.723
Border	.104	.126	.171	.539	.648	.555
South	.125	.175	.243	.408	.517	.538
Midwest	.092	.100	.144	.831	.867	.832
West	.192	.310	.399	.901	.926	.914
U.S.	.132	.169	.226	.609	.670	.660
Two-year public						
Northeast	.108	.130	.215	.658	.716	.746
Border	.169	.155	.165	.572	.712	.670
South	.247	.233	.298	.694	.704	.690
Midwest	.097	.121	.145	.412	.550	.626
West	.241	.344	.416	.706	.765	.814
U.S.	.197	.235	.300	.644	.698	.722
Four-year private						
Northeast	.101	.155	.220	.899	.819	.788
Border	.096	.122	.160	.654	.630	.719
South	.100	.141	.212	.232	.336	.364
Midwest	.105	.129	.161	.732	.757	.764
West	.226	.277	.351	.922	.924	.921
U.S.	.111	.139	.216	.694	.708	.674

Sources: 1976: Higher Education General Information Survey (HEGIS); 1978: Fall Enrollment, 1978 (electronic, ICPSR 2066); 1986: Integrated Postsecondary Education Data System (IPEDS): Fall Enrollment, 1986 (electronic, ICPSR); 1998: IPEDS, Fall Enrollment, 1998 (electronic); author's calculations. See methodological appendix.

Note: Definitions of regions are given in the methodological appendix.

[a]Proportion nonwhite weighted by white enrollment.
[b]Proportion nonblack weighted by black enrollment.

The subsector that experienced the biggest change in white-nonwhite exposure was private four-year institutions. For the United States as a whole, the nonwhite percentage in the typical white undergraduate's college just about doubled, rising from 11.1 percent in 1976 to 21.6 percent in 1998.[41] Except for the West, the patterns and increases in exposure rates were remarkably similar by region. Exposure doubled in the North-east, the Border, and the South and increased by more than half in the other two regions. By 1998, private institutions in the West had the highest white-nonwhite exposure rate of any region, as was the case with the other groups of institutions, again reflecting that region's high per-centage of Hispanics and Asian American students.

The last three columns in the table present exposure rates focusing on the experience of black students. To the extent that blacks attend colleges whose student bodies are largely black, they may be thought of as being isolated racially. Whether or not this may be a good thing or a bad thing—a prominent argument in favor of HBCUs, after all, rests on their perceived advantages to blacks as compared to predominantly white colleges—it is instructive to see how this measure of isolation differs by region and how it changed over time. Looking first at four-year public institutions, blacks were most isolated in the South, in each of the years shown, owing to the importance of HBCUs. But their isola-tion also fell by the most in the South: in 1976 the average black under-graduate in a public four-year institution attended an institution with a 41 percent nonblack percentage, but this had increased to 54 percent by 1998. To be sure, these averages mask a large divide, between the nearly all-black HBCUs and the other, predominantly nonblack colleges and universities. In both years, the region where blacks were least isolated, by this measure, was the West.

In community colleges, the patterns look a bit different, with blacks in the South being comparatively less isolated than elsewhere. Unlike the numerous four-year public HBCUs in the South, two-year HBCUs in the region were rare, leaving black community college students available to attend integrated institutions. The highest degree of isolation for the community colleges was in the Midwest. In the private four-year cate-gory, the isolation of blacks in the South was quite pronounced, with an exposure rate of only 36 percent in 1998. These low rates were no doubt a function of the importance of private HBCUs. The region where blacks experienced the highest exposure rate to non-blacks for all three institu-tion types, and in all three years, was the West.

To translate exposure rates such as these into segregation indices such as those used in the analysis of K–12 schools, it is necessary to adjust for differences in the racial compositions of various states. Since an expo-sure rate of 0.15 of whites to nonwhites (the average white student at-tends a college in which 15 percent of students are nonwhite) would imply much less racial balance in a state where 30 percent of college students were nonwhite than it would in a state where only 17 percent were, it is natural to adjust for differences in racial composition in the same way as was done with K–12 schools, by using the percentage of nonwhites enrolled in a given type of institution.

To measure segregation, I employ the same gap-based index used in previous chapters.[42] This approach assumes that the racial mix of all colleges and universities of a given type within a single state taken together provides the appropriate benchmark for measuring deviations from racial balance in that state. Of the three institutional types identified in this chapter, this assumption applies best to four-year public institutions. By their nature, such institutions are meant to have statewide appeal; thus deviations in racial balance among the public four-year institutions in a state can be associated with segregation of the kind discussed in previous chapters. This index seems less appropriate for two-year public colleges, whose catchment areas are typically much more localized. If every community college student attended the campus closest to home, for example, campuses would not be racially balanced across the state if the racial composition of students was not evenly distributed across the state.[43] Nor is the segregation index for four-year private institutions as appealing a measure as it is for public four-year institutions. To the extent that private colleges and universities appeal to a regional market, and this is surely more true of private than public institutions,[44] an index using the racial composition of a state's private students is not ideal. Nonetheless, granting these difficulties in interpreting the segregation index for two-year public and four-year private institutions, tracing changes in these indices over time should illuminate changes in the tendency of colleges and universities to enroll students more reflective of their states' racial compositions.

Beginning with segregation in four-year public institutions, table 6.5 lists the states with the highest rates of segregation in the earliest and latest year of data. In the fall of 1976, fully two decades after *Brown* and shortly after *Adams*, all of the seven most segregated states were below the Mason-Dixon Line. In each of these states, HBCUs attracted a sizable share of the black college enrollment, while the bulk of the state colleges remained predominantly white. The most segregated of these were North Carolina, Mississippi, and Virginia, states of the former Confederacy that together had ten HBCUs.[45] In North Carolina, for example, five such virtually all-black institutions (North Carolina A&T, North Carolina Central, Fayetteville State, Winston-Salem State, and Elizabeth City State) enrolled 73 percent of all nonwhites attending four-year public

TABLE 6.5
States in Which Four-Year Public Institutions Were Most Segregated,
1976 and 1998

1976		1998	
State	Index	State	Index
North Carolina	.667	South Dakota	.433
Mississippi	.642	Mississippi	.419
Virginia	.641	Delaware	.385
Alabama	.478	North Carolina	.362
Louisiana	.458	Maryland	.324
Maryland	.432	Louisiana	.321
Georgia	.430	New York	.307

Source: See table 6.4.

Note: Segregation indices based on white and nonwhite full-time undergraduate student enrollments.

institutions in the state. At the same time, the state's flagship university, the University of North Carolina, enrolled just 5.8 percent of those college-bound nonwhites, though it enrolled 17.2 percent of all four-year public students in the state.

By 1998, segregation in the public four-year colleges of the South had fallen markedly. North Carolina's index fell by almost half; Mississippi's fell by 35 percent; and Virginia's dropped by more than 60 percent, allowing it to fall out of the top seven states in segregation. The most segregated system of public four-year institutions was in South Dakota, where two of its eight public four-year colleges and universities were predominantly Native American while the remaining six were more than 90 percent white. Interestingly, neither that state nor New York, which ranked seventh in segregation, had any HBCUs.

Table 6.6 gives average segregation indices by region for each of the three types of institutions. Beginning with public four-year colleges and universities, the table makes obvious that in the fall of 1976 the states of the South had by far the most segregated systems of public four-year institutions, with an average segregation index of 0.411. The next most segregated region was the Border, whose states averaged 0.223. Over the twenty-two-year period covered in the table, however, states in those two regions reduced the racial disparities among their four-year public colleges, mainly by increasing the enrollment of blacks in new or histori-

TABLE 6.6

Average State-Level Segregation in Higher Education by Region, Three Types
of Institutions, Fall 1976, 1986, and 1998

Type and Region	1976	1986	1998
Four-year public			
Northeast	.197	.240	.225
Border	.223	.139	.138
South	.411	.312	.259
Midwest	.074	.044	.069
West	.063	.068	.092
U.S.	.213	.178	.177
Two-year public			
Northeast	.419	.402	.369
Border	.238	.160	.152
South	.180	.203	.204
Midwest	.434	.322	.258
West	.187	.170	.171
U.S.	.254	.231	.209
Four-year private			
Northeast	.133	.172	.164
Border	.130	.118	.085
South	.573	.450	.355
Midwest	.167	.158	.129
West	.098	.079	.083
U.S.	.178	.179	.171

Source: See table 6.4.

Note: Indices are weighted by state enrollment. Definitions of regions are given in the methodological appendix.

cally white institutions, leaving the public HBCUs a dwindling share of black enrollments. By 1998, therefore, both the South and Border regions had reduced their segregation indices by more than one-third. Over the period, segregation in four-year public institutions actually increased slightly in the Northeast and the West. Thus, by 1998, the states of the South still had the most segregated systems of public four-year institutions, but the regional differences had diminished markedly.

At the community college level, the patterns and trends in segregation looked very different, as expected due to their localized catchment areas, as noted above. Segregation indices for community colleges outside the

South tended to be higher than for four-year public institutions, whereas the reverse was true in the South.[46] Without the HBCUs as an automatic segregating influence, as they were with four-year institutions, the South's community colleges had the lowest degree of segregation among the regions in 1976. The Midwest, by contrast, had the most segregated systems. Over the twenty-two-year period, however, these regional differences shrank, with measured segregation declining in the Midwest and actually increasing in the South. By 1998, the states of the Northeast had the highest average segregation in community colleges. However, it is worth repeating that these segregation indices take as the benchmark comparison racial balance across all community colleges in a state. Where communities differ in racial composition within states and where there are many such two year colleges, the tendency for students to attend local colleges will show up as segregation, making comparisons across states or between two- and four-year institutions problematic. But changes over time in these indices for a state or a region will reflect, in part, changes in enrollment policy. From this perspective, the increase in segregation in the South may signify a trend contrary to its desegregating tendencies in K–12 public education.

Before turning to private institutions, it is worth noting an additional source of racial segregation among public college students. Because community colleges tend to have higher proportions of nonwhite students than four-year colleges and universities, interracial contact is further reduced, as compared to a world in which all public institutions had the same racial composition. This between-sector segregation is analogous to the between-district segregation at the K–12 level that arises when school districts differ in racial composition. On average, the racial disparity between community colleges and four-year public institutions was about 7 or 8 percentage points. In 1976, the nonwhite percentage was 16 percent in four-year public institutions and 24 percent in two-year institutions. In 1998, the comparable percentages were 27 percent and 34 percent, respectively. Because they measure only the segregation within each sector, therefore, the indices shown in table 6.6 do not account for this sectoral component of segregation.

The bottom portion of table 6.6 presents similar indices for private four-year colleges and universities calculated by state and averaged by region. As with community colleges, the use of state-level segregation indices is less appropriate than in the case of four-year publics, but the reason here is different. To the extent that a private college or university appeals to a regional or national market, using as a benchmark the racial

171

composition of private college students for the state where it is located makes less sense than using the racial composition of the market in which it competes for students. If all private institutions appealed to a national market, for example, the appropriate benchmark would be the racial composition of all students attending private colleges and universities. In truth, only a comparative handful of private colleges have such a national market, so the use of a state benchmark is a reasonable starting point. A glance at the average segregation indices shown in the table reveals one region—the South—standing in stark contrast to the rest of the country, with an index more than three times larger than that of the next-highest region. Probably the bulk of this distinctiveness is due to the South's private HBCUs. Of the forty-seven private four-year historically black institutions, all but two were in the South.[47] Similar to the pattern observed with public four-year institutions, segregation had fallen by 1998 in the South, and in the other regions except for the Northeast, where it increased over the period.

Besides the historically higher levels of segregation in the South, one other regularity is worth noting. This is the generally positive association between rates of segregation in colleges and overall racial composition. States with the highest nonwhite percentages tend to have the highest rates of segregation. The correlation between the segregation index for public four-year institutions and percentage nonwhite in enrollment was 0.66 in 1976 and 0.76 in 1998. Attributable to the existence of HBCUs in the heavily nonwhite states of the South and Border, this positive correlation bears a resemblance to the comparable relationship observed with respect to segregation in K–12 schools.[48] Although this correlation remained high, it is important to note that the size of the effect diminished over time. Whereas a state in which 40 percent of its four-year college students were nonwhite had a predicted segregation index of 0.53 in 1976, the predicted index for that state in 1998 was only 0.38, reflecting the broad decline in segregation that occurred.[49]

CONCLUSION

The racial composition of American colleges and universities changed markedly over the half-century following the *Brown* decision. In 1954 they were a highly segregated set of institutions. Whites attended college in greater numbers, and most of the blacks who did attend enrolled in all-black institutions in the South and Border states. In the years following the desegregation of most public elementary and secondary schools, however, predominantly white colleges and universities began to open their doors to black applicants. Seeking more diverse student bodies and enabled by court decisions favorable to affirmative action, these institutions increased their enrollments of black, Hispanic, and Asian American students. As blacks increasingly moved out of the South, as their college enrollment rates increased, and as the numbers of other nonwhites were swelled by immigration, the proportion of nonwhites attending historically black institutions steadily declined.

At the same time, federal agencies pressured Southern and Border states to desegregate their public four-year institutions. From 1976 to 1998 the national decline in segregation in four-year public institutions was due entirely to the South and Border: the average segregation index for the South fell by 37 percent, and for the Border it dropped 38 percent. In the Northeast and West, segregation in four-year public institutions actually increased. By 1998, segregation in four-year public institutions remained highest in the South, but the differences among regions had been greatly reduced. In the rapidly growing community college sector, the process of desegregation was largely unencumbered by the existence of historically black institutions; those states that invested heavily in these institutions did so on a desegregated basis almost from the start.

Appendix to Chapter 6

TABLE A6.1

Black-White Segregation in Public Four-Year Colleges and Universities, Border and Southern States (Fall of Given Year)

	1961	1965	1970	1976	1986	1998
Border States						
Delaware	.879	—	.463	.459	.432	.525
Kentucky	.481	.516	.306	.225	.136	.147
Maryland	.867	.801	.645	.525	.433	.499
Missouri	—	.355	.201	.201	.152	.115
Oklahoma	—	.532	.349	.259	.172	.292
West Virginia	.397	.284	.137	.089	.041	.024
Median	*.674*	*.516*	*.328*	*.242*	*.162*	*.220*
Southern States						
Alabama	1.000	—	.755	.499	.398	.352
Arkansas	.001	—	.676	.345	.290	.306
Florida	.998	.974	.644	.453	.419	.385
Georgia	.998	—	.782	.493	.324	.271
Louisiana	.911	—	.751	.538	.495	.414
Mississippi	—	.995	.900	.677	.613	.472
North Carolina	.982	—	.881	.721	.513	.462
South Carolina	1.000	.965	.721	.451	.361	.297
Tennessee	.935	.768	.576	.365	.272	.314
Texas	.908	.793	.875	.481	.370	.325
Virginia	.989	.953	.842	.710	.491	.412
Median	*.986*	*.974*	*.782*	*.493*	*.398*	*.352*

Sources: Southern Education Reporting Service (1961, 1965); U.S. Department of Health, Education, and Welfare, Office for Civil Rights (1972, 1974); HEGIS, fall 1976; IPEDS, fall 1986, fall 1988; author's calculations. See methodological appendix.

Note: Segregation indices based on campus-level compositions of four-year institutions, counting white and black students only. Figures for 1961, 1965, and 1970 count total enrollment but exclude institutions primarily devoted to graduate or professional training; figures for other years count full-time undergraduates. Where no data were available for 1970, 1972 figures were used.

TABLE A6.2
Exposure Rates in 175 Large Colleges and Universities, Three Types of Institutions, Various Years

	Number of institutions in sample	1976 enrollment (000s)	Percent nonwhite in typical white student's institution				
			1967[a]	1970[b]	1976	1986	1998
Four-year public colleges and universities							
South	24	339.0	—	.051	.111	.170	.246
Rest of U.S.	39	708.4	—	.091	.149	.203	.293
Two-year public colleges and universities							
South	15	86.6	—	.187	.309	.300	.390
Rest of U.S.	40	245.8	—	.157	.255	.361	.484
Four-year private colleges and universities							
South	13	56.3	.034	.047	.072	.103	.220
Rest of U.S.	44	277.9	.040	.065	.125	.196	.299

Sources: 1967: *Chronicle of Higher Education* (1968); 1970: U.S. Department of Health, Education, and Welfare, Office for Civil Rights (1972); 1976: HEGIS; 1986, 1998: IPEDS. See methodological appendix.

Notes: Sample consists of the 50 largest institutions in each category in 1976, plus institutions in the South that were among the hundred largest in the country in each category. Exposure rates are the percent nonwhite weighted by white enrollment. Definitions of regions are given in the methodological appendix.

[a]Calculations for state institutions in 1967 omitted because data combined enrollments for multi-campus state systems.

[b]1972 data used where 1970 is missing.

TABLE A6.3
State Segregation Indices by Type of Institution, 1976 and 1998

	Public Four-Year		Private Four-Year		Public Two-Year	
	1976	1998	1976	1998	1976	1998
Alabama	.478	.289	.856	.684	.306	.184
Alaska	.000	.001	.000	.006	—	.000
Arizona	.002	.004	.002	.077	.083	.125
Arkansas	.313	.213	.613	.378	.158	.177
California	.071	.110	.099	.084	.195	.182
Colorado	.054	.048	.016	.093	.153	.103
Connecticut	.0004	.002	.023	.121	.195	.145
Delaware	.388	.385	.000	.013	.142	.005
D.C.	.001	.293	.520	.344	—	—
Florida	.334	.248	.313	.262	.129	.216
Georgia	.430	.202	.782	.523	.212	.213
Hawaii	.0003	.031	.089	.006	.040	.017
Idaho	.017	.006	.036	.020	.000	.012
Illinois	.141	.170	.163	.157	.563	.436
Indiana	.037	.029	.037	.066	.060	.142
Iowa	.002	.009	.026	.061	.015	.016
Kansas	.008	.110	.053	.014	.363	.062
Kentucky	.188	.109	.040	.040	.000	.057
Louisiana	.458	.321	.551	.500	.284	.200
Maine	.012	.046	.017	.034	.002	.123
Maryland	.432	.324	.230	.158	.328	.366
Massachusetts	.045	.061	.035	.086	.260	.180
Michigan	.094	.054	.299	.193	.459	.185
Minnesota	.010	.032	.281	.061	.645	.138
Mississippi	.642	.419	.780	.502	.401	.105
Missouri	.169	.068	.042	.050	.300	.237
Montana	.020	.013	.130	.454	.014	.574
Nebraska	.024	.013	.018	.056	.081	.103
Nevada	.014	.023	.000	.000	.052	.035
New Hampshire	.0003	.002	.033	.094	.001	.003
New Jersey	.036	.089	.053	.123	.362	.259
New Mexico	.062	.038	.015	.093	.073	.129
New York	.236	.307	.117	.205	.461	.443
North Carolina	.667	.362	.706	.384	.116	.117
North Dakota	.003	.026	.005	.001	.038	.656
Ohio	.103	.066	.206	.136	.359	.109

TABLE A6.3 *Continued*

	Public Four-Year		Private Four-Year		Public Two-Year	
	1976	1998	1976	1998	1976	1998
Oklahoma	.150	.084	.032	.043	.050	.038
Oregon	.011	.012	.084	.025	.012	.031
Pennsylvania	.231	.172	.251	.115	.386	.217
Rhode Island	.003	.0001	.032	.070	.000	.000
South Carolina	.412	.234	.831	.528	.106	.103
South Dakota	.016	.433	.028	.023	—	.529
Tennessee	.319	.250	.644	.337	.373	.219
Texas	.319	.241	.434	.224	.204	.244
Utah	.001	.008	.315	.167	.007	.026
Vermont	.006	.004	.036	.050	.001	.000
Virginia	.641	.247	.763	.533	.144	.124
Washington	.034	.050	.049	.072	.101	.070
West Virginia	.065	.014	.007	.070	.025	.040
Wisconsin	.016	.029	.026	.042	.135	.169
Wyoming	.000	.000	—	—	.021	.035

Source: See table 6.4.

Note: Segregation indices based on white and nonwhite full-time undergraduate student enrollments.

So What?

We deal here with the right of all of our children, whatever
their race, to an equal start in life and to an equal
opportunity to reach their full potential as citizens. Those
children who have been denied that right in the past deserve
better than to see fences thrown up to deny them that right
in the future. Our Nation, I fear, will be ill served by the
Court's refusal to remedy separate and unequal education,
for unless our children begin to learn together, there is little
hope that our people will ever learn to live together.
Thurgood Marshall, dissenting opinion in
Milliken v. Bradley, 1974[1]

THE PRIMARY PURPOSE of this book is to document how interracial contact changed over the first half-century after *Brown v. Board of Education*. The book's historical perspective seems justified by the generally agreed-upon status of the decision as a landmark in both U.S. constitutional law and social policy. The book's focus on interracial contact, particularly its emphasis on measurable aspects of that contact, may be somewhat more debatable. My reason for adopting this approach lies largely in my own comparative advantage as an economist. But I was also motivated by a belief that contact is a truly important aspect of student desegregation, albeit an intermediate aspect, lying between policy implementation and socially significant outcomes. Although my training and previous research leave me unprepared to speak authoritatively on how those ultimate outcomes come to be, it is nevertheless fitting to attempt to close the circle by discussing how desegregation might have affected these outcomes, drawing evidence from the published research by other social scientists. Accordingly, after reviewing the book's findings, this concluding chapter draws on the research of others to consider the implications of the changes that occurred in interracial contact. The chapter concludes by noting several important policy questions.

OVERVIEW OF FINDINGS

The preceding chapters present evidence on interracial contact for public school districts, private schools, and colleges and universities. Expressed as exposure rates, segregation indices, and measures of racial isolation, the information is organized variously by school district, metropolitan area, region, state, and type of institution. For some measures it is possible to cover most or all of the fifty-year span following the *Brown* decision, but data limitations in most cases require examining shorter time periods. Taken together, the findings collected here can be summarized by two themes: interracial contact increased dramatically as a result of post-*Brown* desegregation, but contrary forces restrained the extent of this increase.

Interracial Contact Increased Dramatically

The overriding fact that emerges about post-1954 developments is the radical change in school environments. For the 40 percent of the nation's public school students who lived in states under de jure segregation at the time of the *Brown* decision, this transformation was the most dramatic. Measured segregation in the South and Border regions declined from its maximum value to rates that by 1972 made schools in those regions the least segregated in the country. In many communities across the South, where school districts often covered large geographic areas and court-ordered desegregation plans required a complete overhaul of student assignments, public schools reached nearly perfect racial balance. This kind of racial balance was easily achieved—logistically, at least—in nonmetropolitan counties with only a few schools. In large urban districts such as Charlotte and Louisville, however, racially balancing the schools required elaborate reassignment plans and extensive use of school buses to transport students to schools sometimes many miles from their homes. But the results were dramatic. As a result of court-ordered desegregation, the percentage of black students attending schools that were 90–100 percent minority fell in Charlotte from 58 percent immediately before its plan was put into effect to 2 percent immediately after, and in Louisville, from 66 percent to 2 percent. For the South as a whole, the comparable percentage declined from 78 percent in 1968, the highest of any region in that year, to 25 percent in 1972, the lowest.

Less precipitous but significant all the same were the declines in seg-

179

regation experienced in other regions. Next to the South, the Border region experienced the next largest change. These six states plus the District of Columbia, where slavery had been practiced up to the Civil War but which had remained in the Union, had practiced de jure segregation in their elementary and secondary schools until 1954. All of them ended this policy shortly after the *Brown* decision, but actual segregation failed to decrease as rapidly or completely as it did in the South. Perhaps surprisingly, average segregation also declined in districts across the Midwest and West. Public school districts in the Midwest were in fact fairly well segregated at the time of the *Brown* decision and stayed that way for another decade and a half, after which segregation there gradually declined until about 1990. In the West, estimates based on unpublished data from a sample of districts suggest that segregation increased during the 1960s but then fell markedly thereafter, leaving districts in that region, along with those in the South, as the least segregated in the country at the turn of the century. Only in the Northeast did segregation not clearly decline. In that region, measures of racial isolation based on all districts showed no decrease in segregation, but measures based on metropolitan area data suggest that segregation within districts did decline between 1970 and 2000.

In addition to public schools, interracial contact also increased in private schools and in colleges and universities. Based on the sparse data available, the exposure of whites to blacks increased in the Catholic schools of most regions between 1970 and 2000. The average change was not large, however, leaving interracial exposure rates generally quite low. Similarly, the ranks of non-Catholic private schools became racially more diverse, though again by degrees quite modest in comparison to the changes occurring in public schools. By 2000, counting public and private schools, the average white student attended a school that was 74 percent white, the average black student attended a school that was 31 percent black, and the average Hispanic student attended a school that was 25 percent Hispanic.[2] Although schools were far from being racially integrated, these figures show that, on average, students were in schools with significant shares of those of other races or ethnic groups. In short, by the end of the twentieth century, interracial contact in schools was common.

In the nation's colleges, the five decades after *Brown* brought profound change in interracial contact. Aside from the historically black colleges and universities, college in 1954 was an almost all-white experience. By the turn of the century, the racial composition of these predominantly white institutions had changed quite significantly. In four-year institutions, both public and private, in all regions of the country, white college students encountered student bodies of increasing racial diversity. For example, a sample of eleven private universities, whose black enrollments averaged just 0.3 percent of all undergraduates in 1951, by 1998 had increased that share to 7.0 percent. The overall nonwhite percentage over that period rose from 1.0 percent to 32.2 percent.

This evidence based on school enrollments is an outward manifestation of a radical transformation of the educational experience of young Americans in the fifty years following the *Brown* decision. While the change has differed by region and community, for the nation as a whole, the opportunities for students of various races and ethnic groups to interact with each other in comfortable, often cooperative settings have multiplied enormously compared to the years before 1954 or, indeed, 1968. This is true at every level of education, including—perhaps, especially—higher education. One indicator of the extent of this change is suggested by results gleaned from an annual survey of high school seniors, summarized in figure 7.1. When asked how often they did things—such as having a conversation, eating together, or playing sports—with people of other races, the percentage of white students who said they did this "a lot" increased over time between 1976 and 2000, approximately doubling. For black students, the percentages were higher but increased only a little. For white students, at least, the world changed during the second half of the post-*Brown* era, and it seems reasonable to believe that it had begun to change before that. Schools represented the most important source of contact for these young people. Two-thirds of blacks and more than one-third of whites said they had gotten to know people of other races a lot in school. Next most important as venues for this contact were employment, sports teams, and clubs, in that order.[3]

Contrary Forces Restrained the Increase in Interracial Contact

As great as the increases were in interracial contact that accompanied school desegregation, they were smaller than they might otherwise have been. Four forces served to retard the increase in interracial contact in schools. First, and most important, was a tendency for whites to avoid racially mixed schools and the things that were associated with those schools. This tendency was especially pronounced where the actual or potential percentage of nonwhites was large.

Second, whites often had at their disposal multiple options for mini-

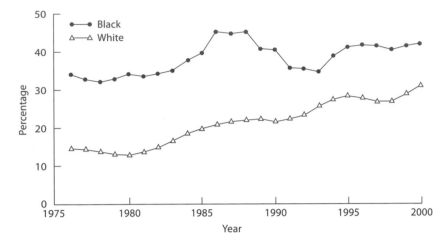

Figure 7.1. Percentage of High School Seniors Who Report Doing "a Lot" with People of Other Races, 1976–2000

> *Sources*: Monitoring the Future survey of high school seniors, Tuch, Sigelman, and MacDonald (1999, appendix); Johnston, Bachman, and O'Malley (various years); author's calculations.
>
> *Note*: Figures are three-year moving averages. Question was: "How often do you do things (like having a conversation, eating together, playing sports) with people of other races?"

mizing the impact of desegregation. Not only were private schools an option that usually promised smaller shares of nonwhites than public schools, so were suburban schools. Most of the white parents living in central cities could feasibly reduce the nonwhite share in their children's school by moving to a nearby suburban school district. Wherever that suburban option did not exist or was inconvenient, entrepreneurial and civic initiative being what it is, the private school option tended to spring up. Another commonly available option for white parents who sought to cushion the effects of desegregation was the possibility of enrolling their children in classes that offered larger shares of white students, made available due to academic tracking. Beyond the choice of school, whites also had ways of blunting the effect of desegregation on the extracurricular life of students by way of segregation in school activities. The social world of the public school, especially the public high school, could have been turned on its head by desegregation. Through various means, whites, the more powerful group in most schools, were able to preserve some of the elements of the previous social order, thus moderating the extent of change in social relations. An interesting by-product created by this multiplicity of avenues of escape was that it provided something like moral cover for white avoidance. It allowed whites to favor racial integration in principle while avoiding it in practice. Reflecting on the growing support for academic tracking in 1958, the psychologist Bruno Bettelheim noted:

> Large numbers of the intelligentsia can advocate desegregation of the public schools all the more freely as their own children (the "gifted" children) are already segregated, either by placement in special classes for the gifted, or in the suburbs. It is not that these groups who fight *against* segregation and *for* special facilities for the gifted wish to establish a new color line. On the contrary, they want to do away with the old-fashioned color line, to replace the "white color" elite by a more up-to-date "white collar" elite, composed of all highly educated persons of all colors.[4]

A third factor retarding interracial contact was that this white avoidance imperative was accommodated and in many cases actively supported by state and local governments, in particular by local school officials. Before the active intervention of federal courts, many districts, North and South, gerrymandered school attendance zones, allowed pupil transfers, and strategically expanded schools or located new ones so as to minimize the extent of racial mixing. These techniques gave way to more subtle approaches, including academic tracking. If track assignments were based on objective criteria such as achievement test scores, such an approach could lead to racially identifiable tracks. If, in addition, parental pressure or outright discrimination came to influence assignments to tracks and special classes, the classrooms could become even more racially demarcated. Outside of the classroom, some school officials looked the other way or endorsed segregated school activities, although this was no means a predominant stance.

Fourth, desegregation's impact was blunted because its initial sponsors gradually lost their resolve to press the case. No doubt influenced by the intensity of white opposition to urban busing orders—opposition that was no means confined to the South—as well as the success of Republican presidents in appointing conservative jurists, the Supreme Court began to back away from aggressive desegregation measures after just two decades. Beginning with the *Milliken* decision in 1974, which limited desegregation efforts in Detroit to its central city district, the court increasingly limited the scope of allowable remedies and turned away from racial balance as a measure of compliance. As the new century began, federal courts in much of the South had not only begun to release local school districts from continuing scrutiny of racial balance but had forbidden the use of race in making student assignments.[5] Meanwhile, the support that black leaders had traditionally given to school desegregation steadily weakened. Frustrated by white resistance to desegregation and disappointed by the perception that blacks had borne the bulk of desegregation's costs—including longer bus rides, inferior teaching assignments, and the closing of black schools—leaders increasingly stressed school quality over desegregation.[6]

The consequences of these four forces are readily apparent in the evidence presented in the book. Of perhaps greatest importance was the movement of whites out of central city school districts into predominantly white suburban districts. Thus, although most school districts brought the schools within them much closer to racial balance, racial disparities *between* districts remained, and even widened. Comparisons of school segregation between 1970 and 2000 clearly show the effect of these two opposing forces. Although segregation declined in virtually all metropolitan areas, these declines were the net result of decreases in within-district segregation offset by increases in between-district segregation (see figure 2.2). This latter, offsetting effect can be associated at least in part with avoidance behavior by white households. The most important form of avoidance behavior was residential location. As the years after initial desegregation passed, white families found ways to minimize their children's exposure to racially mixed schools. In the short run they could pick up and move from one district to another. But the more important force was the gradual relocation of white families with children. Where whiter suburban school districts existed in close proximity to central cities with large nonwhite enrollments, white families over time found their way into those suburbs, aided by a housing industry ready to accommodate demand wherever it was strongest. In metropolitan areas where the central city school district covered a large portion of residential neighborhoods, this kind of separation was more difficult to achieve, leading those metropolitan areas to experience greater declines in residential segregation.

Private schools, of course, offered an alternate means of avoidance. Although the demand for private schools is influenced by many factors, the racial composition of public schools is consistently found to be one of them. The region where desegregation had the largest effect on the racial composition of public schools attended by white students—the South—was also the region with the largest increase in private school enrollment. Although this higher rate of private enrollment did not have a large effect on overall school segregation in most metropolitan areas, it did in a few places in the South. And in the nonmetropolitan South, private schools became the vehicle for the virtual abandonment of public schools in some counties with high proportions of nonwhite students. Private enrollment by whites was subject to a tipping point close to 50 percent nonwhite, beyond which the rate of white exit from public schools accelerated.

Another factor also restrained the increase in interracial contact: segregation within schools. Although contemporary nationwide data on within-school segregation has not been collected, evidence for the state of North Carolina shows its extent at four grade levels. As a percentage of total segregation in North Carolina's districts (measured here at the classroom level), within-school racial disparities are much more important in the upper grades than in elementary schools. Whereas the within-school portion accounted for only one-fifth of total segregation in the first grade, it was almost two-thirds of total segregation in the tenth grade, where the latter is based on English classes. This large share results from grouping tenth-grade students into English classes according to various academic levels.

Racial disparities are evident as well in extracurricular activities, ranging from school newspapers to sports teams. Based on data obtained from almost two hundred high school yearbooks, disparities between the racial compositions of organizations and student bodies arose because of lower participation by nonwhites and the uneven distribution of those who did participate. Even in quite racially mixed schools, all-white groups occasionally appeared, as did groups with no whites. White students were rarely in groups where they were greatly outnumbered by nonwhites. It is worth noting the possibility that within-school segregation in classrooms or student activities could have had a secondary effect favoring interracial contact. It may have had the effect of holding some whites in desegregated schools who would otherwise have left for suburban or private schools.

At the college level, the phenomenon that stands in starkest contrast to the marked increase in interracial contact is the continued existence of historically black institutions. A vestige of the Jim Crow era seemingly oblivious to the desegregation occurring all around them, they enrolled a steady number, but a declining percentage, of black college students through the first fifty years of the post-*Brown* era.

185

CONSEQUENCES OF CONTACT

Given the attention paid to interracial contact, it is fair to raise the question of just what difference contact makes. This section reviews the relevant social science research on the effects of desegregation and interracial contact, research that has been amassed for more than thirty years. But it is instructive to begin by recalling how social science research was used in the original *Brown* decision. A statement of social scientists submitted as an appendix to the appellants' briefs in the segregation cases in 1952 summarized the prevailing consensus, at least among the thirty-two prominent social scientists who signed it. Significantly, this statement concerned the effects not of the mere lack of interracial contact but of racial segregation that was enforced by authority of government. In the social scientists' view, such de jure segregation caused the children being segregated to have low self-esteem and a defeatist attitude; for children in the privileged caste, it perpetuated odious stereotypes. Using words later echoed in Earl Warren's decision, they stated, "regardless of the facilities which are provided, enforced segregation is psychologically detrimental to the members of the segregated group."[7] Bolstered by the famous footnote 11 referring to research by the psychologist Kenneth Clark and other social scientists, the *Brown* decision approvingly quoted a lower court's judgment, "'Segregation with the sanction of law . . . has a tendency to [retard] the educational and mental development of Negro children.'"[8]

Clearly, there is little policy relevance today in the effect of de jure segregation. The question has become whether interracial contact has real effects. Research has identified effects that can be divided into four areas: academic achievement, self-esteem, intergroup relations, and long-term effects on educational attainment and employment.

Achievement

Among the effects of desegregation, perhaps none has been looked to more automatically than achievement. Because of its findings regarding the importance of peers in predicting achievement levels, the Coleman Report of 1966 offered the hope that desegregation would raise the achievement levels of black children. Indeed, this hope was bolstered by a steady decline in the black-white gap in the National Assessment of

Educational Progress (NAEP) after 1971.[9] But whether this narrowing could be attributed to desegregation is another matter. Studies that have sought to determine the effect of desegregation on the achievement of blacks have come up with a decidedly mixed set of results. In general, the research suggests no effect on mathematics achievement for blacks and some modest positive effect on reading for blacks. The achievement of whites does not appear to be harmed.[10] Among the possible explanations for the failure to find a clear connection between desegregation and black achievement is a theory that posits an anti-achievement, "oppositional" orientation among black students, making academic success subject to disapproval among peers.[11] Although some recent research appears to be consistent with this idea,[12] research that has explored aspects of this hypothesized behavior directly has failed to find behavior among black students consistent with it.[13]

Self-Esteem

Certainly the most prominent social science research in the short history of legal challenges to segregation were the doll studies done by Kenneth and Mamie Clark, referred to in footnote 11 of the *Brown* decision. This research, confirmed by subsequent studies, showed that both black and white children preferred white dolls over black ones and that they associated with the white dolls more desirable traits. These findings were taken as evidence that enforced segregation created in blacks feelings of inferiority, and it lay at the center of the commanding statement by social scientists written in 1952 listing the evil effects of official segregation in schools.[14] Thus the effect of desegregation on black self-esteem is one of the potential effects that social scientists paid special attention to in later work. But this subsequent research failed to discern a clear link between desegregation and black self-esteem. In fact, it suggested that blacks do not tend in general to have low self-esteem at all.[15] If desegregation had any effect on black self-esteem, at least the short-term effect was likely to be negative, as black children were exposed to more demanding academic standards or discrimination or both.[16] The failure of later research to find a positive effect should not, after all, be surprising, considering that the early doll research was fundamentally about the effects of officially enforced segregation, not about de facto segregation in a regime in which segregation could not carry the force of law.

Intergroup Relations

In contrast to the relatively limited number of studies examining the effects of school desegregation on self-esteem, psychologists, sociologists, and anthropologists have devoted considerable effort to exploring patterns of interaction between students of different races and the consequences of those interactions. In light of the high degree of residential segregation that characterizes most urban areas of the country, schools are for most children the first opportunity to have significant contact with individuals of other racial and ethnic groups. Thus if interracial contact has any effects, those effects are likely to show up in schools.[17] In evaluating the effect of desegregation on students, social scientists have started by asking what it implies for actual contact. This contact, in turn, is seen as having a two-step effect, wherein contact begets acquaintance and acquaintance influences attitudes.

Like adults, students seek out as friends others who are similar to them: similarity produces an automatic basis for same-race friendships, and socioeconomic status adds an additional reason when it is correlated to race. Contact in school, in the classroom as well as the playing field, has an additional effect on friendships, through the power of propinquity. Psychologists Maureen Hallinan and Richard Williams describe the effect of propinquity this way: "Interaction, whether by chance or by choice, generally leads to positive sentiment, . . . students who are assigned or choose to belong to the same instructional groups or participate in joint cocurricular and extracurricular activities are more likely to become friends than those who are in different groups."[18] That said, racially mixed schools obviously offer an opportunity for interracial contact that single-race schools cannot. Although the tendency to choose same-race friends varies across schools, the chance of cross-race friendship is first and foremost affected by a school's overall racial composition: it increases as the share of other-race students in a student's school increases.[19] One consequence of this is that minority students are more likely to name a cross-race friend than are whites, simply because whites have numerically more opportunities to form same-race friendships. One nationwide survey of students in grades 7–12 found that, on average, about 40 percent of Hispanics and 20 percent of blacks named as best friend a student of another race, whereas only one-tenth of whites did.[20] This racial composition effect on friendships is of obvious relevance to school desegregation because of its impact on interracial contact. Other things being equal, therefore, school desegregation has had the effect of expanding—in some cases dramatically—the extent of interracial acquaintances and friendships.

But ratios alone do not determine the chances for such friendships to arise. Academic tracking, for example, can greatly reduce opportunities for routine contact across races and thus friendships if the tracks differ systematically in racial composition. In contrast, some organizational approaches taken in schools appear to foster cross-race contact. In schools using teams and emphasizing cooperative work, for example, cross-race friendships are more common.[21] Research also suggests that tendencies toward self-segregation vary according to schools' racial mix, with more self-segregation occurring in schools with approximately equal numbers of white and nonwhite students.[22]

A recent study covering more than one hundred middle and high schools analyzed factors affecting the degree of racial segregation observed in friendship patterns, that is, how the propensity of students to name as friends those from other races compared to the proportion of students of other races.[23] Two findings emerged. First, friendship segregation increased with a school's racial heterogeneity up to a point, after which it declined.[24] An increase in friendship segregation does not mean that the number of cross-race friendships declines, but only that their share of all friendships declines. This positive association between friendship segregation and heterogeneity can be understood by seeing that an increase in a minority group's share in a school increases for the students in that group opportunities to have same-race friendships. But it means that racial diversity in a school will not automatically lead to cross-race friendships. The study's second finding was that the extent of a school's friendship segregation was associated with aspects of the school's organization. Segregation was less in schools with cross-race extracurricular activities, those where minority students were not disproportionately assigned to nonacademic tracks, and those without much cross-grade mixing in classes. Opportunities for students in different grades to take the same classes turned out to be opportunities for students to find more same-race friends; thus, limiting cross-grade classes reduced friendship segregation. The finding regarding extracurricular activities seems especially to correspond to Allport's contact theory, which emphasizes the importance for building interracial trust of activities offering equal status and a common goal, characteristics that apply to many high school sports teams and other activities. Given the influence that school authorities have over extracurricular activities—including influence over who participates—the importance attached to these organizational aspects implies that schools can play a significant role in the development of interracial friendships.[25]

Some of the research on intergroup relations in schools emphasizes the importance of contact that is more casual than that implied by friendship. One view is that the criterion of friendship is simply too high a hurdle and that using it to measure interracial relations will understate the extent of significant interracial contact.[26] Another viewpoint stresses the special importance of mere acquaintance, which, according to this view, allows students of one racial group to learn about those of another group without bearing the costs that might be posed by full-fledged friendship. Such "weak ties" are seen as important conduits by which individuals can learn about individuals in other groups. They also become building blocks for social networks, whose importance is noted below.[27]

The most important long-term consequence of these intergroup relations lies in the attitudes formed. Considerable evidence exists that the experience of interracial friendship is associated with more tolerant racial attitudes. Certainly, broad measures of racial tolerance have indicated significant softening of white attitudes over time. Not only have attitudes of adult whites changed, but, as shown in chapter 1, those of white high school seniors have as well. As one writer has put it, the basic norm among white students has shifted over time from one of discrimination to one of equality.[28] An annual survey of high school seniors indicates that, over the period 1976 to 2000, whites became more tolerant while attitudes of blacks toward whites stayed about the same.[29] To illustrate, the percentage of whites who said it would be desirable for their (future) children to have some friends of other races increased from 36 percent in 1976 to 43 percent in 2000 (see figure 7.2). For blacks the percentage fluctuated, ending slightly higher. Exactly what role school desegregation and interracial contact had in these trends is unclear, however, since schools were only one of the forces influencing young people during these years.

Studies seeking to relate contact to the attitudes of students have yielded somewhat mixed results. Some work indicates that the attitudes of whites are associated with the percentage of blacks in a school, being most favorable at the lowest and the highest percentages.[30] But, corresponding to the research on friendships, white attitudes appear to be influenced by more than proportions. Whites tend to have more positive attitudes toward minority students when they associate with them on an equal basis, and their views are more negative in situations where minority

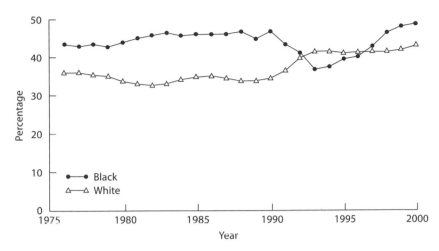

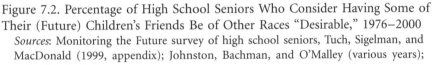

Figure 7.2. Percentage of High School Seniors Who Consider Having Some of Their (Future) Children's Friends Be of Other Races "Desirable," 1976–2000
  Sources: Monitoring the Future survey of high school seniors, Tuch, Sigelman, and MacDonald (1999, appendix); Johnston, Bachman, and O'Malley (various years); author's calculations.
  Note: Figures are three-year moving averages. Question was: "How would you feel about having some of your (future) children's friends be of other races?"

students have low academic performance.[31] Attending diverse schools also appears to affect white students' appreciation for racial and ethnic cultural differences. One ethnographic study comparing the views of white students in two California high schools—one all-white and one racially diverse—found that the whites in the racially diverse school saw much wider differences both within and between racial and ethnic groups. Whereas whites in the all-white school took for granted cultural distinctions associated with whites, white students in the diverse school were fully aware of these distinctions because they were a subject of routine interracial discourse.[32] Among black adults, those who reported having at least one close white friend were much more likely than other blacks to believe that whites are not indifferent to the well-being of blacks, but rather want to help them get ahead.[33]

Interracial contact among adults was the subject of a study published in 1992 by Lee Sigelman, Timothy Bledsoe, Susan Welch, and Michael Combs.[34] Based on surveys in Detroit, the study found that interracial contact had increased over the previous twenty-five years, although it remained modest in this highly segregated metropolitan area. In 1992,

191

27 percent of whites and 43 percent of blacks reported having a good friend of the other race. One big change in the interracial experience of adults in both groups was, not surprisingly, in their school experience: the percentage of adults who reported having attended school with persons of the other race had increased from 56 to 78 percent for whites and from 37 to 79 percent for blacks.[35] Using regression analysis, the authors showed that, for both whites and blacks, the probabilities of having both casual interracial contact and a close interracial friendship were positively and statistically significantly associated with having attended racially mixed schools as a child.[36] Although this finding is not definitive, it is another indication that school desegregation may well have long-term effects on interracial contact in life.

Employment and College Attainment

A final set of consequences to consider are those bearing on students' success in post–high school endeavors. The connection between interracial contact in school and these outcomes lies in the importance of social networks. Networks are vital sources of information about the world beyond high school, information about what kinds of jobs exist, what skills those jobs require, and how one goes about finding a job, as well as similar information about opportunities for post-secondary education. The benefits of networks can even extend to information about specific jobs or colleges, including knowing people who can provide an entree into them. In a classic sociological study, *Getting a Job*, Mark Granovetter shows that personal contacts are a predominant means of finding out about employment openings and landing jobs.[37] Access to these networks can be especially important for urban blacks, whose isolation from mainstream society has been viewed as a major reason for their lack of economic success.[38] A graphic illustration of this isolation is the story of a young Harlem woman who, knowing few people who were employed, dressed for an office job interview in "black evening sheath and wobbly high-heels."[39] Another factor holding minority youths back in both employment and college attendance is what some sociologists have pointed to as a tendency for segregation to perpetuate itself, owing to the reluctance of those in segregated settings to avoid racially mixed ones out of fear of embarrassment or discrimination. According to this view, the associations made in integrated settings allow access to information and modes of behavior that will be helpful in gaining access to jobs and educational opportunities.[40]

To find evidence of these sorts of effects on minority students, sociologists have looked particularly at the association between attendance at desegregated schools and subsequent experiences with respect to college and employment. With the proviso that empirical findings in this area might be especially vulnerable to bias from omitted variables, noted below, research does indeed indicate definite effects from attending such schools. For example, blacks who attended desegregated high schools were more likely to attend college than those who attended all-black schools. Other research, holding constant family background and academic achievement, showed a positive but weak association between attendance at desegregated schools and college attainment for blacks in the North, an association that was absent for blacks in the South.[41] Other work showed that black graduates of desegregated high schools were more likely than other blacks to attend predominantly white colleges or to major in architecture or computer and information sciences.[42] One study in Chicago compared black students who moved within the city to those who moved from city to suburban neighborhoods as part of the large Gatreaux social experiment. As compared to those who stayed in the city, those who moved to suburban schools adapted well to higher disciplinary standards, performed better in sports, and were more likely to attend college, attend four-year colleges, be employed if not attending college, earn a higher wage, and get jobs with benefits.[43]

Segregation at the college level has been found to have effects of its own. For black college students, historically black institutions appear to have at least one kind of advantage. Research covering the 1970s and 1980s suggests that blacks who attended HBCUs were more likely to obtain a bachelor's degree, primarily by drawing them away from two-year institutions. Attendance at an HBCU did not increase the probability of getting an advanced degree, however.[44]

If the ability to work in a diverse workplace is a valuable job skill, this was another advantage blacks from desegregated schools had over blacks who had attended segregated schools. In one study, blacks who attended desegregated schools were more likely a decade after graduation to have white coworkers than blacks who had graduated from all-black schools. The graduates of desegregated schools were also more likely to have found white collar and professional jobs.[45] Residential and social contact with whites was also more likely among those who had been in racially mixed schools: blacks from desegregated schools were more likely to live in integrated neighborhoods and to have white social contacts.[46] Other research based on a nationwide survey of black adults shows that those who had had contact with whites early in life were more likely than other blacks to have whites as friends as adults.[47] These correlations are explained by the access to information and networks and to a lessened reluctance to interact with whites. They may also be the result of higher and more realistic aspirations, which other research has associated with desegregation schooling.[48]

Caveats

A brief review such as the foregoing needs to be accompanied by at least several words of caution, as most of the individual studies in this corpus of research do offer. Two of the most prevalent methodological problems are especially worthy of note. The first of these is the almost ever-present bias that can arise if important explanatory variables are omitted from the analysis, as they almost always are owing to the inherent incompleteness of real-world data sets. Consider the comparison of college attainment between black graduates of desegregated and segregated high schools. If those who attended desegregated schools differ systematically from those who went to segregated schools—if, for example, the parents of those in desegregated schools had higher incomes or more education—then the measured difference in college attendance would reflect not only the effect of the high school experience but also the effect of family background. For this reason, studies that statistically control for family background generally will be more reliable than those that do not. But even that does not solve the potential omitted variable bias problem, especially where the individuals being studied have determined which group they will be in. If students and their parents attend desegregated schools because they have chosen to—such as in programs sending volunteers from cities to suburban schools—almost any comparison between students in desegregated suburban and segregated city schools will be subject to selection bias. Where participants are chosen randomly, however, comparisons can usually be made safely.[49] For studies of desegregation's effects over time, another form of omitted variable bias arises in trying to distinguish the effects of school desegregation from other important changes occurring in society over the same period, including changes in civil rights laws and societywide reductions in discrimination.

The second potential pitfall in doing research on the effects of school desegregation and interracial contact lies in the tremendous diversity of experiences that these terms include. That is, identifying "desegregation" may not be as easy at it might first appear. As a close reading of the research on desegregated schools will reveal, the circumstances applying to desegregated schools differ in a multitude of ways, particularly in the institutional structures applying to the school. Schools that have diversified enrollments, for example, may have highly segregated tracks and classrooms. School administrators also influence much of the environment of a school, including attitudes of teachers toward desegregation or policies followed in choosing the members of sports teams and other school organizations. To quote one careful review of the academic literature, "School desegregation is a many-sided phenomenon."[50] Thus context is important, but it is difficult to reflect adequately in empirical studies. The difficulty of accounting for these important but hard to-measure details generally means that the policy of interest is not well measured, resulting in a tendency in empirical studies to find no statistically significant effect.[51]

Despite these potential problems, the weight of evidence on some questions makes it likely that the interracial contact that has accompanied school desegregation has had important effects. The transformation in intergroup relations that has accompanied school desegregation has surely had an important role in the growth of tolerance of whites toward blacks and other minority groups. For blacks, part of the effect of desegregation has undoubtedly been a certain disillusionment with integration, but desegregation has also had an important hand in making real the educational and vocational opportunities opened up through civil rights legislation. One test of the effects of school desegregation is the simple thought experiment of trying to imagine the current American society the same in all respects but for racially segregated schools and undergraduate colleges in the Border and South regions. The difficulty of imagining this scenario is a testament to the thoroughgoing change that desegregation has brought about.

Judging the success or the desirability of school desegregation is quite another matter. While it is natural for an economist to assess policies in terms of costs and benefits, some of the most important of each in this case defy easy quantification. David Armor has argued that proponents of school desegregation have justified it by similar thinking, by what he terms the "harm and benefit thesis." As he defines it, this notion rests on the propositions that legal segregation harmed minority students and that desegregation based on racially balancing schools (regardless of the origin of previous segregation) will bring benefits.[52] As the legal constraints on local school districts fall away, the question of whether and how to pursue school desegregation as a policy seems destined to rely increasingly on this kind of cost-benefit thinking. And it is quite plain that at least some participants in the debate will not shrink from enumerating the costs of continued efforts to racially balance schools. Nor is it likely that desegregation proponents will end their advocacy for active steps to promote racial balance in schools. This being the case, it is fitting to conclude by considering how interracial contact fits into current policy debates.

POLICY CHOICES

The first half-century following *Brown v. Board of Education* is now prologue. The evil of officially sanctioned public schools is a thing of the past. Indeed, the America of 2004 is in many important ways radically different from that which received the *Brown* proclamation in 1954. Thanks to a massive and sustained civil rights movement and a thoroughgoing transformation of laws regarding access and opportunity, the legal status of racial and ethnic minorities in most realms of social and political life has been profoundly changed. Yet in some respects the America of 2004 bears a striking resemblance to that previous time. Racial segregation remains an ever-present fact, demarcating neighborhoods, urban jurisdictions, and thus many public schools. Middle schools and high schools that are desegregated often include classrooms and school activities that reveal obvious racial disparities. Although official segregation has ended, therefore, actual segregation still exists in various forms.

Public policy surrounding interracial contact in public schools is shaped first and foremost by the Supreme Court, through its evolving interpretation of the Constitution and federal law. Consequently, public policy discussions about segregation are inevitably constrained by the court's decisions. Just as *Brown* started the engine and *Green* and *Swann* stepped on the accelerator, *Milliken* and *Dowell* applied the brakes. By virtue of these decisions, the policy setting of 2004 is manifestly different from that which existed in 1964, or even 1984. Viewing the growing judicial reluctance to push desegregation further, some commentators have written with alarm about the "dismantling" of desegregation, one concluding that Republican appointees to the Supreme Court "undermined desegregation."[53] As it led the process of ending judicial supervision over numerous school districts by declaring them "unitary," the Supreme Court returned control over interracial contact in the schools to local authorities.[54] Once a school district was deemed to be unitary, almost any race-neutral and otherwise nondiscriminatory method of assigning students appeared acceptable, including traditional neighborhood schools. The 2003 *Grutter* decision may leave the door open to assignment plans designed to foster racial diversity, but at this writing the practical implications of that decision are anything but obvious. What does seem clear is that the era of federally mandated plans based on achieving racially balanced schools is over.

Despite the atrophy of judicial activism in pursuing school desegregation, state and local policy makers, including local school boards, nevertheless still have some policy options at their disposal. Indeed, in the post-unitary era to come, the degree to which public schools will be racially mixed will be largely a local policy decision, constrained of course by each district's demographic makeup. Options exist in at least three areas. The first and most important realm of choice lies in the assignment of public school students to schools. As the preceding discussion makes clear, the federal courts have left it up to local school districts to decide how to assign students. Given the preference of most whites for predominantly white schools, and the continuing reality of neighborhood segregation, the use of neighborhood attendance zones will produce at least moderate levels of school segregation. For most districts, the only way not to end up with many racially identifiable schools will be through proactive pupil assignment policies. One such proactive policy is to modify the kind of assignment plans previously used for racial balance by substituting other assignment criteria, such as free-lunch eligibility or test scores, in place of race. This approach is likely to achieve some degree of racial balance, but not as much as under a race-sensitive plan.

Other approaches appear less likely to increase interracial contact beyond what neighborhood schools would produce. For example, magnet schools, again stripped of explicit reference to race, may be used to offer programs likely to appeal to white families in schools located in neighborhoods with higher nonwhite proportions. An alternative to the magnet school approach is "controlled choice," which allows or requires all parents to choose specific schools for their children, subject perhaps to geographical limitations on the set of schools available to each family or to some overall balance constraint. Bolstered by the notion that they will foster competition among schools, such choice plans are similar to voucher proposals, only restricted to public schools within a single district.[55]

The impact that pupil assignment plans can have in this post-unitary era is amply illustrated by the example of three of North Carolina's largest districts. As noted at the beginning of this book, Winston-Salem/Forsyth adopted a choice plan giving wide latitude to parents in selecting schools, eventually doing away with any racial balance requirement. Under this plan, the percentage of black students enrolled in schools that were 90–100 percent minority rose from zero in 1994 to 22.0 percent in the fall of 2002. A similar policy was adopted in Charlotte-Mecklenburg. After being released from its thirty-year-old racial-balance desegregation plan and being challenged in federal court for using race in making assignments to magnet schools, Charlotte-Mecklenburg created a choice plan that ultimately had the effect of guaranteeing suburban whites places in predominantly white suburban schools.[56] As a result, the comparable percentage of blacks in 90-plus percent minority schools there rose from 9.6 percent in the fall of 2001 to 20.5 percent in 2002 after the plan's first year of implementation. In contrast, Wake County (which contains Raleigh), decided to replace its racial balance assignment with a policy that roughly balanced schools by socioeconomic status and achievement.[57] By devising a plan emphasizing balance over parental choice, Wake County continued to have very low rates of segregation, illustrated by the fact that no school in the district had a minority enrollment as high as 90 percent.[58]

Other policy options related to school assignment may affect interracial contact as well. One is the option of permitting voluntary transfers between school districts, as has been done, for example, in Boston, Hartford, and St. Louis, where minority students in central cities can volunteer to be bused to suburban schools.[59] Though likely to be small in scale, such programs can bring a degree of interracial contact into the school experience of students from both suburban and central city neighborhoods. Another policy option with a less obvious racial aspect is year-round schools. Their adoption can lead to unintended racial segregation, if the various schedules that divide the school's year-round enrollment receive disparate proportions of various racial and ethnic groups.[60] Where such self-segregation is likely, local school officials who wish to minimize it can design the rules for placement into the various schedule tracks to make them more racially balanced.

The second set of policy options open to state and local officials applies to organization and practice at the school level. Of greatest importance is probably the set of policies regarding academic grouping and academic tracks. In any elementary classroom, the teacher chooses from among a variety of approaches to organize her classroom and carry out instruction. Pupils can be grouped by ability or not; assignments can include cooperative group work or not. In middle schools, students can be organized to emphasize teamwork rather than individual assignments. In high schools, classes in English, math, and other academic subjects can be differentiated by level, and this differentiation can be modest or highly developed. School officials also decide what criteria they will use to assign students to special education classes or to suspend students for disciplinary problems or how students will be selected for sports teams and student organizations. With regard to all these choices, school principals and other local school officials have considerable influence. And, not incidentally, principals usually have substantial control over classroom assignments, especially in elementary schools. In high schools, they and other local officials make decisions affecting how much interaction there will be among students in different grades. The research on intergroup relations suggests strongly that these aspects of school organization affect the likelihood that students of different races will become acquainted and whether these acquaintances will affect attitudes.

The third set of policy questions apply to higher education. One issue with obvious importance for interracial contact is that of the historically black colleges and universities. Despite some attempts to integrate these institutions, there has been only limited success in doing so at the undergraduate level. Indeed, there remains ambivalence about the desirability of integrating these institutions, as they are viewed by many as a hospitable and effective alternative to predominantly white colleges and universities. Whatever their merits, they undoubtedly limit the degree of interracial contact in the South and Border regions by their very existence. This is by no means a novel proposition, and it has probably been a consideration in the ongoing efforts of federal and state higher education officials to determine policy regarding HBCUs.

The broader set of policies affecting interracial contact at the college level relates to admissions and financial aid. Due to the generally greater financial need of minority students, enrollment decisions will be influenced by the amount and nature of financial aid. Not only will federal financial aid programs have this effect, but so will federal tax provisions and state financial aid policies. One of the most significant new trends in financial aid in public higher education is the use of merit aid programs such as Georgia's HOPE scholarships. As originally designed, this Georgia program gave aid preponderantly to middle-class students, since it lacked any need-based provision and was reduced for Pell Grant recipients.[61] Because of their large effects on college-going behavior, programs such as this have the potential to affect interracial contact.

Policies and practices related to admission decisions are obviously important as well in determining the racial composition of colleges and universities. Few topics in higher education have been more contentious than affirmative action in college admissions. Motivated by their desire to enroll more racially diverse student bodies, most colleges and universities, both public and private, have pursued this goal by giving preferential consideration to minority applicants in much the same way that many of them favor children of alumni or prospective varsity athletes. Although permitted by the 1978 *Bakke* decision, such preferences came under increased scrutiny in the 1990s, leading state university systems in Texas and California to stop the practice altogether. An alternative mechanism for maintaining racial diversity was the percent plan, whereby the top few percent of every high school's graduating class in a state is guaranteed admission to one of its public colleges or universities.[62] This approach, exemplified by the Texas Ten Percent Plan, effectively exploits the existing racial segregation in high schools to guarantee college entrance to some portion of minority high school graduates. In 2003 the Supreme Court settled the constitutional question in *Grutter* by giving a conditional green light to racial preferences in admissions decisions. While the ruling disallowed their use in the kind of large-scale, computer-based admissions processes operated by most state universities, it allowed them to remain a part of a detailed and holistic evaluation of individual applicants.[63] Thus the question for states and state institutions will be whether they are willing to devote the resources necessary to establish admissions processes that will pass judicial scrutiny under this standard.

In considering these policy alternatives at all levels of education, policy makers must weigh various considerations, only one of which is the effect on interracial contact. What then will matter most will be the likely effect of the policies on such contact and the value placed on incremental change. To the extent that the effects are large and racial diversity for its own sake is valued, these policy choices will be significant considerations.

Methodological Appendix

MEASURING INTERRACIAL CONTACT AND SEGREGATION

In legal and social science research on racial patterns of school enroll-ment, the term *segregation* has been used in two ways—as the name of a deliberate government policy and as a descriptive characteristic of actual patterns of enrollment. Segregation in the first sense, commonly associ-ated with the terms *de jure segregation* in the case of the American South and *apartheid* in the South African case, was the explicit policy, backed up by law, of keeping racial groups separate in a variety of settings. Although segregation-as-policy in the United States was declared uncon-stitutional in the *Brown* decision, segregation-as-description remains a public policy issue of profound importance. As commonly used in social science research on schools, segregation in this latter sense refers to dis-parities, or unevenness, in racial compositions across districts, schools, or classrooms.[1] Although one might suspect sinister motives underlying such patterns, *segregation* used in this descriptive sense does not neces-sarily carry with it the same kind of moral indictment that is commonly associated with explicit policies of segregation.

A natural starting point in measuring segregation is to consider the degree to which members of different racial groups have contact with each other. In the case of education, contact is usually taken to mean enrollment in the same school, although the grouping unit could also be districts, classrooms, sports teams, or friendship groups. One common measure of interracial contact is the *exposure rate*, which is defined as the racial composition encountered by the typical member of a given racial group.[2] For example, the exposure rate of whites to nonwhites may be defined as the percentage nonwhite in the typical white student's school. Mathematically, this is calculated as:

$$E = [\Sigma\ W_j\ n_j]\ /\ \Sigma\ W_j, \qquad (1)$$

where W_j is the number of whites in school j and n_j is its nonwhite percentage. This exposure rate is simply a weighted average of the racial compositions of schools, where the shares of white enrollments are used as the weights. If all schools in a district were racially balanced, the exposure rate would reach its maximum value, which is equal to the nonwhite percentage in the district. At the other extreme, if whites and nonwhites attended entirely separate schools, the exposure rate would be zero, indicating that the average white student attended a school with no nonwhites. These two extreme cases—racial balance on the one hand and complete separation on the other—suggest a basis for calculating an index based on the gap between the actual exposure rate and the hypothetical maximum exposure rate (the nonwhite percentage).

A second, closely related measure of interracial contact is based rather on its absence, or what is sometimes termed *racial isolation*. One commonly used measure of racial isolation, for example, is the percentage of black students who are in schools with enrollments between 90 and 100 percent nonwhite. Obviously, higher values indicate more intense racial isolation. Another variant is the percentage of blacks enrolled in majority nonwhite schools. Needless to say, measures of this sort can be defined for different racial groupings and different percentage categories. Measures such as these have the virtue of being easily understood. To attend a school that is more than 90 percent nonwhite, for example, is to have virtually no contact with white students. A disadvantage of these measures of racial isolation, however, is that they are inevitably influenced by the overall racial composition of a school district. Districts with relatively few nonwhites, no matter how students are arranged between schools, will tend not to have students classified as isolated. On the other end, those with high proportions will have large shares of its students so classified, no matter what assignment policies are adopted.

To correct for differences in district racial composition, social scientists have turned to measures of unevenness, or dispersion. Such measures of segregation, typically expressed in the form of indices bounded by 0 and 1, assess the degree of unevenness of racial compositions across constituent units of organization such as schools. Among the indices that have been used in this way are the dissimilarity index, the Gini coefficient, and the gap-based segregation index used in this book.[3] All of these indices measure the degree to which the actual distribution of students diverges from a racially balanced distribution. The gap-based index, based on the gap between actual and maximum exposure rate, is fairly easy to use and explain, and it produces patterns similar to those based on other measures. In mathematical terms, it is calculated as:

$$S = (n_k - E) / n_k. \tag{2}$$

For a district in which all schools reflect the overall racial composition of students, S takes on its minimum value of zero. By contrast, when schools are completely segregated, so that E = 0, the index takes on its maximum value of 1.

To see how the concepts of interracial contact and segregation can be measured in practice, it is helpful to consider a simplified example. Table MA.1 sets out the enrollments, by race, for the five schools in a hypothetical school district under three policy scenarios related to the distribution of students by race. The first case is readily recognized as one of complete racial segregation: two schools in the example, Washington and Kennedy, are entirely nonwhite, while the remaining schools are all-white. At the other extreme is the case of racially balanced schools, with each school's racial composition exactly matching that of the district as a whole. In between these two polar cases exist any number of middling distributions, one of which is shown in the example.

The primary application of the exposure rate in this book is that of whites to nonwhites, which is interpreted as the nonwhite percentage in the typical white student's school. Applying this measure to the hypothetical cases shown in the table shows that the exposure rate where schools are entirely separate must be zero because the average white student attends a school with 0 percent nonwhites. In the intermediate case shown in the table, although schools still vary from as little as 0 percent to as high as 100 percent nonwhite, some whites do attend schools with nonwhites, and it turns out that the average white student is in a school that is 12.6 percent nonwhite, as indicated by the exposure rate of 0.126. The highest value this exposure rate could possibly reach for this hypothetical district, given its racial makeup, is 25 percent, as shown by the 0.25 value in the racial balance case. These three cases illustrate how the exposure rate can measure interracial contact. Because it is an average, it does not in itself reflect the variety of experiences of individual students, but only the "typical" student of a particular group. Another feature of this measure illustrated by this example is that it is necessarily limited by the overall racial composition of a school district. This basic fact becomes relevant in comparing districts with different demographic makeups.

The segregation index standardizes for a district's overall racial composition. Its maximum value of 1, signifying completely segregated schools, is illustrated by case 1 and its minimum value of 0, signifying racially balanced schools, is shown in case 3. For any configuration between these two poles, the index produces a value between 0 and 1. In the middle case shown in table MA.1, for example, the segregation index is calculated to be 0.50.[4]

An important feature of the segregation index is that it is a "pure"

TABLE MA.1

Measuring Exposure and Segregation in a Hypothetical School District: Three Illustrative Enrollment Patterns

School	1. Complete segregation			2. Some segregation			3. Racial balance		
	White students	Nonwhite students	Proportion nonwhite	White students	Nonwhite students	Proportion nonwhite	White students	Nonwhite students	Proportion nonwhite
East	900	0	0.00	500	0	0.00	500	167	0.25
Washington	0	450	1.00	400	100	0.20	400	133	0.25
Kennedy	0	550	1.00	0	550	1.00	600	200	0.25
Frost	900	0	0.00	900	200	0.18	900	300	0.25
West	1,200	0	0.00	1,200	150	0.11	600	200	0.25
Total	3,000	1,000	0.25	3,000	1,000	0.25	3,000	1,000	0.25
Exposure rate of whites to non-whites (E)			0.000			0.126			0.250
Segregation index (S)			1.00			0.50			0.00

Note: $S = (n - E)/n$, where n is the portion nonwhite in the district (0.25).

measure of unevenness; it is independent of a district's racial composition. This allows ready comparisons between enrollment patterns of various school districts of metropolitan areas no matter what their underlying racial mix might be. In this regard, the segregation index is like the widely used index of dissimilarity, which is defined as

$$D = 0.5 \, \Sigma \mid N_j \, / \, N \, - \, W_j \, / \, W \mid,$$

where N and W are total nonwhite and white enrollment in a district, and N_j and W_j are the nonwhite and white enrollment in school j. Like S, the dissimilarity index has a maximum of 1, indicating complete segregation, and a minimum of 0, indicating racial balance. It can be interpreted as the proportion of students who would have to change schools to achieve racially balanced enrollments. In practice, calculated values of D tend to be larger than corresponding values of S, but the two measures are highly correlated with each other. For example, for the 715 public school districts with enrollments of ten thousand or more in the fall of 1999, D had a mean value of 0.29 compared to 0.10 for S, but their correlation was 0.86. The segregation index is used in this book because it lends itself naturally to decomposition, which allows the contributions to segregation to be separately measured.

Extrapolating Regional Measures of Racial Isolation

Table 2.1 in chapter 2 presents summary measures of racial isolation by region for two periods before 1968: the early 1950s (roughly 1950–1954) and the early 1960s (roughly 1960–1961). Information of two kinds was used to produce measures of racial isolation for years before 1968: unpublished enrollment data by school and tabulations based on elementary schools published in U.S. Commission on Civil Rights (1967, appendix table A.3). The former was collected by calling 192 districts to ask if such information were available. Two measures of racial isolation were used: the percentage of black students who attended schools that were 90–100 percent minority or nonwhite (*pb91m*), and the percentage who attended 50–100 percent minority schools (*pb51m*). The regional figures were derived by extrapolating backward from 1968 using trends in these two measures for a group of forty-nine individual school districts. This extrapolation consisted of two steps. The first was to estimate values for the two measures for thirty-nine of these districts. For these districts, tabulations in the U.S. Commission on Civil Rights (1967, appendix table A.3) provide information on very similar indices covering elementary schools only: the percentage of black students attending schools that were 90–100 percent black (*pb91be*) and 50–100 percent black (*pb51be*). These measures will tend to differ from those above to the extent that secondary schools are more racially balanced than elementary schools and districts have significant numbers of nonblack nonwhites. Because both of these factors differ among districts but probably change rather slowly for any given district over time, it is reasonable to use the relationship between the pairs of measures in 1968 to adjust the observed measures for the earlier years. Thus, for the districts for which the racial isolation measures based only on elementary schools were available for the earlier years, estimates of the two measures of racial isolation, denoted by asterisks, were derived as follows:

$$pb91m_t{}^* = pb91be_t + (pb91m_{68} - pb91be_{68}), \text{ and}$$

$$pb51m_t{}^* = pb51be_t + (pb51m_{68} - pb51be_{68}),$$

where t represents pre-1968 data covering either the 1950–1954 or the 1960–1961 period.[5] If these calculations produce proportions outside the 0–1 range, they are set equal to the corresponding extreme value.

The second step in the extrapolation begins with the assumption that the trends in the forty-nine observed districts are representative of the trends of their respective regions. Accordingly, a weighted average of the percentage change in each index was calculated for each region and for each of the two pre-1968 periods, and these percentage changes were applied to the region's 1968 values of the two indices to produce corresponding values for the earlier years. For example, the average value of *pb91m* for the fifteen districts in the Midwest in 1960–1961 (weighted by their 1968 enrollments) was 57.5; the weighted average in 1968 for those same districts was 59.4; the 1960–1961 value was thus about 97 percent of its 1968 value. Applying this same ratio to the Midwest region's index of 58.0 based on the complete set of districts in the region covered in the national survey (see table 2.1) yields the extrapolated value of 56 given in table 2.1. Table MA.2 gives actual and estimated figures for racial isolation for the districts used for extrapolation.

DECOMPOSITION OF THE SEGREGATION INDEX

The segregation index for a metropolitan area (or a nonmetropolitan county) can be decomposed into components representing different

TABLE MA.2
Districts Used for Regional Extrapolations

Region and District	Period 1950-54		Period 1960-61		Proportion of Black Students in Schools: 90-100% Minority			50-100% Minority		
	School Year	K-12 Data	School Year	K-12 Data	1950-54	1960-61	1968	1950-54	1960-61	1968
South										
Miami, FL	50–51		60–61		1.00*	1.00*	0.00	1.00*	1.00*	0.00
Charlotte-Mecklenburg Co., NC	50–51		60–61		1.00*	1.00*	0.59	1.00*	1.00*	0.72
Dallas, TX	50–51		60–61		1.00*	1.00*	0.88	1.00*	1.00*	0.98
Richmond, VA			60–61		1.00*	1.00*	0.85	1.00*	1.00*	0.94
Border										
Wilmington, DE	50–51		60–61		1.00*	0.31	0.47	1.00*	0.86	0.88
Washington, DC	50–51		60–61		1.00*	0.84	0.30	1.00*	0.99	0.00
Louisville-Jefferson Co., KY			60–61	Y	1.00*	0.68	0.50	1.00*	0.78	0.80
Baltimore, MD	54–55		60–61		1.00*	0.78	0.00	1.00*	0.91	0.92
Kansas City, MO	50–51		60–61		1.00*	0.59	0.79	1.00*	0.80	0.86
Oklahoma City, OK	50–51				1.00*		0.83	1.00*	0.88	
Northeast										
New Haven, CT			63–64			0.14	0.31		0.66	0.78
Boston, MA			63–64	Y		0.38	0.43		0.73	0.77
Springfield, MA			63–64	Y		0.15	0.08		0.52	0.40
Camden, NJ			62–63	Y		0.29	0.00		0.79	0.00
Newark, NJ			61–62			0.57	0.86		0.93	0.98
Albany, NY			62–63	Y		0.00	C.02		0.48	0.42

TABLE MA.2 Continued

Region and District	Period 1950–54 School Year	Period 1950–54 K–12 Data	Period 1960–61 School Year	Period 1960–61 K–12 Data	Proportion of Black Students in Schools: 90–100% Minority 1950–54	90–100% Minority 1960–61	90–100% Minority 1968	50–100% Minority 1950–54	50–100% Minority 1960–61	50–100% Minority 1968
Buffalo, NY			61–62			0.81	0.63		0.89	0.73
Syracuse, NY			62–63			0.31	0.00		0.44	0.32
Chester County, PA			63–64			0.71	0.00		0.86	0.00
Harrisburg, PA			63–64			0.36	0.35		0.76	0.65
Philadelphia, PA	50–51		60–61		0.59	0.66	0.67	0.84	0.78	0.91
Pittsburgh, PA	50–51		60–61	Y	0.27	0.45	0.53	0.47	0.69	0.79
Midwest										
East St. Louis, IL	54–55		62–63		0.86	0.82	0.75	0.95	0.98	0.95
Peoria, IL	50–51				0.00		0.00	0.38		0.00
Fort Wayne, IN	50–51	Y	60–61		0.00	0.00	0.32	0.21	0.72	0.73
Gary, IN	51–52	Y	61–62	Y	0.81	0.84	0.00	0.96	0.87	0.00
Indianapolis, IN	51–52		60–61		0.67	0.55	0.58	0.76	0.67	0.78
South Bend, IN			60–61			0.00	0.16		0.50	0.70
Topeka, KS			55–56			0.46	0.00		0.46	0.00
Wichita, KS	52–53	Y	60–61	Y	0.71	0.65	0.47	0.85	0.76	0.55
Ann Arbor MI			63–64			0.00	0.00		0.28	0.00
Detroit, MI			60–61			0.59	0.69		0.87	0.91
Flint, MI	50–51		59–60		0.21	0.23	0.37	0.82	0.93	0.76
Akron, OH			60–61			0.04	0.24		0.61	0.62
Cincinnati, OH	50–51		60–61		0.29	0.48	0.42	0.64	0.71	0.78
Cleveland, OH	52–53		62–63		0.56	0.81	0.86	0.85	0.96	0.95

City									
Columbus, OH	50–51	60–61		0.28	0.16	0.41	0.59	0.66	0.71
Milwaukee, WI	50–51	60–61		0.48	0.64	0.63	0.64	0.84	0.88
West									
Berkeley, CA	47–48	58–59	Y	0.52	0.16	0.00	1.00	0.32	0.80
Oakland, CA	49–50	59–60		0.10	0.18	0.58	0.69	0.79	0.93
Pasadena, CA	50–51	61–62		0.16	0.00	0.44	0.14	0.49	0.74
Sacramento, CA		63–64			0.13	0.04		0.63	0.30
San Francisco, CA		62–63			0.20	0.34		0.89	0.85
Denver, CO		63–64	Y		0.40	0.56		0.82	0.80
Portland, OR		63–64			0.53	0.21		0.23	0.43
Salt Lake City, UT	60–61				0.00	0.00		0.00	0.00
Seattle, WA		62–63			0.10	0.38		0.91	0.50

Note: Indices were calculated for districts where K–12 data were available, indicated by Y under "K–12 Data" column. Indices indicated by an asterisk were assumed based on official policy of segregation. All others were extrapolated as explained in the appendix text. School years given in the table indicate year for which data were available. Extrapolation was required where sufficient data were not available to calculate proportion of black students in 90–100 percent and 50–100 percent minority schools, based on all schools. Most of these cases come from U.S. Commission on Civil Rights (1967, table A.3).

identifiable aspects of segregation. In chapter 4, it is decomposed into four components. Chapter 2 presents a modification of this approach, necessitated by the absence of school-level enrollment data for private schools in 1970. In this section, the full approach employed in chapter 4 is described, followed by the modification used in chapter 2. To see how the four-part decomposition is accomplished, it is helpful to begin by comparing the actual exposure rate in the metropolitan area to four hypothetical exposure rates. The actual exposure rate is simply a weighted average of the exposure rates of public and private schools. Because the exposure rate as defined earlier refers to the average racial composition of schools attended by white students, the numbers of white students then serve as the weights in this broader exposure rate:

$$E = (E_1 W_1 + E_2 W_2) / (W_1 + W_2),$$

where W_1 and W_2 are the number of whites in public and private schools, respectively, and E_1 and E_2 are the corresponding exposure rates in both sectors.

Now consider what the exposure rate would be in four hypothetical cases:

I: *Racially balanced public school districts.* Every public school in each district has the same racial composition. Thus the exposure rate for public schools in each district is raised to $E_{1k}^* = n_{1k}$ and the average for public school whites would then be $E_1^* = \Sigma W_{1k} E_{1k}^*$. For all public school students in the metropolitan area, the exposure rate is raised to E_1^*, which is a weighted average of district racial compositions.

$$E^* = (E_1^* W_1 + E_2 W_2) / (W_1 + W_2)$$

II. *Metropolitanwide racial balance in public schools.* Every public school throughout the metropolitan area has the same racial composition. Thus the exposure rate for public schools is raised to n_1, the nonwhite proportion in the public schools.

$$E^{**} = (n_1 W_1 + E_2 W_2) / (W_1 + W_2)$$

III. *Racial balance in private schools; racial balance in public schools; existing racial disparity in overall racial composition between public and private schools.* Although public and private schools may have different overall racial compositions, all private schools have the same racial composition, and all public schools have the same racial composition. Thus the exposure rate for private schools is raised to n_2, the proportion of private school students who are nonwhite.

$$E^{***} = (n_1 W_1 + n_2 W_2) / (W_1 + W_2)$$

IV. *Racial balance with a common racial composition in all schools, public and private.* Every school throughout the metropolitan area has the same racial composition. Thus the exposure rate for all schools is raised to n.

Using these hypothetical cases as markers, it is possible then to divide the segregation index $S = (n - E)/ n$ into four parts:

Portion due to racial disparities within districts	$(E^* - E)/ n$
Portion due to racial disparities between districts	$(E^{**} - E^*)/ n$
Portion due to segregation among private schools	$(E^{***} - E^{**})/ n$
Portion due public-private racial disparity	$(n - E^{***})/ n$
Total segregation	$(n - E)/ n$

MODIFIED DECOMPOSITION USED IN 1970, 2000 COMPARISONS

Owing to the absence of school-level enrollment data for private schools in 1970, it was necessary to modify the decomposition described above. In effect, all private schools in each metropolitan area were combined. For 1970, private enrollment was based on census data; for 2000, it was based on data from the Private School Universe, 1999–2000.

1970 Calculations

Segregation in public schools was calculated by combining census data and detailed school-level enrollments from the Office of Civil Rights (OCR) surveys.

STEP 1: CENSUS

T_{1k} = total public enrollment in district k;

N_{1k} = nonwhite public enrollment in district k

These totals were calculated as

K–12 enrollment for districts of type 1 (containing elementary and high schools)

K–8 enrollment for districts of type 2 (containing only elementary schools)

9–12 enrollment for districts of type 3–4 (containing only high schools)

STEP 2: OCR

Those enrollments were replaced with OCR enrollment for all districts for which OCR data were available, first using 1969–1970, then 1970–1971 if the first were not available. For each district, values of T_{1k}, N_{1k}, and E_{1k} were recorded.

STEP 3: ESTIMATION OF E FOR DISTRICTS NOT INCLUDED IN OCR

For each OCR district, calculate $q_k = E_{1k}/n_{1k}$

For all OCR districts in a metro area, calculate average q:
$q' = [\Sigma\ T_{1k}\ q_k]/\Sigma\ T_{1k}$

For all missing districts, estimate E_{1k} as $E_{1k}' = q'\ n_{1k}$

When these three steps are done, all districts in every metro area have data on T_{1k}, N_{1k}, W_{1k}, n_{1k}, and E_{1k} or E_k'. In what follows, E_{1k} represents E_{1k} or E_{1k}', whichever is relevant.

2000 Calculations

Data for every public district were used to calculate these measures: N_{1k}, W_{1k}, n_{1k}, and E_{1k}.

PRIVATE SCHOOL ENROLLMENTS AND "EXPOSURE"

Because school-level racial composition for private schools was unavailable for 1970, it was necessary for the sake of comparability to assume $E_2 = n_2$ for both 1970 and 2000, where all private school students in the metro area are taken together. This approach will understate segregation to the extent that private schools were racially segregated. From the census, we know T_{2p}, N_{2p}, W_{2p}, and n_{2p} from each public comprehensive or elementary school district. Summing over all the districts in the metro area yields T_2, N_2, W_2, and n_2.

DECOMPOSITION FOR THE METROPOLITAN AREA

Exposure rates for the two sectors are:

$$E_1 = (\Sigma\ W_{1k}\ E_{1k})/(\Sigma\ W_{1k})$$

$$E_2 = n_2$$

For the metropolitan area, the average exposure rate is:

$$E = (E_1 W_1 + E_2 W_2) / (W_1 + W_2),$$

where W_1 and W_2 are the number of whites in public and private schools, respectively, and E_1 and E_2 are the corresponding exposure rates in both sectors.

Now consider what the exposure rate would be in three hypothetical cases:

I: *Racially balanced public school districts.* Every public school in each district has the same racial composition. Thus the exposure rate for public schools in each district is raised to $E_{1k}^* = n_{1k}$ and the average for public school whites would then be $E_1^* = (\Sigma W_{1k} n_{1k})/(\Sigma W_{1k})$. For all public school students in the metropolitan area, the exposure rate is raised to E_1^*, which is a weighted average of district racial compositions.

$$E^* = (E_1^* W_1 + E_2 W_2) / (W_1 + W_2)$$

II. *Metropolitanwide racial balance in public schools.* Every public school throughout the metropolitan area has the same racial composition. Thus the exposure rate for public schools is raised to n_1, the non-white proportion in the public schools.

$$E^{**} = (n_1 W_1 + E_2 W_2) / (W_1 + W_2)$$

III. *Racial balance with a common racial composition in all schools, public and private.* Every school throughout the metropolitan area has the same racial composition. Thus the exposure rate for all schools is raised to n. (Note: case III in the complete decomposition is excluded here because of the absence of school-level private school data. See previous section regarding 1999–2000.)

Using these hypothetical cases as markers, it is possible then to divide the segregation index $S = (n - E)/ n$ into parts:

Portion due to racial disparities within districts	$(E^* - E)/ n$
Portion due to racial disparities between districts	$(E^{**} - E^*)/ n$
Portion due public-private racial disparity	$(n - E^{**})/ n$
Total segregation	$(n - E)/ n$

REGION DEFINITIONS

Following Orfield and Monfort (1992, p. 2), regions are defined as follows: *Northeast*: Connecticut, Maine, Massachusetts, New Hampshire, New Jersey, New York, Pennsylvania, Rhode Island, Vermont; *Midwest*: Illinois, Indiana, Iowa, Kansas, Michigan, Minnesota, Nebraska, North Dakota, Ohio, South Dakota, Wisconsin; *Border*: Delaware, District of Columbia, Kentucky, Maryland, Missouri, Oklahoma, West Virginia; *South*: Alabama, Arkansas, Florida, Georgia, Louisiana, Mississippi, North Carolina, Tennessee, Texas, South Carolina, Virginia; *West*: Arizona, California, Colorado, Idaho, Montana, Nevada, New Mexico, Oregon, Utah, Washington, Wyoming.

DESCRIPTION OF DATA SETS

Elementary and Secondary Schools

Two separate data sets were created to obtain enrollment and segregation index data for the 1969–1970 and 1999–2000 school years. For 1969–1970, data from the Census's School District state data sets were combined into one data set and then merged with information from the Office for Civil Rights Desegregation Trends data at the school district level. Where district enrollment information (and exposure rates) were available, the OCR public school data were substituted for Census data. When 1969–1970 data were not available, data for 1970–1971 or 1968–1969 were used in that order. For the metropolitan area analyses, 1990–1991 Common Core of Data (CCD) School District Data were used to assign 1990 metropolitan area codes to the combined 1969–1970 district data.

For 1999–2000, public school enrollment was based on data in the CCD, which was downloaded from the NCES Web site, http://nces.ed.gov/ccd/ccddata.asp, and combined into one data file. Due to incomplete information for 1999–2000 for two states, Idaho and Tennessee, 1998–1999 data were used for Tennessee and 2000–2001 data for Idaho. These data were then combined with 1990–1991 CCD School District data to assign 1990 metropolitan area codes in order to combine metropolitan data according to the 1990 definitions of metropolitan areas. To correct some miscoding of metropolitan areas, an additional step combined the CCD information with a file downloaded from the U.S. Census of 1990 metropolitan areas by county. The public school data file was then combined with private school data from the NCES 1999–2000 Private School Universe Survey at the metropolitan area level (or county level for nonmetropolitan area analysis). Private school enrollments for 1999–2000 were weighted using the weighting variable SFNLWT. Although necessary to obtain appropriately weighted national and regional totals, these weights produce implausibly large private enrollments in a few metropolitan areas and nonmetropolitan counties, causing segregation indices based on weighted and unweighted enrollments to differ noticeably in those areas. Among metropolitan areas, these differences amounted to more than 0.01 in four areas: Albany, Georgia; Jackson, Mississippi; Knoxville; and Wichita. Weighting made little difference in regional or national averages, however. For example, in table 4.4, average segregation in 2000 in metropolitan areas was 0.354 using unweighted enrollments, compared to 0.360 using weighted enrollments. For nonmetropolitan areas, average segregation using unweighted enrollments of 0.094, compared to 0.095 weighted. The weighting of private enrollments increased only the components of segregation due to private schools. For all metropolitan areas, the unweighted calculation implies that private schools accounted for about 13 percent of all segregation, compared to 14 percent for the weighted calculations.

For 1970 census data, Spanish ancestry is assumed to equate to Hispanic and Negro to black. White was calculated as total minus Spanish ancestry and Negro. These calculations apply to private school enrollment and public school districts not included in any OCR survey. For most public school districts, where OCR data could be used, racial categories exactly comparable to those used in 1999–2000 data were available. The 1970 census generally excluded districts with fewer than three hundred students. For the sake of comparability, districts smaller than three hundred were also dropped in 1999–2000.

Colleges and Universities

For the higher education analysis in chapter 6, data from the 1976 HEGIS Survey and 1986 and 1998 IPEDS were used. Higher education enrollment data generally include only full-time undergraduates and cover the academic years beginning in 1970, 1976, 1986, and 1998. The 1976 fall enrollment data were downloaded from the ICPSR Web site at the University of Michigan, http://www.icpsr.umich.edu:8080/IAED-STUDY/07650.xml, study no. 7650. This is the first year that HEGIS reported enrollment by race. Previously, enrollment by race was collected separately by the Office for Civil Rights. By 1986, IPEDS replaced HEGIS. The 1986 data are from study no. 2221, downloaded from http://www.icpsr.umich.edu:8080/IAED-STUDY/02221.xml. The source for the 1998 IPEDS data is http://nces.ed.gov/Ipeds/ef9899/, available on the NCES Web site.

The 1970 data were hand-entered from the Office for Civil Rights, *Racial and Ethnic Enrollment Data from Institutions of Higher Education* (1972). The institutions were selected based on size of enrollment. Included in the 1970 data are the fifty institutions with the largest full-time undergraduate enrollment in 1976 for each of three types of institutions—public two-year, public four-year, and private four-year. In order to expand the sample of Southern institutions, those in the South were included if they were among the top one hundred in terms of enrollment. In total, 175 institutions were selected. These data differ from those reported in the HEGIS and IPEDS in that the race category "other" is included and there is no category for "white." "Other" includes nonresident aliens, but since this is likely to be a very small portion of enrollment, I assumed all students in the "other" category were white.

For universities located in the South and Border states, data for 1959–1960 and 1964–1965 were collected from the Southern Education Reporting Service (1961, 1965). These data include, in general, only black and white enrollment; therefore it was impossible to calculate nonwhite as in other years. Data for 1951 and 1976 (1976a) for thirty-two institutions of higher education were collected from unpublished College and Beyond data obtained from the Andrew W. Mellon Foundation. Data for these thirty-two institutions in 1967 were taken from the table "White, Negro Undergraduates at Colleges Enrolling 500 or More, as Compiled from Reports to U.S. Office for Civil Rights," *Chronicle of Higher Education,* April 22, 1968, p. 3.

* *Notes* *

Introduction

1. *Brown v. Board of Education*, 347 U.S. 483 (1954).

2. Dahleen Glanton, "Separate Proms Stir Questions on Integration," *Raleigh News and Observer*, May 11, 2003, p. 9A.

3. In 2001–2002, 53 percent of Taylor County High School's students were black. U.S. Department of Education, National Center for Education Statistics Common Core of Data 2001–2002. Web site visited 2/29/03.

4. *Scott v. Winston-Salem/Forsyth County Board of Education*, 317 F. Supp. 453 (1970).

5. For accounts of the Winston-Salem/Forsyth Schools of Choice plan, see Susan Abramson, "School Redistricting Plan Would Let Parents Choose," *Winston-Salem Journal*, March 21, 1995, pp. B1, B3; Kristin Scheve, "Time to Choose for 22,000 Students in Forsyth County," *Winston-Salem Journal*, March 7, 1999, p. A8; Dawn Ziegenbalg, "Civil-Rights Inquiry into Schools Ending No Major Redistricting Changes Expected," *Winston-Salem Journal*, January 7, 2000, p. A1; and the district's Web site (http://mts.admin. wsfcs.k12.nc.us/prospect/zoneover.html, visited 7/25/03).

6. Author's calculations from North Carolina Department of Public Instruction data provided by the North Carolina Education Resource Data Center and statistics provided by the Winston-Salem/Forsyth County Schools. Calculations do not include charter schools.

7. In 1950 elementary and secondary enrollment in the eleven states of the South, the six border states, and Washington, DC, was 39 percent of the U.S. total. (See the methodological appendix for a list of states in each region.) In addition, most public schools in Arizona, Nebraska, and New Mexico were segregated, adding another 2 percent. U.S. Bureau of the Census, *Statistical Abstract of the United States*, 1953, table 132, p. 120.

8. In documenting interracial contact, the book makes use of the concept of segregation as a statistical description, as opposed to a legally enforced policy. Used in this way, the term *segregation* refers to unevenness, and is typically measured in social science research by numerical indices that range from zero (signifying perfect racial balance across all schools) to one (for entirely separate schools by race). Throughout the book, the term *race* is used as a shorthand to refer to groups that are widely recognized as different from each other, by virtue of physical markers or ethnic background, and in practice often distinguished from one another in both everyday life and policy discussions. Thus, the term *race* is meant to include ethnic groupings and is used in the spirit of Loury (2002, p. 21), whose definition emphasizes physical traits or bodily markings, not easily changed, that "are taken to signify something of import within an historical context."

In referring to racial and ethnic groups, I adopt terminology commonly, though not universally, employed in scholarly, journalistic, and everyday writing and speaking. I use *white* to refer to non-Hispanic whites or European Americans, *nonwhite* (or *minority*) to refer to all other groups, and *black* to refer to African Americans. I use the term *Hispanic* rather than *Latino* because it is the more commonly used term in statistical and academic references. To be sure, great heterogeneity exists within all of the groupings used here, but the simplification achieved through this aggregation does not, I believe, obscure essential patterns or trends.

9. Allport (1954); Schofield (1982, pp. 10–13).

10. See, for example, Boger and Orfield (forthcoming).

11. See Orfield and Eaton (1996).

12. See Fiske and Ladd (2000); also Fuller and Elmore (1996).

13. See Oakes and Guiton (1995), for example; also Loveless (1999).

14. Clotfelter, Ladd, and Vigdor (2003b); Lankford, Loeb, and Wyckoff (2002).

15. Myrdal ([1944] 1962).

16. For a discussion of these measures, see the methodological appendix.

17. Arizona, Kansas, and New Mexico permitted segregation as a local option, and districts in each state did adopt it. Wyoming law also provided for segregation by local option, but this option was apparently never elected (Ashmore 1954, p. 2; Knox 1954, p. 290).

18. The issue of white preferences regarding interracial contact is discussed in more detail in chapter 3. See also Henig (1996) and Schneider, Teske, and Marschall (2000).

Chapter 1: Walls Came Tumbling Down

1. 1963 inaugural address, *Life*, December 26, 1969, quoted in *Simpson's Contemporary Quotations*, 1988 (www.bartleby.com/63/52/552.html, visited 3/7/03).

2. 391 U.S. 430 (1968).

3. See, for example, Sarratt (1966), Kluger (1976), and Patterson (2001).

4. For a description of the unwritten rules that circumscribed daily contact between the races in the rural South, see Johnson (1941, pp. 276–280). See also Dollard ([1937] 1957).

5. Myrdal ([1944] 1962, p. 660) states, "Negroes adjust and have to adjust to this situation. They become conditioned to patterns of behavior which not only permit but call for discriminatory observance on the part of whites."

6. Ervin (1956, p. 32).

7. Myrdal ([1944] 1962, p. 660).

8. Bond (1934).

9. Alexander (1947, pp. 375, 377).

10. See table Al.1; Picott, Wright, and Knox (1950, pp. 27, 64, 65, 77, 110).

11. As would be shown by the Coleman Report in 1966, by the mid-1960s the gap in measurable facilities in the schools attended by blacks and whites had mostly disappeared, suggesting that this process of narrowing had continued, and indeed accelerated, in the decade after *Brown*. For an analysis of the declining racial gap before 1954, see, for example, Margo (1990, pp. 18–28).

12. This lack of data is probably not merely the result of chance. As Ming (1952, p. 266) reported, school officials in the North were reluctant to release data on the racial composition of schools that might reveal segregation. He states, "a worthy social science project would be the assembly of detailed information with respect to the extent to which segregated schools exist in the North and West."

13. Knox (1954, pp. 290–292).

14. Ibid. (p. 294).

15. Eick (2001, p. 31); Knox (1954, p. 292).
16. Ashmore (1954, pp. 3, 67). In Wyoming, segregation was authorized if the number of black pupils was at least fifteen, but Ashmore (p. 67) notes that no district exercised that option.
17. Williams and Ryan (1954, pp. 25–27).
18. Bustard (1952, pp. 278–280). In 1947–1948, the state had 561 school districts (U.S. Office of Education 1951, "Statistics of State School Systems, 1947–48," table 3, p. 34).
19. Ming (1952, p. 268).
20. Valien (1954, p. 304); Ashmore (1954, pp. 72–74); Shagaloff (1954, pp. 330–336).
21. Greenberg (1959, p. 248n).
22. Ming (1952, p. 267).
23. Jacobs (1998, p. 14).
24. Hillsboro, Ohio, required its seventeen black students to attend the two-classroom Lincoln Elementary School, even though some of those students lived closer to one of the two all-white schools. *Clemons v. Board of Education of Hillsboro, Ohio*, 228 F. 2nd 853 (1956). See also Greenberg (1959, p. 222).
25. According to the NAACP, the practice "was deeply imbedded in the customs and practices of practically all the communities along the northern bank of the Ohio River; in all of central and southern New Jersey; in such Pennsylvania cities as Philadelphia, Chester and Coatesville; as well as in Hillburn, Hempstead and Freeport, N.Y." (National Association for the Advancement of Colored People 1962, p. 3). Among these states was Indiana, where state law had until 1949 allowed local school boards the option of operating segregated schools at all levels (Culver 1954, pp. 296–297).
26. Willie and Greenblatt (1981, p. 303).
27. Farley, Danziger, and Holzer (2000, pp. 147–148) report that about 80 percent of properties beyond Grand Boulevard in Detroit were covered by restrictive covenants in the late 1940s. Grand Boulevard envelopes the most central area of Detroit, about fifteen square miles, extending northwest from the Detroit River.
28. *Shelley v. Kraemer*, 334 U.S. 1 (1948).
29. That local policy makers can have chutzpah is illustrated by one defense offered for such exclusion: that there were no schools for blacks in the town (Ming 1952, p. 267). See also Farley, Danziger, and Holzer (2000, p. 157).
30. Farley, Danziger, and Holzer (2000, table 6.1, p. 160).
31. Ming (1952, p. 273).
32. Yinger (1953, pp. 4, 8, 12).
33. Ibid.
34. Ibid. (pp. 22–23).
35. Ming (1952, p. 273) writes: "Negroes generally inhabit the oldest portions of cities. Schools located there share the general deterioration of the surrounding neighborhood. Limited budgets prevent even honest, decent school officials from making extensive alterations, and the others treat these schools as 'Negro schools,' that is, to be maintained on a submarginal basis."
36. New York Public Education Association (1955, p. 8).
37. Ming (1952, p. 273).
38. Cited in Donato (1997, p. 13).

39. According to Donato (1997, pp. 13–14), these districts included San Bernardino, Orange County, Los Angeles, Imperial, Ventura, Santa Barbara, and Riverside.

40. Gonzalez (1990, p. 137).

41. *Mendez v. Westminster School District*, 64 F. Supp. 544 (S.D. Cal. 1946), 161 F. 2nd 774 (9th Cir. 1947).

42. Gonzalez (1990, pp. 139–156). The degree of segregation was not complete; Gonzalez estimates that, circa 1945, 80 percent of Mexican American grade school students in Santa Ana attended segregated schools (p. 137).

43. According to Hendrick (1975, pp. 28–29, 42), the Hispanic school, Casa Blanca, served as a cultural center and its principal an "unofficial mayor" for the city's Hispanic population.

44. Williams and Ryan (1954, chapter 8, especially pp. 165–166).

45. *Delgado v. Bastrop Independent School District*, Civil no. 388 (W.D. Tex.) unreported decision.

46. San Miguel (1987, pp. 121–133). In Driscoll, Texas, all Mexican American children were compelled to spend four years in grades one and two, after which they were allowed into regular third-grade classes (p. 133).

47. *Briggs v. Elliot*, 132 F. Supp. 776 (E.D.S.C. 1955); Armor (1995, p. 24).

48. See Peltason (1961, pp. 46–55) and Patterson (2001, pp. 81–82) for discussions of Eisenhower's views and inaction. Exemplifying his refusal to endorse court-ordered desegregation, he denied at a press conference on August 26, 1958, that he disagreed with the *Brown* decision with this lukewarm neutrality:

> I have said here I think that I would never give an opinion about my conviction about the Supreme Court decisions because such a statement would have to indicate either approval or disapproval, and I was never going to do it about any of their decisions.
>
> Now, with respect to the other one, it might have been that I said something about "slower," but I do believe that we should—because I do say, as I did yesterday or last week—we have got to have reason and sense and education, and a lot of other developments that go hand in hand as this process, if this process is going to have any real acceptance in the United States. (*New York Times*, August 27, 1958, p. 10)

49. The Manifesto denounced the Supreme Court's decision and promised to use "all lawful means" to reverse it. All but three of the Southern states' twenty-two U.S. Senators signed it. The exceptions were Lyndon Johnson and Tennessee's Estes Kefauver and Albert Gore (Patterson 2001, p. 98).

50. Southern Regional Council (1960). For example, in 1959 Durham, North Carolina, received 225 applications for transfer; eight of these were approved (p. 36). For a description of North Carolina's use of this tactic, see also Cecelski (1994, p. 25).

51. Sarratt (1966, pp. 352–353 and table 2).

52. Quoted in Bayor (1996, p. 233).

53. Sarratt (1966, pp. 350–352 and table 2).

54. National Association for the Advancement of Colored People (1962, p. 3).

55. U.S. Commission on Civil Rights (1967, pp. 44–45).

56. See, for example, ibid. (pp. 50–51), Barndt, Janka, and Rose (1981, p. 245), and Mihelich and Welch (1981, p. 264).

57. Milwaukee and Boston were two such districts. See Barndt, Janka, and Rose (1981, p. 245) and Bullard, Grant, and Stoia (1981, p. 33).

58. For example, whites in the attendance area of Cleveland's Washington Irving Elementary School, which was 98 percent black in 1951, had the option of transferring to Woodland School, which was 96 percent white at the time (U.S. Commission on Civil Rights 1967, p. 52). For other examples, see Mihelich and Welch (1981, p. 265), Bullard, Grant, and Stoia (1981, p. 35), and Barndt, Janka, and Rose (1981, p. 244).

59. *United States Statutes at Large*, vol. 78, 88th Congress, Public Law 88-352 (July 2, 1964).

60. Orfield (1969, pp. 46, 77). See also Patterson (2001, p. xxi). For an analysis of the delays inherent in enforcement by the Department of Health, Education, and Welfare, see Rodgers and Bullock (1972).

61. U.S. Commission on Civil Rights (1977, table 21.1, p. 16).

62. *Green v. County School Board of New Kent County*, 391 U.S. 430 (1968).

63. *Alexander v. Holmes County [Mississippi] Board of Education*, 396 U.S. 19 (1969).

64. *Swann v. Charlotte-Mecklenburg Board of Education*, 402 U.S. 1 (1971).

65. See table 2.1.

66. Welch and Light (1987, pp. 23-28).

67. In response to such recitations from senator John Stennis, Connecticut senator Abraham Ribicoff stated, "the North is guilty of monumental hypocrisy in its treatment of the black man. . . . Perhaps we in the North needed the mirror held up to us by the Senator from Mississippi, in order to see the truth." *New York Times*, February 15, 1970, sec. IV, p. 2.

68. *Keyes v. Denver School District No. 1*, 413 U.S. 189 (1973). See also Armor (1995, pp. 34-38).

69. See Armor (1995, pp. 65-66).

70. To illustrate the study's findings, table A1.2 presents some of the measures used in the survey to compare high schools. Comparisons are made by computing weighted means showing the characteristic of the average student of a given racial group in the specified region, divided into metropolitan and nonmetropolitan areas. Thus 48 percent of Mexican American students in the country's public high schools attended a school that was newer than twenty years old, while only 33 percent of blacks in Midwest metropolitan areas did. Each of the table's first five columns contain comparable percentages, and each indicates a feature of high schools that is presumably good to have. The last column gives the pupil-teacher ratio in the average student's school, and in that column only, larger numbers indicate poorer facilities. Except for the relative size of libraries, the measures shown in the table reveal no consistent racial disparities; this was a finding that surprised researchers and policy makers in 1966.

71. Taped conversation, September 18, 1971, quoted in Dean (2001, pp. 46-47).

72. *Milliken v. Bradley*, 418 U.S. 717 (1974). One area where the conditions were met was Louisville, where the city district and that of the surrounding Jefferson County ended up consolidating (Welch and Light 1987, p. 29).

73. See McDermott, Bruno, and Varghese (2002).

74. Keung Hui, "Magnet Schools Work, Maybe Too Well," *Raleigh News and Observer*, March 23, 2003, p. 5A.

75. *Spangler v. Pasadena*, 375 F. Supp. 1304 (1974). See Armor (1995, pp. 49-50).

76. *Board of Education of Oklahoma v. Dowell*, 498 U.S. 237 (1991); *Freeman v. Pitts*,

503 U.S. 467 (1992). See also Orfield and Eaton (1996, p. xxiii) and Armor (1995, pp. 50–54). For a district to be deemed "unitary," it must conform to the criteria set out in *Green v. New Kent County* (1968). See Armor (1995, pp. 48–49) for a brief explanation.

77. *Belk v. Charlotte-Mecklenburg Schools*, 269 F. 3d 305 (2001). The district court ruling was *Capacchione v. Charlotte-Mecklenburg Schools*, 57 F. Supp. 2nd 228 (1999).

78. For a discussion of plans not based on racial balance, see Sara Rimer, "Schools Try Integration by Income, Not Race," *New York Times*, May 8, 2003, p. A1.

79. See Perlmann and Waters (2002).

80. U.S. Bureau of the Census (1975, pp. 24–37); U.S. Bureau of the Census, *Statistical Abstract of the United States* 1970, table 28; 2001, table 24.

81. Farley, Danziger, and Holzer (2000, p. 30).

82. Chiswick and Sullivan (1995, pp. 227, 229). The rate of immigration in the 1990s was the highest of any decade since 1910–1920 (U.S. Bureau of the Census, *Statistical Abstract of the United States* 2001, table 5, p. 10.

83. Calculation based on U.S. Bureau of the Census, *Statistical Abstract of the United States* 2001, table 23.

84. U.S. Bureau of the Census, *Statistical Abstract of the United States*, 1978, table 734; 2002, table 659.

85. See Wilson (1987).

86. Calculated from U.S. Bureau of the Census, *Statistical Abstract of the United States*, 1970, table 11; 1987, table 725; 2001, tables 24, 652.

87. U.S. Bureau of the Census (1975, part 1, series A276–287, p. 40).

88. Author's calculations. The relative college completion rate is best measured by the odds ratio, or $[p_n / (1 - p_n)] / [p_w / (1 - p_w)]$, where p_n and p_w are the proportion of each group with four or more years of college. This ratio increased from 0.32 to 0.56 between 1950 and 2000. 1950 data calculated from: U.S. Bureau of the Census, *Statistical Abstract of the United States*, 1953, table 127, p. 115. 2000 data from: U.S. Bureau of the Census, *Statistical Abstract of the United States*, 2002, table 208, p. 139.

89. Author's calculations. 1954 data calculated from: U.S. Bureau of the Census, *Statistical Abstract of the United States*, 1956, table 372, p. 309. 2000 data calculated from: U.S. Bureau of the Census, *Statistical Abstract of the United States*, 2002, table 658, p. 436.

90. Schuman et al. (1997, table 3.1A, p. 104).

91. Ibid. (pp. 126–127).

92. For analysis of these equalization policies, see Wyckoff (1992).

93. For an analysis of these patterns, see Clotfelter, Ladd, and Vigdor (2003b).

CHAPTER 2: THE LEGACIES OF *BROWN* AND *MILLIKEN*

1. *Congressional Record—Senate*, April 20, 1971, p. 10959. See also David E. Rosenbaum, "Javits Accused by Ribicoff of 'Hypocrisy' on Schools," *New York Times*, April 21, 1971, p. 1.

2. Boozer, Krueger, and Wolkon (1992, pp. 279–282).

3. See table A2.1 for calculated averages by decade.

4. These estimates are all subject to error, of course. For example, the standard deviation of the 32.9 percent figure for the Rest of the United States in the 1940s is 5.2 percent, meaning that there is a 95 percent chance that the true percentage is between 23 and 43 percent, surely a wide range. By comparison, the standard deviation of the 96.3 percent figure is 1.3 percent, implying a corresponding range of 94 to 99 percent.

5. The proportion of blacks in a respondent's school was based on categories and was assumed to be 100 percent for schools described as all black, 75 percent for mostly black, 50 percent for half black, 25 percent for mostly white, and 5 percent for almost all white.

6. U.S. Bureau of the Census, *Statistical Abstract of the United States*, 1970, table 28, p. 27.

7. In contrast to the definition used in this book, the definition of the South in the Coleman Report excludes Texas and includes Kentucky and West Virginia.

8. See table A.2.

9. An exposure rate of 0.03 would be obtained by the weighted average: $0.03 = 0.99$ $(1/33) + 0 (32/33)$.

10. See table A2.1 for more detailed calculations based on the Survey of Black Americans.

11. For a tabular summary of the Coleman Report's findings on racial segregation in schools, see table A2.2.

12. See Orfield (1983), Orfield and Monfort (1992), Orfield, Bachmeier, James, and Eitle (1997), and Orfield and Gordon (2001).

13. Actually, the Office for Civil Rights undertook a study for the fall of 1967, but it has not been used extensively because it employed different racial categories than the subsequent studies (only white, Negro, and other) and because it was apparently not circulated in electronic form.

14. Calls were made to a total of 192 school districts, asking whether they had enrollment data by school, by race for any school year between 1950 and 1954 or between 1960 and 1961. Such enrollment data were entered into spreadsheets and summary statistics calculated. See the methodological appendix for a description of how these data were used to estimate regionwide measures of racial isolation and for an explanation of the methods used to analyze these data.

15. All of the calculations presented are based on the combined enrollments from both pairs of districts.

16. U.S. Commission on Civil Rights (1962); James T. Wooten, "Parents in Charlotte, Even Those Who Favor Integration, Deeply Resent Racial Busing," *New York Times*, October 7, 1970, p. 34; Welch and Light (1987, appendices A3, C).

17. U.S. Commission on Civil Rights (1962, pp. 25–37); William K. Stevens, "Louisville, Suburbs Integrate Schools," *New York Times*, September 5, 1975, pp. 1, 7; Welch and Light (1987).

18. Indiana Advisory Committee to the U.S. Commission on Civil Rights (1977); Indiana Advisory Committee to the U.S. Commission on Civil Rights (1979); Welch and Light (1987).

19. U.S. Commission on Civil Rights (1977, pp. 3–12); Welch and Light (1987). For a discussion of school desegregation in the larger context of civil rights in Wichita, see Eick (2001, especially pp. 180–183).

20. "Denver Schools Told to Integrate," *New York Times*, April 9, 1974, p. 28; "Thousands are Bused in Denver as School Desegregation Begins," *New York Times*, August 31, 1974, p. 32; Welch and Light (1987).

21. Where data were available for more than one school year for a given school district, the year was chosen (where the year denotes that in which the school year began) on the basis of this ordering: for 1950–1954: 1950, 1951, 1952, 1953, 1954, 1949, 1955; for 1960–1961: 1960, 1961, 1962, 1959, 1963, 1958, 1957.

For the districts shown in the figure, data for the 1950–1954 period were taken from

1950–1951 for Fort Wayne, and 1952–1953 for Wichita. There is more uniformity for the second observation: 1960–1961 for Wichita, 1961–1962 for Denver and Jefferson County, and 1962–1963 for Fort Wayne.

22. One school in Louisville, presumably serving a special population, had a racially mixed student body before 1954. For the case of Charlotte in 1950–1954 and 1960–1961, the strict segregation reflected in the measure shown is based on official policy, not school-level enrollment data.

23. See chapter 7 for a description of a new pupil assignment plan adapted by the Charlotte-Mecklenburg schools in the fall of 2000.

24. As is well known to researchers familiar with both, they are highly correlated and almost always yield the same qualitative results, as they do in the present case. For an explanation of how these indices are calculated, see the methodological appendix.

25. Orfield (1983).

26. See methodological appendix for details of the extrapolation.

27. In 1960–1961 0.16 percent of blacks attended schools with whites in the South, and in 1961–1962 the percentage was 0.24 percent (Sarratt 1966, table 2, p. 361).

28. According to the Census Bureau (U.S. Bureau of the Census 2001, p. 892), "The general concept of an MA [metropolitan area] is that of a core area containing a large population nucleus, together with adjacent communities having a high degree of economic and social integration with that core." Specific criteria regarding population and urbanized area are applied to determine each area's geographical definition.

29. For a fuller discussion of this theme, see Clotfelter (1999).

30. This ignores a fourth possible component, dealt with in chapter 4, and a fifth, discussed in chapter 5. For a mathematical description of the decomposition used in the present chapter, see the methodological appendix.

31. For 1970, enrollment data for most public school districts were obtained from the surveys conducted by the U.S. Office for Civil Rights (1978); for the remaining districts and private schools they were taken from the U.S. Bureau of the Census, (1973). For 2000, public school enrollment data were taken from the U.S. Department of Education, National Center for Education Statistics (2001a); and private school enrollment data were based on weighted enrollments from the U.S. Department of Education, National Center for Education Statistics (2001b). See the methodological appendix for more detail on weighting of private enrollments for 2000.

33. For details on the method of estimation, see the methodological appendix.

34. As noted in the text, the sample included only districts with three hundred or more students. The number of districts fell from 5,582 in 1970 to 5,399 in 2000.

34. The difference in these two tables may mean that the low rates of segregation ascribed to Southern districts depends in large part on racially balanced nonmetropolitan districts, or it may be due to the use of different measures.

CHAPTER 3: RESIDENTIAL SEGREGATION AND "WHITE FLIGHT"

1. Coleman (1975, pp. 3–12)

2. William K. Stevens, "Louisville, Suburbs Integrate Schools," *New York Times*, September 5, 1975, p. A1; Stevens, "Violence Breaks Out in Louisville after 2d Peaceful Day of Cross-District Busing," *New York Times*, September 6, 1975, p. 16; Stevens, "50 Per-

sons Are Injured and 200 Arrested in Clashes over School Busing," *New York Times*, September 7, 1975, p. A1.

3. Author's calculations from Kentucky Department of Education, *Educational Bulletin, Kentucky Public School Directory*, vols. 18 (November 1950, pp. 969–971), 19 (November 1951, pp. 699–701), 20 (November 1952, pp. 425–425), 21 (November 1953, pp. 795–797), and 22 (December 1954, pp. 570–572); Thompson (1976, pp. 336–347); U.S. Department of Health, Education and Welfare, Office for Civil Rights (1969, 1970); U.S. Department of Health, Education, and Welfare, U.S. Office for Civil Rights (1978); U.S. Department of Education, Office for Civil Rights (n.d.); U.S. Department of Education, National Center for Education Statistics (2001a); Jefferson County Public Schools (2003). The unpublished enrollment totals in Thompson (1976) were consistently smaller than comparable figures in the federal survey, suggesting that the former excluded kindergarten. Thus, the unpublished figures were adjusted by multiplying them by the average ratio of the two sources in years both were available, 1.0344. The exponential growth rate was calculated from white enrollment of 105,538 in 1974 and 65,973 in 1982.

4. Coleman, Kelly, and Moore (1975).

5. Coleman et al. (1966).

6. See, for example, Mark R. Arnold, "A Scholar Who Inspired It Says Busing Backfired," *National Observer*, June 7, 1975, pp. 1, 18. See also Walter Goodman, "Integration, Yes; Busing, No," *New York Times Magazine*, August 24, 1975, pp. 10–11, 42, 46–47; Diane Ravitch, "Busing: The Solution That Has Failed to Solve," *New York Times*, December 21, 1975, p. 3; and Pettigrew and Green (1976).

7. For descriptions of voluntary desegregation plans, see, for example, Eaton (2001) or McDermott, Bruno, and Varghese (2002).

8. Massey and Hajnal (1995, p. 528).

9. U.S. Bureau of the Census (1975), part 1, series A264–275, p. 39.

10. For an early comparison of segregation indices, see Duncan and Duncan (1955).

11. Originally published in 1965, the book was revised in 1972 (Taeuber and Taeuber [1965] 1972, pp. 37–38).

12. Ibid. (pp. 56–57).

13. Johnson (1943, pp. 174–175). The nation's first residential segregation ordinance was in San Francisco, however, a short-lived attempt to segregate Chinese (p. 173).

14. U.S. Commission on Civil Rights (1967, p. 21). For a description of residential patterns in the South, see Johnson (1943, pp. 8–10); Taeuber and Taeuber ([1965] 1972, p. 45) notes the extreme example of Charleston, where whites and blacks traditionally lived in close proximity.

15. Massey and Denton (1993, pp. 28–29).

16. Ibid. (p. 45).

17. Farley, Danziger, and Holzer (2000, pp. 157, 160). See also Farley and Frey (1994, p. 24).

18. U.S. Commission on Civil Rights (1967, pp. 20–25), Farley, Danziger, and Holzer (2000, pp. 148–157), Denton (1996, p. 803). See also Newman et al. (1978, chapter 5), and Farley and Frey (1994, p. 26).

19. U.S. Commission on Civil Rights (1967, table 3, p. 9).

20. Taeuber and Taeuber (1964, p. 381). The calculation is based on the dissimilarity index.

21. See Farley (1991, p. 288), which shows that residential segregation by race in

Chicago was much stronger than that by income. See also, for example, Alba and Logan (1993), which presents a study of the New York City metropolitan area in 1980.

22. Wilger and Farley (1989, p. 9).

23. See Denton (1996, p. 804). Massey and Hajnal (1995, p. 536) argues that the law had little effect, however.

24. Farley and Frey (1994, p. 30).

25. Wilger and Farley (1989 pp. 4, 6).

26. Frey (1994, table 1).

27. Glaeser and Vigdor (2001, table 2). This dissimilarity index was calculated for blacks and nonblacks, using census tracts. The average was weighted by black population.

28. Cutler, Glaeser, and Vigdor (1999).

29. Farley, Danziger, and Holzer (2000, p. 213). Also see Frey and Farley (1996).

30. Farley and Frey (1994, table 3, p. 39).

31. Glaeser and Vigdor (2001, table 5).

32. Ibid. (table 5, pp. 3, 12).

33. Massey and Hajnal (1995, table 2, p. 535).

34. See Frey's (1979, p. 444) argument that "flight" is an inappropriate term since most locational change is effectuated by whites who were already going to move. He emphasizes the centrality of the locational choices made by that group.

35. A less extensive survey was undertaken also in the fall of 1967. For a description of the sampling plan followed in the Office for Civil Rights' surveys, see Coleman, Kelly, and Moore (1975, appendix 1).

36. Welch and Light (1987, table 18, p. 53).

37. Clotfelter (1979).

38. One modification was to define the hypothetical exposure rate that would have obtained had there been no white losses. The other was to employ instrumental variables estimation. These approaches yielded similar results.

39. Farley, Richards, and Wurdock (1980).

40. Ibid. (Table 2, p. 132).

41. Ibid. (Figure 3, p. 135).

42. Ibid. (p. 137).

43. For example, for a district with a desegregation plan implemented in 1976, this previous trend would be based on changes in white enrollment between 1968 (the first year of data) and 1974.

44. Welch and Light (1987, pp. 27–28). A considerably more intricate pairing plan was ordered in Louisville, involving a predetermined schedule of reassignments of randomly selected classes in grades 2–12, based on clusters containing previously white and minority schools.

45. Welch and Light (1987, p. 27).

46. *Morgan v. Kerrigan* (Boston School Committee), 401 F. Supp. 216 (D. Ma. 1975), June 5, 1975; *Newburg Area Council, Inc. v. Gordon* (Board of Education of Jefferson County, Kentucky), 521 F. 2nd 578 (6th Cir. 1975), July 17, 1975.

47. Rossell and Armor (1996).

48. Actual percentage change in whites (the dependent variable) is used for districts without a plan. (Email correspondence, May 12, 2002, from Christine Rossell).

49. In economic terminology, it need only apply to the "marginal" household.

50. Clotfelter (1975a, p. 450).

51. Bogart and Cromwell (2000).

52. Ibid. (p. 296).

53. Pearce (1980, pp. 13–17).

54. Estimated equations are shown in table A3.1. Equation (1) implies that an increase in the exposure rate from zero to 0.20 would decrease the percentage of whites fourteen or younger by 1.4 percentage points (out of a mean of about 25 percent); equation (2) implies a decline of 0.8 percentage points. Although the equations feature coefficients of the expected sign for all but one of the remaining explanatory variables, the positive sign for percent nonwhite in the tract is contrary to expectations; this sign may reflect differences in income among white families. For an earlier study using a similar model, see Clotfelter (1975b).

55. This view is expressed in Orfield (1981, p. 213).

56. See Cutler, Glaeser, and Vigdor (1999).

57. The estimated regressions are shown in table A3.2.

58. Massey and Hajnal (1995, p. 539).

59. Henig (1996, p. 105).

60. Rice and Betts (2003).

61. Author's calculations based on enrollment and utilization rates given in *Educate!* March 6, 2003, p. 6, www.educateclt.org.

62. Armor (1995, p. 207).

63. Based on surveys of mothers whose children moved from city to suburban schools in the Chicago Gautreaux program between 1976 and 1981, city schools compared unfavorably to suburban schools with regard to physical environment, class size, safety, discipline, teacher commitment, and parental involvement (Rubinowitz and Rosenbaum 2000, pp. 129–147).

64. Henig (1996, p. 112).

65. Foley (1981, p. 192).

66. Scherer and Slawski (1979, pp. 141, 143).

67. Henig (1996, p. 135).

68. Lukas (1986, p. 297).

69. That school quality can differ markedly is illustrated graphically by Anyon's (1997, pp. 26–27, 93) description of education in a poor and predominantly black urban school. The school she describes featured dramatically lower academic standards, teachers who used nonstandard English, and a high percentage of substitute teachers.

70. Henig (1996, p. 109).

71. Taylor (1986, p. 60).

72. See chapter 1.

73. Schneider, Teske, Marshall (2000, chapter 4).

74. For a discussion of this concept, see McConahay (1982).

75. Sears, Hensler, and Speer (1979, p. 382).

CHAPTER 4: THE PRIVATE SCHOOL OPTION

1. Merrill (1967, p. 37).

2. Derby Academy Web site, www.derbyacademy.org, visited 12/12/02.

3. Central Hinds Academy Web site, http://www.centralhinds.com, visited 12/4/02.

4. Our Lady of Lourdes Web site, http://www.ololschool.org/, visited 4/25/03.

5. U.S. Department of Education, National Center for Education Statistics (2001b, table 1).

6. Author's calculations from U.S. Department of Education, National Center for Education Statistics (2001b, 2001a).

7. For a discussion of this achievement gap, see Jencks and Phillips (1998).

8. Grogger and Neal (2000, pp. 185, 187).

9. Patterson (2001, p. 99).

10. Table A4.1 provides the percentages from which the figure was constructed.

11. See table A4.1.

12. By way of comparison, U.S. Department of Education, National Center for Education Statistics (2001c, tables 40, 59) gives estimates that total 51,269,000 for total fall 1999 K–12 enrollment, 10.1 percent of which was in private schools. The totals implied in table 4.1 understate the published numbers for public enrollment by 2.1 percent and private enrollment by 0.1 percent, owing to the omission of Alaska and Hawaii and schools that did not provide a racial breakdown of enrollment, including schools operated by military bases. Using comparable data for public and private schools for 1997–1998, Reardon and Yun (2002, table 1, p. 16) understates private enrollment by 4.1 percent compared to the published figures for that year. The authors calculate the private enrollment share for the nation as 9.7 percent, somewhat smaller than the 10.0 percent share implied by the published figures.

13. 1970: author's calculations from 1970 Census of Population; 1999 public: U.S. Department of Education, National Center for Education Statistics (2002, table 42, p. 58); 1999 private: U.S. Department of Education, National Center for Education Statistics (2001c, table 16, p. 20).

14. The categories specified in the survey were all black, mostly black, mixed, mostly white, and all white, corresponding to these percentages of blacks: 98–100, 80–98, 20–80, 2–20, and 0–2. Calculations using published tabulations revealed, however, that the actual racial compositions of schools did not always conform to these definitions. Calculated exposure rates were based on the racial compositions within the published categories. Assuming that schools were roughly categorized correctly, the use of actual enrollments should result in reasonably accurate approximates of exposure rates. See National Catholic Educational Association (1971).

15. See table 4.2 for definitions used in the survey.

16. This definition of the Southeast excludes Texas and includes Kentucky and Oklahoma.

17. The Great Lakes region used in this survey included Illinois, Indiana, Michigan, Ohio, and Wisconsin.

18. The 1969 survey of schools belonging to the Association of Independent Schools covered 752 schools and reported the number of schools by percentage of black students. This tabulation was replicated using the U.S. Office of Education, National Center for Education Statistics (2001b) for the fall of 1999, for the 845 schools belonging to this association. The percentage of schools by category for 1969 and 1999, respectively (where ranges exclude the lower bound and include the upper bound) were: no blacks: 13.2 percent, 5.1 percent; 0–5 percent: 67.2, 51.8; 5–10 percent: 15.3, 30.8; 10–20 percent: 3.5, 9.0; 20–30 percent: 0.7, 1.4; more than 30 percent: 0.2, 1.9. National Association of Independent Schools Minority Report 1969–1970, cited in Kraushaar (1972, p.

240n); U.S. Office of Education, National Center for Education Statistics (2001b); author's calculations.

19. See, for example, Long and Toma (1988). To illustrate the correlation of private enrollment with household income, the percentage of elementary-age children in private school in 1998 rose from less than 6 percent among families with incomes less than $20,000 per year to almost 20 percent for those in families making $75,000 or more. (U.S. Bureau of the Census, *Current Populations Reports*, series P-20, no. 521, *School Enrollment—Social and Economic Characteristics of Students*, October 1998 [Washington, DC: Government Printing Office, September 1999], table 6). Illustrating the quantitative importance of income and socioeconomic status in determining private enrollment, Betts and Fairlie (2001) estimated models attempting to explain the observed differences in private enrollment rates by race and immigration status. The authors find that family income explains about 30 percent of the observed difference in elementary private enrollment between native whites and all other groups and 36 percent of the difference in private secondary enrollment. Differences in parental education explain an even greater share. Whether it is measured on a current or a permanent basis, then, income is an important predictor of private enrollment.

20. See Tiebout (1956).

21. See Martinez-Vasquez and Seaman (1985) and Schmidt (1992) for studies examining this relationship.

22. See, for example, Clotfelter (1976a), Long and Toma (1988), Figlio and Stone (2001, table 1).

23. In 1999–2000, more than 78 percent of private schools in the United States had some religious orientation. The most frequently named were Roman Catholic (30 percent of all private schools) and conservative Christian (18 percent) (U.S. Department of Education, National Center for Education Statistics 2001b, p. 2).

24. Clotfelter (1976b, p. 30) and U.S. Department of Education, National Center for Educational Statistics, *Digest of Education Statistics 1989* (Washington, DC: Government Printing Office, 1989), table 37, p. 48.

25. Among the private schools founded in 1974 and 1975 in Louisville were the Farmdale Christian School, the Evangel School, Faith Baptist Temple School, First American Christian Academy, Shively Christian School, St. John's Academy, and the Walden School. Of these, only the Walden School was not religious (Reichert 1977, p. 14).

26. Most of these schools held classes in church buildings. The Walden School used the campus of a former military school (Reichert 1977).

27. Reichert (1977, pp. 21–27).

28. Clotfelter (1976b) and Conlon and Kimenyi (1991).

29. Giles and Gatlin (1980).

30. Lankford, Lee, and Wyckoff (1995) and Fairlie and Resch (2002).

31. Betts and Fairlie (2003).

32. See Schelling (1972) for an analysis of racial tipping points.

33. Estimated functions using all counties were very similar to those using only nonmetropolitan counties. The implied tipping points for Mississippi and the South for the full samples were 0.49 and 0.46, respectively, compared to 0.48 and 0.49 shown in the figure and table A4.2.

34. Although individual white families may base their decisions on the actual or

anticipated percentage of students in public schools who are nonwhite, that percentage at the county level is naturally dependent on the decisions of white families, making it an inappropriate explanatory variable. An appropriate independent variable, or instrument, is the racial composition of all students in the county. Because the sample is composed of nonmetropolitan counties, this composition is unlikely to be subject to residential relocation.

35. These "spline" functions are based on inflection points that fit the data best. In each case, they exhibited better fits than a quadratic function. See table A4.2 for estimated regressions.

36. See table A4.2 for the regression equation estimated for all U.S. nonmetropolitan counties.

37. The percentage of white families with incomes of $50,000 or more in 1990 was associated with higher private enrollment rates in all three samples, but the estimated effect was statistically insignificant for Mississippi. See table A4.2.

38. See Bond (1934).

39. Blackmon (1992).

40. These counties (and the percentage of their students who were nonwhite) were: Alabama: Sumter (89 percent), Wilcox (82), Greene (93), Bullock (93), Loundes (89), and Perry (86); Mississippi: Noxubee (88), Wilkinson (65), Claiborne (90), and Holmes (82). Except for Holmes, which had two, all counties were served by a single school district.

41. Reardon and Yun (2002, pp. 7–8) argues that private enrollment is not driven by "white flight." As evidence against the notion that private enrollments are motivated by the desire to avoid desegregated public schools, the authors cite the historically higher private enrollment rates in regions with lower rates of interracial contact in public schools (the Northeast and Midwest) and the stability of private enrollment during the 1970s, the period of the most intense desegregation activity. In fact, these observations simply confirm that avoidance of desegregation is not the exclusive or primary motivation for private enrollment. The dominance of Catholic parochial schools in some regions, and their decline everywhere, largely explain these observations. Abundant evidence supports the importance of avoidance motives in private enrollment, including the explanatory power of the percentage black in Reardon and Yun's regressions explaining white private enrollment rates (table D1).

42. Conlon and Kimenyi (1991). To test the same hypothesis, I included in regressions of the form shown in table A4.2 the ratio of nonwhite family income to white family income, but this variable was in all cases not significantly different from zero.

43. Mathew D. Staver, "What Do Super Bowl Sunday and the ACLU Have in Common?" *The Liberator* 11 (March 2000) pp. 1–2; William J. Murray Report (http://www.rfcnet.org/wjmreport/march2000.htm, visited 12/6/02). For a description of the ACLU suit, see Americans United for Separation of Church and State press release, http://www.au.org/press/pr12173.htm, visited 12/6/02.

44. U.S. Department of Education, National Center for Education Statistics (2001, table 63, p. 72).

45. Calculations based on income and population figures, U.S. Bureau of the Census, *Statistical Abstract of the United States*, 1970 (table 11, p. 12); 1987 (table 725, p. 449); 2000 (table 652, p. 426); 2001 (table 24, p. 26).

46. Information on public schools comes from the Common Core of Data (CCD),

which is based on data reported by state departments of education. Data for two states, Idaho and Tennessee, were not included in the 1999–2000 CCD. Thus public school enrollment data for the 1998–99 year were used for Tennessee, and data for 2000–2001 were used for Idaho. Data on private schools are taken from the National Center for Education Statistics' Private School Universe Study, a periodic survey most recently undertaken for the 1999–2000 year. Private school enrollment data exclude special education schools, include kindergartens in schools whose highest grade was kindergarten, and were weighted to reflect nonresponses using the weight variable SFNLWT.

47. Metropolitan statistical areas (MSAs) and primary metropolitan statistical areas (PMSAs) were used. Those that had components in more than one region were assigned to the region containing the larger enrollment.

48. All MSAs and PMSAs, for those metropolitan areas that are part of consolidated metropolitan statistical areas, using 1990 definitions of components, were included. Excluded were metropolitan areas in Idaho, for which no data were available in the CCD, as well as Alaska and Hawaii. Public school enrollment data were taken from the National Center for Education Statistics, *Common Core of Data, Public School Universe, 1999–2000*, and private school enrollment data were based on weighted enrollments from the National Center for Education Statistics, *Private School Universe Survey, 1999–2000*. See the methodological appendix for more detail on weighting of private enrollments for 2000.

49. The index of .522 was calculated as $S = (27.6 - 13.2)/27.6$.

50. To illustrate, the first component is calculated as $(0.143 - 0.132)/0.522 = 0.040$. The details of these calculations are spelled out in the methodological appendix.

51. In New England, metropolitan areas are defined as aggregations of towns and cities rather than counties, so nonmetropolitan counties in New England were defined as the remaining portions of counties not part of metropolitan areas.

52. Even less appealing is the nation, which was the implicit unit of comparison used by Coleman, Hoffer, and Kilgore (1982).

53. Calculated metropolitan segregation indices for 1994–1995 for five of the large metropolitan areas shown in table 4.3 appear in Clotfelter (1999, table 3, p. 494). The indices in that study are quite similar to those shown in table 4.3 of this book, but generally tend to be a little larger. For example, the within- and between-district components for Detroit in 1994–1995 were 0.03 and 0.68, respectively. For Atlanta, the corresponding components were 0.15 and 0.36, respectively. These components are not strictly comparable. The calculations in the present study employ exposure rates that are weighted averages that include private schools, and the percentage gap is based on the racial composition of all students, not just public school students. The indices calculated in this chapter also differ from those in chapter 2, which do not reflect racial differences between private schools, as do those in this chapter.

54. Coleman, Hoffer, and Kilgore (1982).

55. They base this conclusion on a comparison of two segregation indices: the actual segregation index (incorporating private schools in the calculation) and the segregation index in public schools alone. They argue that the segregation index of public schools is the same index that would be achieved if all private schools were closed and the private schools' students enrolled in public schools in proportion to the numbers of blacks and whites already attending public schools. This assertion turns out to be almost, but not quite, correct. More problematical is their calculation of segregation indices based on

gaps between actual and potential interracial exposure using national racial compositions. Although this approach was necessitated by their reliance on a relatively small sample of schools and students, the resulting segregation indices do not incorporate the kinds of gaps that are involved in segregation as it is normally thought of. To the degree that different regions of the country have different racial compositions, a significant amount of "segregation" would show up even if every metropolitan area were to racially balance its schools. For this reason, calculations of segregation indices made at the local level contain a more realistic implicit benchmark than those calculated at the national, or even regional, level.

CHAPTER 5: INSIDE SCHOOLS: CLASSROOMS AND SCHOOL ACTIVITIES

1. Quoted in Deever (1994, p. 279).
2. Tyson, Darity, and Castellino (2002, table 4).
3. Schofield (1982, p. 100).
4. Kimball and Wagley (1974, p. 181).
5. Wells and Crain (1997, p. 329).
6. Based on examination of the school's yearbook for 1997–1998. See Clotfelter (2002) for a description of the methodology.
7. Gamoran's (1992) study of placement in ninth-grade honors English classes in several Midwestern school districts reveals significant underrepresentation of minority students, even when achievement test scores were controlled for. For a study of within-class grouping in elementary school, see Epstein (1985). For a summary of the arguments against tracking, including its racial aspects, see Oakes (1987), for example.
8. McNeal (1998, p. 187).
9. Ingersoll (1999, table 2, p. 30) found that, among teachers in grades 7–12, the percentage without an appropriate major or minor in college was highest in low-track classes in each of five subject areas. For example, among English teachers, the percentage without a major or a minor in a English was 24.7 percent in low-track, 11.8 percent in medium-track, and 11.2 percent in high-track classes.
10. Epstein (1985, p. 39) argues, for example, "the sorting mechanisms used in the elementary grades may begin a cumulative process of differentiation that, in high school, results in the exclusion of many black students from college-preparatory tracks." See also Oakes (1987) and Oakes and Guiton (1995).
11. Loveless (1999).
12. The decision stated: "The court concludes as a matter of law, that the RSD [Rockford school district] engaged in intentional and purposeful discrimination in regard to the operation of the District's purported desegregation programs, tracking system, Bilingual Education Program, magnet school program and its various alternative educational programs. This intentional conduct resulted in systemwide segregation." *People Who Care v. Rockford Board of Education, School District # 205*, 851 F. Supp. 905, 1026 (1994).
13. See Allport (1954). For discussion of its implications for school integration, see St. John (1975, p. 85) and Schofield (1982, pp. 10–16).
14. Damico, Bell-Nathaniel, and Green (1981); see also Hallinan and Williams (1989, p. 77).
15. See Hallinan and Williams (1989, p. 68) for a discussion of the importance of groups for fostering friendships among students. Similarly, Ellison and Powers (1994)

sees contact as important chiefly to the extent that it leads to friendships, which in turn are central to positive effects on attitudes. Also see Schofield (1979) for similar findings.

16. See Granovetter (1986, pp. 83–87). Interracial contact may also have an important role in integrating students into the social networks that play a large role in generating subsequent job opportunities. As Arrow (1998, p. 98) has noted, "social segregation can give rise to labor market segregation through network referrals." By the same token, increased interracial contact has the potential to exert the opposite effect. See also Schofield (1995, p. 610) for a discussion of these effects.

17. See San Miguel (1987, p. 121).

18. Barndt, Janka, and Rose (1981, p. 243). Milwaukee's schools were highly segregated, with 72 percent of its black elementary students attending schools that were 90–100 percent black in 1965–1966 (U.S. Commission on Civil Rights 1967, appendix table A.3, p. 18).

19. American Friends Service Committee et al. (1970, pp. 31–38).

20. American Friends Service Committee et al. (1970, p. 35); Deever (1994, p. 284).

21. *Moses v. Washington Parish School Board*, 330 F. Supp. 1340 (E.D. La. 1971).

22. The district and its policies are described in Clement, Eisenhart, and Harding (1979, pp. 20–21).

23. "Thus the prevalence of a major form of differentiation, the practice of tracking, seems to be correlated with the ethnic composition of urban schools." Persell (1977, p. 85).

24. Meier, Stewart, and England (1989, p. 25).

25. Persell (1977, p. 87).

26. 851 F. Supp. 905, 1011 (1994).

27. 851 F. Supp. 905, 1012, 1026 (1994).

28. Rebell and Block (1985, pp. 67–68, 114–115).

29. Ibid. (p. 115).

30. Gamoran (1992, tables 4 and 6, pp. 197 and 200).

31. Hollingshead's (1949) case study offers evidence of the influence that middle-class parents have over the operation of a public high school. Rosenbaum (1976, pp. 9, 154–155) elaborates on the point. Sieber (1982) offers an ethnographic study of a New York City elementary school where gentrifying middle-class parents succeeded in placing all their children in the top classroom regardless of the usual meritocratic criteria. Gamoran (1992) found that the influence of parental pressure differed among the five school systems he analyzed but had a quantitatively significant effect for students with average achievement levels.

32. Ability grouping also heightened status differences by drawing attention to the black-white achievement gap. See Schofield (1982, pp. 79–84).

33. The indices have the form $S = (b - E)/b$, where b is the school's percent black and E is the exposure of whites to blacks. They differ from those used in the analysis of North Carolina schools below in two respects: the use of school rather than district racial composition as the benchmark for comparison and the use of black-white rather than nonwhite-white racial groupings. Morgan and McPartland (1981) calculate segregation indices in two ways, counting other nonwhites and ignoring other nonwhites, and then averaging the resulting exposure rates.

34. Morgan and McPartland (1981, table 3, p. 21). They note that these indices are much smaller than those based on differences between schools, but this comparison is

problematic, in that their measure of between-school segregation uses racial disparities across the country rather than within districts or metropolitan areas. As noted in chapter 2, the use of disparities in such broad geographical areas implicitly sets an unrealistic benchmark of racial balance and thus overstates commonsense notions of between-school segregation.

35. Ibid. (p. 9).

36. Ibid. (table 5A, p. 23; p. 9).

37. Ibid. (table 3, p. 21; table 4, p. 22).

38. See Clotfelter, Ladd, and Vigdor (2003a).

39. For grades 1 and 4, these were based on the student's primary classroom. For students in grades 7 and 10, exposure rates were based on the racial composition of English classes. For details on the methodology, see Clotfelter, Ladd, and Vigdor (2003a, appendix C).

40. A simulated random assignment of students to schools and classrooms within districts yielded school racial compositions that were generally very close to racial balance, but yielded distributions that deviated noticeably from racial balance within some schools. For the state as a whole, the simulation suggests that random distribution of students in 2000–2001 would have produced within-school segregation indices of 0.04 in grades 1 and 4, 0.05 in grade 7, and 0.06 in grade 10. By contrast, random assignment would have produced between-school indices of 0.01 in grades 1 and 4 and 0.00 in grades 7 and 10. If random assignment rather than racial balance were adopted as the benchmark for measuring segregation, therefore, the within-school portion would be smaller than what is implied by the calculations reported in the text.

41. For the most part, the calculated segregation indices and their components would not differ by much if other racial groupings had been employed in place of the white-nonwhite division. Black-white segregation tended to be slightly higher, but in no case was the difference more than 0.02. Between white and Hispanic students, between-school segregation was less than white-nonwhite segregation at all grade levels, and within-school segregation was greater. Within-school segregation at the tenth grade was particularly high (0.29, compared to 0.15 for white-nonwhite), reflecting in part the existence of ESL (English as a second language) classes. Patterns of black-Hispanic segregation followed the white-Hispanic patterns closely. See table A5.1.

42. These are Fayetteville, Jacksonville, Goldsboro, and Greenville.

43. The calculations for this comparison ignore students from other racial groups. In their study, Morgan and McPartland actually calculated the index two ways and averaged them. For a fuller description, see Clotfelter, Ladd, and Vigdor (2003a, p. 1493n.).

44. See Meier, Stewart and England (1989). The authors also found that blacks were expelled at higher rates than whites.

45. Gamoran (1992, tables 4 and 6, pp. 197, 200).

46. Oakes (1993, tables 11 and 12).

47. Mickelson (2001, table 3, p. 237).

48. See Deever (1994, p. 282).

49. Epstein (1985, pp. 28–29).

50. *United States v. City of Yonkers*, 833 F. Supp. 214, 218 (1993).

51. See Rosenbaum (1976, pp. 154–155), citing Hollingshead.

52. See Oakes and Guiton (1995, pp. 14, 30). The authors note that, once placed in a track or ability level, students tended to be placed similarly in succeeding years, or lower.

53. Meier, Stewart, and England (1989) presents an analysis of several techniques to discriminate against and segregate blacks in desegregated schools. For tracking, see especially pp. 82, 98–99. Placing blacks in gifted classes is a function of percentage of black teachers, white poverty, black education, black-white income ratio, and district size (all with positive coefficients) and Southern region (negative). The techniques used are designed to act as a substitute for segregation and serve to limit white flight. The authors also emphasize the importance of black teachers and administrators.

54. "Georgia Superintendent Battles a Subtle Racism," *New York Times*, February 14, 1995, p. A6.

55. Wells and Crain (1997, p. 327).

56. Meier, Stewart, and England (1989, p. 131).

57. Yinger (1953, p. 9).

58. See American Friends Service Committee et al. (1970). In one Florida high school, elections were held by making the top vote-getter president, and then giving the vice presidency to the student of the other racial group receiving the most votes. The cheerleading squad in that school was made racially balanced as part of the selection process (Kimball and Wagley, 1974, p. 181).

59. Deever (1994, p. 278).

60. For a discussion of the role of school authorities in student interactions, see Quiroz, Gonzalez, and Frank (1996, pp. 104–117). The authors argue that schools exert influence in the creation of the resulting social networks.

61. See Scherer and Slawski (1978, p. 145).

62. Collins (1979, p. 105).

63. Deever (1994, p. 283).

64. See Scherer and Slawski (1978), Collins (1979, pp. 100–108), and Sullivan (1979, pp. 209, 222). These patterns may change over time, as suggested by Hall and Gentry (1969), which found that blacks' participation rates rose over time after being assigned to predominantly white schools (p. 161).

65. Collins (1979, pp. 109–113).

66. Scherer and Slawski (1978).

67. Sullivan (1979, p. 209).

68. Data for the study were obtained from a detailed examination of a sample of 1997–1998 high school yearbooks taken from a collection of sample copies produced by Jostens, Inc., a large yearbook publisher in Winston-Salem, North Carolina. The sample of schools covered was heavily weighted toward the South, East, and Midwest. By type of school, the percentage of schools in the sample that are private is close to that of all high schools in the nation, but the average size of the sample schools is larger than average. For every sports team or other organization having a formal group picture in the yearbook, a count was made of the white, black, Hispanic, and other students. Information on each school's overall racial composition was calculated from the National Center for Education Statistics (NCES) Common Core of Data for 1997–1998, the year corresponding to the yearbooks, and the NCES Private School Universe Survey for 1997–1998. For a fuller description of the methodology, see Clotfelter (2002).

69. If yearbooks systematically tend to picture whites at a higher rate than nonwhites, the calculations of nonwhite underrepresentation would be understated, as would be the actual gap in exposure. Comparisons using a ten-school subsample showed a slight tendency to include nonwhites less completely than whites in yearbook photos of individual

students. If this tendency extended to pictures of school organizations, then the calculated rates of nonwhite participation would tend to overstate the true degree of underrepresentation.

70. Using data from a national survey of high school students, McNeal found that whites participated in most types of extracurricular activities at a higher rate than black or Hispanic students, the exceptions being cheerleading and vocational activities. The rate for Asian Americans exceeded that for whites in academic clubs, publications, and, to a small degree, in athletics. In multivariate analysis, using two national surveys, he found that participation rises with socioeconomic status and performance on standardized tests. Holding those and other factors constant, the partial effect on participation is actually positive for blacks for most types of activities. See McNeal (1998, p. 187; 1999, pp. 300–301).

71. This index is defined as:

$$S = 100(n - E)/n,$$

where n is the overall proportion nonwhite in organizations.

72. For a discussion of tipping points in the context of school desegregation, see Clotfelter (1976b).

73. Collins (1979, p. 103).

74. See Hallinan and Williams (1989) and Joyner and Kao (2000).

75. Clotfelter, Ladd, and Vigdor (2003b, table 7) shows that, within schools, seventh-grade students in remedial and standard classes are more likely to be taught by a novice teacher than students in advanced classes and, within each type of class, nonwhite students are more likely than whites to be taught by such a teacher. See also Ingersoll (1999) [note 9 in this chapter] for evidence that teachers in low-track classes are less likely to have formal training in the subject they are teaching.

CHAPTER 6: HIGHER LEARNING AND THE COLOR LINE

1. DuBois (1973, p. 100).

2. Harvard College (1954, 1964).

3. See slide titled "Minorities—2006" at www.fas.harvard.edu/~admisweb/stats/ Prof06—files /frame.htm, visited 5/19/03.

4. For discussions of these changes, see Lemann (1999) and Hoxby (n.d.).

5. Compared to Harvard, the 2002 entering classes at Duke and Virginia had higher percentages of blacks (11 percent and 9 percent, respectively) and lower percentages of Asian Americans (12 percent and 11 percent). Their proportions of Hispanic Americans were 7.5 percent and 3 percent, respectively. (Email correspondence from Christoph Guttentag, director of Duke admissions, and University of Virginia web page, www. virginia.edu/undergradadmission/profile02-03A.html, visited 6/18/03).

6. For a discussion of the college earnings advantage, see Clotfelter (1996).

7. See, for example, Bowen and Bok (1998).

8. *University of California Regents v. Bakke*, 438 U.S. 265 (1978); *Hopwood v. Texas*, 78 F. 3d 932 (5th Cir. 1996); *Grutter v. Bollinger*, 71 U.S.L.W. 4498 (2003); *Gratz v. Bollinger*, 71 U.S.L.W. 4480 (2003). For a description of Proposition 209, see Solmon, Solmon, and Schiff (2002, p. 64). See also Tierney and Chung (2002).

9. *Sweatt v. Painter*, 339 U.S. 629 (1949); and *McLaurin v. Oklahoma State Regents for Higher Education*, 339 U.S. 637 (1949).

10. Of the 102 HBCUs existing in 1982, 47 were affiliated with religious groups, 12 were independent nonprofits, and 43 were operated by states. Sixteen of the state-controlled HBCUs were land-grant institutions, made possible by the requirement of the Second Morrill Act of 1890 that states operating dual systems had to establish land-grant institutions for blacks as well as whites (U.S. Department of Education, National Center for Education Statistics 1985, table A1.2, pp. 78–80; p. 2).

For a discussion of the role of HBCUs in training blacks, see Allen and Jewell (2002).

11. Southern Education Reporting Service (1961, 1965).

12. A notable exception was Kentucky's Berea College, which has been open to blacks since its founding in 1855 (www.berea.edu/Publications/History-of-Berea.html, visited 9/9/02). Early in the twentieth century, this violation of the region's racial norms was challenged, unsuccessfully, by the state of Kentucky. See *Berea College v. Commonwealth of Kentucky*, 211 U.S. 45 (1908).

13. Oberlin was the first college to admit students on a racially nondiscriminatory basis, in 1835. See Wiggins (1966, p. 1).

14. Author's calculations. U.S. Bureau of the Census, *Statistical Abstract of the United States*, 1971, table 28.

15. Three of these had been established prior to the Civil War: Cheyney (1837), Lincoln (1854), and Wilberforce (1856) (U.S. Department of Education, National Center for Education Statistics 1985, p. 2). See also Plaut (1954, p. 313) and Morris (1979, p. 302).

16. Plaut (1954, p. 310).

17. U.S. Bureau of the Census, *Statistical Abstract of the United States*, 1970, table 28; 1998, table 24.

18. Author's calculations based on population by state, 1950 and 2000. U.S. Bureau of the Census, *Statistical Abstract of the United States*, 1970, table 28; and 2000, table 24.

19. For comparisons of attendance rates by socioeconomic class over time, see Clotfelter, Ehrenberg, Getz, and Siegfried (1991, table 2.11, p. 41).

20. See ibid. (chapter 4).

21. As summarized by Morris (1979, p. 338 n. 2), the cases are *Adams v. Richardson*, 351 F. Supp 636 (D.C.D.C. 1972, amended 1973); *Adams v. Richardson*, 356 F. Supp 92 (D.C.D.C. 1973); *Adams v. Richardson* 480 F. 2d 1159 (C.A.D.C. 1973); *Adams v. Califano*, 430 F. Supp 118 (D.C.D.C. 1977). See also Brown (1999, pp. xvi–xvii, 26, 59, 128 n. 10). Three guidelines were set down in *Adams v. Califano*, although they were by no means achieved in every state: equal proportions of black and white high school graduates attending college, annual increases in the percentage of blacks attending predominantly white state institutions, and increases in the percentage of whites attending HBCUs (Teddlie and Freeman 2002, p. 83).

22. *United States v. Fordice*, 505 U.S. 717 (1992); Susan Chira, "Ruling May Force Changes at Colleges," *New York Times*, June 27, 1992, p. 10; Days (1998, pp. 146–148); Ehrenberg, Rothstein, and Olsen (1999, p. 173). Among the policies that have been used to desegregate these institutions is specialization, wherein duplications in graduate programs are eliminated. A full consideration of this issue therefore must include attention to graduate enrollments.

23. *University of California Regents v. Bakke*, 438 U.S. 265 (1978).

24. *Hopwood v. Texas*, 78 F. 3d 932 (5th Cir. 1996).

25. *Grutter v. Bollinger*, 71 U.S.L.W. 4498 (2003); *Gratz v. Bollinger*, 71 U.S.L.W. 4480 (2003).

26. U.S. Department of Health, Education, and Welfare, National Center for Education Statistics (1970, table 87, p. 67).

27. U.S. Department of Education, National Center for Education Statistics (2001c, table 173, p. 202).

28. One form this pressure took was from private foundations. For an account of the deliberations by five prominent private universities in the South over the admission of black students, see Kean (2000).

29. For a discussion of the educational value of diversity, see Bowen and Bok (1998, chapter 8).

30. Writing about institutions outside the South and Border states, Plaut (1954, pp. 313–314) notes a tendency for blacks to become segregated when their numbers rise above a token representation on college campuses: "Where they are present in large numbers, there is often a tendency for them to build their own social ghettoes. The observation has been made again and again that in large universities, particularly in the Middle West, where Negro enrollment is counted in the high hundreds, a 'Negro corner' is conspicuous the university dining-halls and cafeterias."

31. For 1976 the table shows the racial breakdown using both data sets: the College and Beyond data are used in the column headed 1976a, and the federal survey (covering all students) is the basis for the percentages under 1976b. These are reasonably close except in the case of public universities.

32. Table A6.1 gives the underlying calculated indices. Owing to differences in the data used, the figures for the earlier years are not entirely comparable with those in the later years, but the resulting errors are not likely to be large. For 1961 and 1965, racial categories were white and black except in Texas, where they were total and black; for other years, the breakdown was white and nonwhite. For the states shown, this change is likely to affect the comparability of data over time most in Florida and Texas, owing to large Hispanic enrollments in those states. Less significantly, data for 1961 and 1965 include graduate enrollments (except in freestanding professional campuses, which were dropped), slightly raising the exposure rates in those years. Also, figures for the first three years include part-time students, whereas those for the last three cover only full-time.

33. See chapter 2 and the methodological appendix for an explanation of the segregation index.

34. See table A6.1.

35. American Association of Community and Junior Colleges (1988, table 2, p. 8).

36. In the fall of 1998, ten states had higher public two-year enrollments than public four-year enrollments. In addition to Florida and Texas, they were Hawaii, Illinois, and six Western states: Arizona, California, Nevada, New Mexico, Oregon, and Washington. U.S. Department of Education, National Center for Education Statistics (2001c, table 197, p. 226).

37. Smith (1998).

38. The sample consisted of the fifty largest institutions in each of the three categories (two-year public, four-year public, and four-year private), plus all institutions in the South that were among the hundred largest in each category. Two of the top fifty listings for community colleges were actually entire state systems (Kentucky and Wisconsin), not campuses, so they were dropped from the sample. This approach yielded a sample of 55, 63, and 55 institutions in the three categories, respectively, for a total of 175. Of these, 15, 24, and 13, respectively, were in the South.

For four-year institutions, the decision to use only the largest institutions does not appear to create any pronounced bias, but for two-year institutions it may. In 1976, 46 of the 55 community colleges in the sample came from four states: California, New York, Florida, and Texas. Since these states also have high proportions of nonwhites, exposure rates of whites to nonwhites may well overstate actual national averages, as is suggested by a comparison of figure 6.3 and table 6.4. Nevertheless, the trends shown in figure 6.3 are instructive because they are based on a fixed panel of institutions over a long period.

39. The South–non-South gap in exposure rates for public four-year institutions evident in the sample of 175 institutions disappeared in the full sample of institutions for 1986 and 1998.

40. Author's calculations based on HEGIS 1976 and IPEDS 1998.

41. This increase was somewhat smaller than that experienced by the predominantly white private colleges and universities depicted in table 6.3. The average nonwhite percentage in 1976 was 12.4 percent in the private universities and 10.4 percent in the private colleges summarized in table 6.3. For 1998 the comparable shares were 32.2 and 26.4 percent.

42. Comparable to the index used in previous chapters, the gap-based segregation index in this case is $S_{lm} = (n_{lm} - E_{lm})/n_{lm}$, where n_{lm} is the proportion of nonwhites enrolled in institution type l in state m and E_{lm} is the corresponding exposure rate of whites to nonwhites. For a more detailed explanation of the calculation of these measures, see the methodological appendix.

43. The tendency of two-year institutions to reflect the racial mix of their immediate vicinity and the tendency of local areas within a state to vary in racial composition explain the higher segregation indices found by Thomas, McPartland, and Gottfredson (1981) for two-year institutions outside the South and Border.

44. See Hoxby (n.d.) for an analysis of the increasingly national character of the market for higher education, especially for selective institutions.

45. U.S. Department of Education, National Center for Education Statistics (2001c, table 222, pp. 260–261).

46. See Thomas, McPartland, and Gottfredson (1981).

47. U.S. Department of Education, National Center for Education Statistics (1985, appendix 2).

48. See Clotfelter, Ladd, and Vigdor (2003a).

49. Author's calculations, based on data from HEGIS and IPEDS.

CHAPTER 7: SO WHAT?

1. *Milliken v. Bradley*, 418 U.S. 717, 783 (1974).

2. Author's calculations, U.S. Department of Education, National Center for Education Statistics (2001a and 2001b).

3. Johnston, Bachman, and O'Malley (1999, appendix, p. 190, question A07). The series of questions began with: "The next questions are about race relations. How much have you gotten to know people of other races?"

4. Bettelheim (1958, p. 337).

5. See Boger (2000).

6. See, for example, Allen and Jewell (1995), Bell (1980), Minow (1990) and Glenn C. Loury, "Integration Has Had Its Day," *New York Times*, April 23, 1997, p. A23.

7. Allport et al. (1953, p. 72).

8. *Brown v. Board of Education*, 347 U.S. 483, 494 (1954).

9. Grissmer, Flanagan, and Williamson (1998, pp. 221–222). See also Gerard and Miller (1975) for a careful study of achievement under desegregation, which finds no beneficial achievement effect.

10. U.S. Department of Health, Education, and Welfare (1976, p. 49); Schofield (1995, pp. 599–602). Similarly, a more recent study by Cook and Evans (2000) finds that little if any of the convergence in NAEP scores of blacks and whites can be attributed to any changes in school quality brought about by school desegregation.

11. Fordham and Ogbu (1986).

12. Hanushek, Kain, and Rivkin (2002).

13. Cook and Ludwig (1997); Tyson, Darity, and Castellino (2002).

14. See Clark and Clark (1950) and an assessment by Schofield (1991, pp. 341–342). See also U.S. Department of Health, Education, and Welfare (1976, p. 51).

15. Schofield (1995, p. 607) believes research on self-esteem "may have been out of proportion to the problem" and believes there is no reason to expect that desegregation would increase the self-esteem of blacks.

16. U.S. Department of Health, Education, and Welfare (1976, p. 95) gives a review of studies. See also Epstein and Karweit (1983), which found self-esteem among blacks to be generally lower after desegregation, the effects also depending on aspects of school environment, such as the use of cooperative learning techniques; and Wells (1996, p. 46), which reports examples of black students in St. Louis feeling rejected by whites in predominantly white high schools.

17. Schofield (1995, p. 608).

18. Hallinan and Williams (1989, p. 68).

19. Joyner and Kao (2000, p. 823).

20. Ibid. (p. 824).

21. Damico, Bell-Nathaniel, and Green (1981, pp. 390–391) reports that there is no simple relationship between school racial mix and cross-race friendships. In schools that are team-organized, white students reported having more black friends than in traditional schools; poor academic performance by blacks may reinforce stereotypes rather than lead to positive interactions.

22. Hallinan (1982, p. 56).

23. Moody (2001).

24. Heterogeneity was measured by $h = 1 - \Sigma p_k^2$, where p_k is the proportion of group k in the school. Note that the probability of naming other-race students as friends can increase with exposure to other-race students at the same time that friendship segregation is increasing, if that probability rises less rapidly than the proportion of other-race students.

25. Other researchers emphasize the importance of extracurricular activities. For example, Epstein and Karweit (1983, p. 132) argues that participation in extracurricular activities may provide an opportunity for friendships to develop, although the environment in the school matters. Granovetter (1986, p. 83) writes:

> Though it may account for a quantitatively small part of the day, time spent out of classrooms in school is opportunity for spontaneous, unsupervised social interaction among children, and may thus be more important for shaping

social relations than what happens in the classroom, particularly when teaching is carried out in traditional lecture style, each student interacting with the teacher, and with one another only at the risk of penalties for deviant behavior.

In junior high and high school settings, extracurricular activities become a particular focus of out of-class student interaction, and may take on greater significance for many students than the formal educational process. Though it is frequently noted that these activities tend to sort by race and sex—so that segregation is recreated at the small-group level—we have little insight into how this occurs.

26. Schofield (1995, p. 609) makes this argument, preferring a measure such as willingness to associate with those of another race to friendship as an indicator of cross-race relations.

27. See Granovetter (1986) for an exposition of this theory.

28. Stephan (1986, p. 197). For evidence that racial prejudice among whites in general has declined over time, see Schuman, Steeh, Bobo, and Krysan (1997) and Hanssen and Andersen (1999).

29. MacDonald, Sigelman and Tuch (2000).

30. Stephan (1986, p. 185).

31. See Damico, Bell-Nathaniel, and Green (1981, pp. 390–391) and Schofield and Sagar (1983, pp. 93–94). For an example of the effects of tracking on stereotypes, see Perry (2002, p. 59).

32. Perry (2002, pp. 100–101).

33. Ellison and Powers (1994, pp. 385, 394).

34. Sigelman, Bledsoe, Welch, and Combs (1996).

35. Ibid. (p. 1310).

36. Ibid. (table 1, p. 1321, and table 2, p. 1323). Other variables included in the regressions included age, gender, education, socioeconomic status, percentage black in neighborhood, location of work, church attendance, and early life neighborhood composition.

37. Granovetter (1995, pp. 4, 11).

38. See Wilson (1987).

39 Felicia R. Lee, "On a Harlem Block, Hope Is Swallowed by Decay," *New York Times*, September 8, 1994, p. A1.

40. Wells notes three strands in the sociology literature relevant to these long-run effects: networks, social inertia or perpetuation theory, and "weak ties," the associations opening up channels of information. On the basis of her review of twenty-one studies, Wells (1995, p. 699) concluded, "interracial exposure in school can indeed reduce blacks' tendency to avoid whites while penetrating barriers between African-American students and networks of information and sponsorship."

41. Schofield (1995, pp. 605, 606).

42. Astin (1982, p. 95); Schofield (1995, p. 606); Wells (1995, pp. 700–701).

43. Rubinowitz and Rosenbaum (2000, pp. 155, 158, 163).

44. Ehrenberg and Rothstein (1994, p. 131) and Ehrenberg, Rothstein, and Olsen (1999, pp. 171, 187).

45. Stephan (1986, p. 195); Wells (1995, p. 701).

46. Schofield (1995, p. 610).

47. Ellison and Powers (1994, p. 397).

48. See Wells (1995, p. 699).

49. Plans based on voluntary city-suburban transfers, such as those in Boston and Hartford, present this kind of sample-selection problem. In contrast, a program based on random assignments would avoid selection bias.

50. St. John (1975, p. xi).

51. The statistical term for this effect is *errors-in-variables*. When an explanatory variable such as desegregation is measured with error, its estimated effect will tend to be biased toward zero. Schofield (1995, p. 609) notes this as one of the reasons militating against statistically significant findings in studies of desegregation's effects.

52. Armor (1995, pp. 8–9).

53. See Orfield and Eaton (1996) and Chemerinsky (2003, quotation from p. 1601).

54. Boger (2003, pp. 1394–1395) argues that the courts gradually shifted the burden of proof away from the defendant school districts and onto minority plaintiffs, lessening the prospect for judicial interventions to increase racial balance in schools. See chapter 1 for the definition of *unitary.*

55. For a thorough discussion of the rationale underlying choice plans, see Chubb and Moe (1990).

56. *Capacchione v. Charlotte-Mecklenburg Bd. of Educ.*, 57 F. Supp. 2d 228 (1999); *Belk v. Charlotte-Mecklenburg Bd. of Educ.*, 269 F. 3d 305 (4th Cir. 2001). In September 2001 the Fourth Circuit Court of Appeals affirmed that the district had achieved unitary status and ordered it to institute an assignment plan without regard to race by the fall of 2002. For descriptions of the district's Family Choice Plan, see Mickelson (2003, p. 1524) and the district's Web page, www.cms.k12.nc.us/discover/ history.asp, visited on 7/24/03.

57. For a description of the Wake County assignment plan and the history that preceded its adoption, see Silberman (2002).

58. Author's calculations, based on data from the Common Core of Data for 1999–2000 and 2001–2002 and from the individual school districts for 2002–2003. The indices of segregation for the three years, respectively, were: Winston-Salem/Forsyth: 0.167, 0.204, and 0.277; Charlotte-Mecklenburg: 0.240, 0.252, and 0.246; Wake County: 0.069, 0.080, and 0.087.

59. For descriptions, see Eaton (2001), McDermott, Bruno, and Varghese (2002), and Wells and Crain (1997, chapter 2).

60. For a study of the effect of year-round schooling on racial segregation, see Mitchell and Mitchell (2003).

61. See Dynarsky (2000) and Cornwell, Mustard, and Sridhar (2000) for analyses of this Georgia program.

62. For an analysis of the Texas Ten Percent Plan, see Kain and O'Brien (2001).

63. *Grutter v. Bollinger*, 71 U.S.L.W. 4498 (2003); *Gratz v. Bollinger*, 71 U.S.L.W. 4480 (2003).

Methodological Appendix

1. James and Taeuber (1985, p. 4) defines the term this way: "We understand *segregation* to refer to the differences in the distribution of social groups, such as blacks and whites, among units of social organization such as schools. School segregation indexes

measure the unequal assignment of students to schools by race; they quantify the deviation of a set of schools from a condition of no segregation."

2. See James and Taeuber (1985, p. 4). This index is sometimes written in the form $_wP_N^*$; see Massey and Denton (1988, p. 288).

3. For thorough comparisons of these and other segregation indices, see Zoloth (1976) and James and Taeuber (1985). What is referred to here as the gap-based segregation index was used by Coleman, Kelley, and Moore (1975) (their r) and described by Zoloth (1976) (her S). James and Taeuber (1985, pp. 6–7) shows that it is equivalent to the variance ratio index used in earlier sociological studies. Reardon and Yun (2002, table 14, p. 32) refers to it as a "normalized exposure index."

4. $S = (.25 - .126) / .25 = .496$, which is rounded to 0.50.

5. Where data were available for more than one school year for a given school district, the year chosen (where the year denotes that in which the school year began) followed this order: for 1950–1954: 1950, 1951, 1952, 1953, 1954, 1949, 1955; for 1960–1961: 1960, 1961, 1962, 1959, 1963, 1958, 1957.

The calculation of these racial isolation indices can be illustrated for the case of Philadelphia in the 1950–1951 year. In 1968, the values for $pb91m$ and $pb91be$ in the Philadelphia district were .672 and .709, respectively. Applying that difference to the percentage of elementary school blacks attending schools that were 90–100 percent black in 1950–1951, .63 (U.S. Commission on Civil Rights 1967, appendix table A.3), yields the estimate that 59.3 percent of blacks in all schools attended schools that were 90–100 percent minority.

* References *

Books, Articles, Reports, and Printed Sources

Alba, Richard D., and John R. Logan. 1993. "Minority Proximity to Whites in Suburbs: An Individual-Level Analysis of Segregation." *American Journal of Sociology* 98 (May): 1388–1427.

Alexander, Florence O. 1947. "The Education of Negroes in Mississippi." *Journal of Negro Education* 16 (September): 375–380.

Alexander, George J. 1963. *Civil Rights U.S.A.: Public Schools Cities in the North and West, 1963: Buffalo.* Staff report submitted to the U.S. Commission on Civil Rights.

Allen, Walter R., and Joseph O. Jewell. 1995. "African American Education since *The American Dilemma.*" *Daedalus* 125, no. 1: 77–100.

———. 2002. "A Backward Glance Forward: Past, Present, and Future Perspectives on Historically Black Colleges and Universities." *Review of Higher Education* 25 (Spring): 241–261.

Allport, Floyd H., et al. 1953. "The Effects of Segregation and the Consequences of Desegregation: A Social Science Statement." *Journal of Negro Education* 22 (Winter): 68–76. Also published in *Minnesota Law Review* 37 (1953): 427–439.

Allport, Gordon W. 1954. *The Nature of Prejudice.* Cambridge, MA: Addison-Wesley.

American Association of Community and Junior Colleges. 1988. *Community College Fact Book.* New York: American Council on Education.

American Friends Service Committee et al. 1970. *The Status of School Desegregation in the South, 1970.* Pamphlet.

Anyon, Jean. 1997. *Ghetto Schooling: A Political Economy of Urban Educational Reform.* New York: Teachers College Press.

Armor, David J. 1995. *Forced Justice: School Desegregation and the Law.* New York: Oxford University Press.

Arrow, Kenneth J. 1998. "What Has Economics to Say about Racial Discrimination?" *Journal of Economic Perspectives* 12 (Spring): 91–100.

Ashmore, Harry S. 1954. *The Negro and the Schools.* Chapel Hill: University of North Carolina Press.

Astin, Alexander W. 1982. *Minorities in American Higher Education.* San Francisco: Jossey-Bass.

Barndt, Michael, Rick Janka, and Harold Rose. 1981. "Milwaukee, Wisconsin: Mobilization for School and Community Cooperation." In *Community Politics and Educational Change: Ten School Systems under Court Order,* ed. Charles V. Willie and Susan L. Greenblatt, pp. 237–259. New York: Longman.

Bayor, Ronald H. 1996. *Race and the Shaping of Twentieth-Century Atlanta.* Chapel Hill: University of North Carolina Press.

Bell, Derrick. 1980. "*Brown v. Board of Education* and the Interest-Convergence Dilemma." *Harvard Law Review* 93 (January): 518–533.

Berkeley Board of Education. 1959. *Interracial Problems and Their Effect on Education in the Public Schools of Berkeley, California.* October 19.

Bettelheim, Bruno. 1958. "Sputnik and Segregation: Should the Gifted Be Educated Separately?" *Commentary* 26: 332–339.

Betts, Julian R., and Robert W. Fairlie. 2001. "Explaining Ethnic, Racial, and Immigrant Differences in Private School Attendance." *Journal of Urban Economics* 50: 26–51.

———. 2003. "Does Immigration Induce 'Native Flight' from Public Schools into Private Schools?" *Journal of Public Economics* 87: 987–1012.

Blackmon, Douglas A. 1992. "The Resegregation of a Southern School." *Harper's Magazine*, September, pp. 14–21.

Bogart, William T., and Brian A. Cromwell. 2000. "How Much Is a Neighborhood School Worth?" *Journal of Urban Economics* 47: 280–305.

Boger, John Charles. 2000. "Willful Colorblindness: The New Racial Piety and the Resegregation of Public Schools." *North Carolina Law Review* 78 (September): 1719–1796.

———. 2003. "Education's 'Perfect Storm'? Racial Resegregation, High Stakes Testing, and School Resource Inequities: The Case of North Carolina." *North Carolina Law Review* 81 (May): 1375–1462.

Boger, John Charles, and Gary Orfield, eds. Forthcoming. *The Resegregation of Southern Schools?* Chapel Hill: University of North Carolina Press.

Bond, Horace Mann. 1934. *The Education of the Negro in the American Social Order.* New York: Prentice-Hall.

Boozer, Michael A., Alan B. Krueger, and Shari Wolkon. 1992. "Race and School Quality since *Brown v. Board of Education.*" *Brookings Papers on Economic Activity: Microeconomics*, pp. 269–338.

Bowen, William G., and Derek Bok. 1998. *The Shape of the River: Long-Term Consequences of Considering Race in College and University Admissions.* Princeton, NJ: Princeton University Press.

Bracey, John H. Jr., and August Meier. 1997. "Papers of the NAACP, Part 23: Legal Department Case Files, 1956–1965." University Publications of America.

Braunstein, Albert P. 1963. *Civil Rights U.S.A.: Public Schools, Cities in the North and West, 1963: Camden and Environs.* Staff report submitted to the U.S. Commission on Civil Rights.

Brown, Christopher M. 1999. *The Quest to Define Collegiate Desegregation: Black Colleges, Title VI Compliance, and Post-Adams Litigation.* Westport, CT: Bergin and Garvey.

Bullard, Pamela, Joyce Grant, and Judith Stoia. 1981. "Boston, Massachusetts: Ethnic Resistance to a Comprehensive Plan." In *Community Politics and Educational Change: Ten School Systems under Court Order,* ed. Charles V. Willie and Susan L. Greenblatt, pp. 31–63. New York: Longman.

Bustard, Joseph L. 1952. "The New Jersey Story: The Development of Racially Integrated Public Schools." *Journal of Negro Education* 21, no. 3 (Summer): 275–285.

Cecelski, David. 1994. *Along Freedom Road: Hyde County, North Carolina, and the Fate of Black Schools in the South.* Chapel Hill: University of North Carolina Press.

Chemerinsky, Erwin. 2003. "The Segregation and Resegregation of American Public Education: The Court's Role." *North Carolina Law Review* 81 (May): 1597–1622.

Chiswick, Barry R., and Teresa A. Sullivan. 1995. "The New Immigrants." In *State of the Union: America in the 1990s,* ed. Reynolds Farley, vol. 2, pp. 211–270. New York: Russell Sage Foundation.

Chronicle of Higher Education. 1968. "White, Negro Undergraduates at Colleges Enrolling 500 or More, as Compiled from Reports to U.S. Office for Civil Rights." April 22, p. 3.

Chubb, John E., and Terry M. Moe. 1990. *Politics, Markets, and America's Schools.* Washington, DC: Brookings Institution Press.

Clark, Kenneth B., and Mamie P. Clark. 1950. "Emotional Factors in Racial Identification and Preference in Negro Children." *Journal of Negro Education* 19, no. 3 (Summer): 341–350.

Clement, D. C., M. A. Eisenhart, and J. R. Harding. 1979. "The Veneer of Harmony: Social-Race Relations in a Southern Desegregated School." In *Desegregated Schools: Appraisals of an American Experiment,* ed. R. C. Rist, pp. 15–64. New York: Academic Press.

Clotfelter, Charles T. 1975a. "The Effect of School Desegregation on Housing Prices." *Review of Economics and Statistics* 57 (November): 446–451.

———. 1975b. "Spatial Rearrangement and the Tiebout Hypothesis: The Case of School Desegregation." *Southern Economic Journal* 42 (October): 263–271.

———. 1976a. "The Detroit Decision and 'White Flight,'" *Journal of Legal Studies* 5 (January): 99–112.

———. 1976b. "School Desegregation, 'Tipping,' and Private School Enrollment." *Journal of Human Resources* 22 (Winter): 29–50.

———. 1979. "Urban School Desegregation and Declines in White Enrollment: A Reexamination." *Journal of Urban Economics* 6: 352–370.

———. 1996. *Buying the Best: Cost Escalation in Elite Higher Education.* Princeton, NJ: Princeton University Press.

———. 1999. "Public School Segregation in Metropolitan Areas." *Land Economics* 75 (November): 487–504.

———. 2002. "Interracial Contact in High School Extracurricular Activities." *Urban Review* 34 (March): 25–46.

Clotfelter, Charles T., Ronald G. Ehrenberg, Malcolm Getz, and John J. Siegfried. 1991. *Economic Challenges in Higher Education.* Chicago: University of Chicago Press.

Clotfelter, Charles T., Helen F. Ladd, and Jacob L. Vigdor. 2002. "Segregation between and within Schools: Evidence from North Carolina." Unpublished paper, Duke University (May).

———. 2003a. "Segregation and Resegregation in North Carolina's Public School Classrooms." *North Carolina Law Review* 81 (May): 1463–1511.

———. 2003b. "Who Teaches Whom? Race and the Distribution of Novice Teachers." Unpublished paper, Sanford Institute of Public Policy, Duke University.

Cobb, Deirdre Lynn. 1998. "Race and Higher Education at the University of Illinois, 1945 to 1955." Ph.D. diss., University of Illinois.

Coleman, James S. 1975. "Recent Trends in School Integration." *Educational Researcher* 4 (July–August): 3–12.

Coleman, James S., et al. 1966. *Equality of Educational Opportunity.* Washington, DC: Government Printing Office.

Coleman, James S., Thomas Hoffer, and Sally Kilgore. 1982. *High School Achievement: Public, Catholic, and Private Schools Compared.* New York: Basic Books.

Coleman, James S., Sara D. Kelly, and John A. Moore. 1975. *Trends in School Segregation, 1968–73.* Urban Institute Paper no. 722-03-01 (August).

Collins, Thomas W. 1979. "From Courtrooms to Classrooms: Managing School Desegregation in a Deep South School." In *Desegregated Schools: Appraisals of an American Experiment,* ed. R. C. Rist, pp. 89–113. New York: Academic Press.

Conlon, John R., and Mwangi S. Kimenyi. 1991. "Attitudes towards Race and Poverty in the Demand for Private Education: The Case of Mississippi." *Review of Black Political Economy* 20: 5–22.

Cook, Michael D., and William N. Evans. 2000. "Families or Schools? Explaining the Convergence in White and Black Academic Performance." *Journal of Labor Economics* 18 (October): 729–754.

Cook, Philip J., and Jens Ludwig. 1997. "Weighing the 'Burden of "Acting White"': Are There Race Differences in Attitudes toward Education?" *Journal of Policy Analysis and Management* 16 (Spring): 256–278.

Cornwell, Christopher, David Mustard, and Deepa Sridhar. 2000. "The Enrollment Effects of Merit Aid: Evidence from Georgia's HOPE Scholarship Program." Paper presented at National Bureau of Economic Research Higher Education Meeting (November 10).

Culver, Dwight. 1954. "Racial Desegregation in Education in Indiana." *Journal of Negro Education* 23 (Summer): 296–302.

Cutler, David M., Edward L. Glaeser, and Jacob L. Vigdor. 1999. "The Rise and Decline of the American Ghetto." *Journal of Political Economy* 107, no. 3 (June): 455–506.

Damico, Sandra, Afesa Bell-Nathaniel, and Charles Green. 1981. "Effects of School Organizational Structure on Interracial Friendships in Middle Schools." *Journal of Educational Research* 74: 388–393.

Days, Drew S. III. 1998. "*Brown* Blues: Rethinking the Integrative Ideal." In *Redefining Equality,* ed. Neal Devins and Davison M. Douglas, pp. 139–153. New York: Oxford University Press.

Dean, John W. 2001. *The Rehnquist Choice: The Untold Story of the Nixon Appointment That Redefined the Supreme Court.* New York: Free Press.

Deever, Bryan. 1994. "Living *Plessy* in the Context of *Brown*: Cultural Politics and the Rituals of Separation." *Urban Review* 26, no. 4: 273–288.

Denton, Nancy A. 1996. "The Persistence of Segregation: Links between Residential Segregation and School Segregation." *Minnesota Law Review* 80, no. 4: 795–824.

Dollard, John. [1937] 1957. *Caste and Class in a Southern Town.* Garden City, NY: Doubleday Anchor.

Donato, Ruben. 1997. *The Other Struggle for Equal Schools.* Albany: State University of New York Press.

DuBois, W.E.B. 1973. "The Field and Function of the Negro College." In *The Education of Black People: Ten Critiques 1906–1960,* ed. Herbert Aptheker, pp. 83–102. Amherst: University of Massachusetts Press.

Duncan, Otis D., and Beverly Duncan. 1955. "A Methodological Analysis of Segregation Indexes." *American Sociological Review* 20, no. 2 (April): 210–217.

Dynarski, Susan. 2000. "Hope for Whom? Financial Aid for the Middle Class and Its Impact on College Attendance." *National Tax Journal* 53 (September): 629–661.

Eaton, Susan E. 2001. *The Other Boston Busing Story: What's Won and Lost across the Boundary Line.* New Haven, CT: Yale University Press.

Egerton, John. 1969. *State Universities and Black Americans: An Inquiry into Desegregation and Equality for Negroes in 100 Public Universities.* Atlanta: Southern Education Reporting Service.

Ehrenberg, Ronald G., and Donna S. Rothstein. 1994. "Do Historically Black Institutions of Higher Education Confer Unique Advantages on Black Students? An Initial Analysis." In *Choices and Consequences: Contemporary Policy Issues in Education,* ed. Ronald G. Ehrenberg, pp. 89–137. Ithaca, NY: ILR Press.

Ehrenberg, Ronald G., Donna S. Rothstein, and Robert B. Olsen. 1999. "Do Historically Black Institutions of Higher Education Enhance the College Attendance of African American Youths?" In *A Nation Divided: Diversity, Inequality, and Community in American Society,* ed. Phyllis Moen, Donna Dempster-McClain, and Henry Walker, pp. 171–188. Ithaca, NY: Cornell University Press.

Eick, Gretchen Cassel. 2001. *Dissent in Wichita: The Civil Rights Movement in the Midwest, 1954–72.* Urbana: University of Illinois Press.

Ellison, Christopher G., and Daniel A. Powers. 1994. "The Contact Hypothesis and Racial Attitudes among Black Americans." *Social Science Quarterly* 75 (June): 385–400.

Epstein, Joyce L. 1985. "After the Bus Arrives: Resegregation in Desegregated Schools." *Journal of Social Issues* 41, no. 3: 23–43.

Epstein, Joyce L., and N. Karweit. 1983. *Friends in School: Patterns of Selection and Influence in Secondary Schools.* New York: Academic Press.

Ervin, Sam. 1956. "The Case for Segregation." *Look,* April 3, pp. 32–33.

Fairlie, Robert W., and Alexandra M. Resch. 2002. "Is There 'White Flight' into Private Schools? Evidence from the National Educational Longitudinal Survey." *Review of Economics and Statistics* 84 (February): 21–33.

Farley, Reynolds. 1991. "Residential Segregation of Social and Economic Groups among Blacks, 1970 to 1980." In *The Urban Underclass,* ed. Christopher Jencks and Paul E. Peterson, pp. 274–298. Washington, DC: Brookings Institution Press.

Farley, Reynolds, Sheldon Danziger, and Harry J. Holzer. 2000. *Detroit Divided.* New York: Russell Sage Foundation.

Farley, Reynolds, and William H. Frey. 1994. "Changes in the Segregation of Whites from Blacks during the 1980s: Small Steps toward a More Integrated Society." *American Sociological Review* 59 (February): 23–45.

Farley, Reynolds, Toni Richards, and Clarence Wurdock. 1980. "School Desegregation and White Flight: An Investigation of Competing Models and their Discrepant Findings." *Sociology of Education* 53 (July): 123–139.

Figlio, David N., and Joe A. Stone. 2001. "Can Public Policy Affect Private School Cream Skimming?" *Journal of Urban Economics* 49 (March): 240–266.

Fiske, Edward B., and Helen F. Ladd. 2000. *When Schools Compete: A Cautionary Tale.* Washington, DC: Brookings Institution Press.

Foley, Albert S. 1981. "Mobile, Alabama: The Demise of State-Sanctioned Resistance." In *Community Politics and Educational Change: Ten School Systems under Court Order,* ed. Charles V. Willie and Susan L. Greenblatt, pp. 174–207. New York: Longman.

Fordham, Signithia, and John Ogbu. 1986. "Black Students' School Success: Coping with the Burden of 'Acting White.'" *Urban Review* 18, no. 3: 176–206.

Frankenberg, Erica, Chungmei Lee, and Gary Orfield. 2003. "A Multiracial Society with Segregated Schools: Are We Losing the Dream?" Harvard Civil Rights Project, Harvard University (January).

Frey, William H. 1979. "Central City White Flight: Racial and Nonracial Causes." *American Sociological Review* 44 (June): 425–448.

———. 1994. "Minority Suburbanization and Continued 'White Flight' in U.S. Metropolitan Areas: Assessing Findings from the 1990 Census." *Research in Community Sociology* 4: 15–42.

Frey, William H., and Reynolds Farley. 1996. "Latino, Asian, and Black Segregation in U.S. Metropolitan Areas: Are Multiethnic Metros Different?" *Demography* 33 (February): 35–50.

Fuller, Bruce, and Richard F. Elmore, eds. 1996. *Who Chooses? Who Loses? Culture, Institutions, and the Unequal Effects of School Choice.* New York: Teachers College Press.

Gamoran, Adam. 1992. "Access to Excellence: Assignment to Honors English Classes in the Transition from Middle to High School." *Educational Evaluation and Policy Analysis* 14 (Fall): 185–204.

Gerard, Harold B., and Norman Miller. 1975. *School Desegregation: A Long-Term Study.* New York: Plenum.

Giles, Micheal W., and Douglas S. Gatlin. 1980. "Mass-Level Compliance with Public Policy: The Case of School Desegregation." *Journal of Politics* 42 (August): 722–746.

Glaeser, Edward L., and Jacob L. Vigdor. 2001. "Segregation in the 2000 Census: The Continuing Decline of the American Ghetto." Unpublished paper, Harvard University, the Brookings Institution, and Duke University (April 1).

Gonzalez, Gilbert. 1990. *Chicano Education in the Era of Segregation.* Philadelphia: Balch Institute Press.

Granovetter, Mark. 1986. "The Micro-Structure of School Desegregation." In *School Desegregation Research: New Directions in Situational Analysis,* ed. Jeffrey Prager, Douglas Longshore, and Melvin Seeman, pp. 81–110. New York: Plenum Press.

———. 1995. *Getting a Job.* Chicago: University of Chicago Press.

Greenberg, Jack. 1959. *Race Relations and American Law.* New York: Columbia University Press.

Grissmer, David, Ann Flanagan, and Stephanie Williamson. 1998. "Why Did the Black-White Score Gap Narrow in the 1970s and 1980s?" In *The Black-White Test Score Gap,* ed. Christopher Jencks and Meredith Phillips, pp. 182–226. Washington, DC: Brookings Institution Press.

Grogger, Jeffrey, and Derek Neal. 2000. "Further Evidence on the Effects of Catholic Secondary Schooling." In *Brookings-Wharton Papers on Urban Affairs: 2000,* ed. William G. Gale and Janet Rothenberg Pack, pp. 151–201. Washington, DC: Brookings Institution Press.

Hall, Morrill M., and Harold W. Gentry. 1969. "Isolation of Negro Students in Integrated Public Schools." *Journal of Negro Education* 38 (Spring): 156–161.

Hallinan, Maureen T. 1982. "Classroom Racial Composition and Children's Friendships." *Social Forces* 61 (September): 56–72.

Hallinan, Maureen T., and Richard A. Williams. 1989. "Interracial Friendship Choices in Secondary Schools." *American Sociological Review* 54 (February): 67–78.

Hanssen, F. Andrew, and Torben Andersen. 1999. "Has Discrimination Lessened over Time? A Test Using Baseball's All-Star Vote." *Economic Inquiry* 37 (April): 326–352.

Hanushek, Eric A., John F. Kain, and Steven G. Rivkin. 2002. "New Evidence about *Brown v. Board of Education:* The Complex Effects of School Racial Composition on Achievement." NBER Working Paper 8741 (January).

Harvard College. 1954, 1964. *The Register 1958, 1968.* Cambridge, MA: Harvard Yearbook Publications.

Hendrick, Irving G. 1975. "The Historical Setting." In *School Desegregation: A Long-Term Study,* by Harold B. Gerard and Norman Miller, pp. 25–51. New York: Plenum.

Henig, Jeffrey R. 1996. "The Local Dynamics of Choice: Ethnic Preferences and Institutional Responses." In *Who Chooses? Who Loses? Culture, Institutions, and the Unequal Effects of School Choice*, ed. Bruce Fuller, Richard F. Elmore, and Gary Orfield, pp. 95–117. New York: Teachers College Press.

Heyman, Ira M. 1963. *Civil Rights U.S.A.: Public Schools Cities in the North and West, 1963: Oakland.* Staff report submitted to the U.S. Commission on Civil Rights.

Hollingshead, August B. 1949. *Elmtown's Youth: The Impact of Social Classes on Adolescents.* New York: John Wiley and Sons.

Hoxby, Caroline M. N.d. "The Effects of Geographic Integration and Increasing Competition in the Market for College Education." Unpublished paper, Department of Economics, Harvard University.

Indiana Advisory Committee to the U.S. Commission on Civil Rights. 1977. *Equal Opportunity in the Fort Wayne Community Schools: A Continuing Struggle.* Washington, DC: U.S. Commission on Civil Rights.

———. 1979. *Equal Opportunity in the Fort Wayne Community Schools: A Reassessment.* Washington, DC: U.S. Commission on Civil Rights.

Ingersoll, Richard M. 1999. "The Problem of Underqualified Teachers in American Secondary Schools." *Educational Researcher* 28 (March): 26–37.

Irwin, Mary. 1956. *American Universities and Colleges*, seventh edition. Washington, DC: American Council on Education.

Jackson, James S., and Harold W. Neighbors. 1997. *National Survey of Black Americans, Waves 1–4.* Inter-university Consortium for Political and Social Research (ICPSR), ICPSR 6668, Ann Arbor, Michigan (August).

Jacobs, Gregory S. 1998. *Getting around* Brown: *Desegregation, Development and the Columbus Public Schools.* Columbus: Ohio State University Press.

James, David R., and Karl E. Taeuber. 1985. "Measures of Segregation." In *Sociological Methodology 1985*, ed. Nancy Brandon Tuma, pp. 1–32. San Francisco: Jossey-Bass.

Jencks, Christopher, and Meredith Phillips, eds. 1998. *The Black-White Test Score Gap.* Washington, DC: Brookings Institution Press.

Johnson, Charles S. 1941. *Growing Up in the Black Belt.* Washington, DC: American Council on Education.

———. 1943. *Patterns of Negro Segregation.* New York: Harper and Brothers.

Johnston, Lloyd D., Jerald G. Bachman, and Patrick M. O'Malley. Various years. *Monitoring the Future: Questionnaire Responses from the Nation's High School Seniors.* Ann Arbor: Survey Research Center, Institute for Social Research, University of Michigan.

Joyner, Kara, and Grace Kao. 2000. "School Racial Composition and Adolescent Racial Homophily." *Social Science Quarterly* 81 (September): 810–825.

Kain, John, and Daniel O'Brien. 2001. "*Hopwood* and the Top 10 Percent Law: How They Have Affected the College Enrollment Decisions of Texas High School Graduates." Paper presented at National Bureau of Economic Research Higher Education Meeting (November 9).

Kean, Melissa F. 2000. "'At a Most Uncomfortable Speed': The Desegregation of the South's Private Universities, 1945–1964." Ph.D. diss., Rice University.

Kentucky Department of Education. 1950. *Educational Bulletin* 18, no. 9 (November): 969–971. (*Kentucky Public School Directory, 1950–51*).

———. 1951. *Educational Bulletin* 19, no. 9 (November): 699–701. (*Kentucky Public School Directory, 1951–52*).

————. 1952. *Educational Bulletin* 20, no. 9 (November): 425–426. (*Kentucky Public School Directory, 1952–53*).

————. 1953. *Educational Bulletin* 21, no. 9 (November): 795–797. (*Kentucky Public School Directory, 1953–54*).

————. 1954. *Educational Bulletin* 22, no. 4 (December): 570–572. (*Kentucky Public School Directory, 1954–55*).

Kentucky State Department of Education. 1965. *Annual Survey and Progress Report: Integration in the Public Schools of Kentucky.* October 10.

Kimball, Solon T., and Charles Wagley. 1974. *Race and Culture in School and Community.* Unpublished report, Office of Education, National Institute of Education Project No. 2–2069 (January).

Kluger, Richard. 1976. *Simple Justice: The History of* Brown v. Board of Education *and Black America's Struggle for Equality.* New York: Alfred A. Knopf.

Knox, Ellis O. 1954. "Racial Integration in the Schools of Arizona, New Mexico, and Kansas." *Journal of Negro Education* 23 (Summer): 290–309.

Kraushaar, Otto F. 1972. *American Nonpublic Schools: Patterns of Diversity.* Baltimore: Johns Hopkins University Press.

Lankford, Hamilton, E. S. Lee, and James Wyckoff. 1995. "An Analysis of Elementary and Secondary School Choice." *Journal of Urban Economics* 38: 236–251.

Lankford, Hamilton, Susanna Loeb, and James Wyckoff. 2002. "Teacher Sorting and the Plight of Urban Schools: A Descriptive Analysis." *Educational Evaluation and Policy Analysis* 24 (Spring): 37–62.

Lemann, Nicholas. 1999. *The Big Test: The Secret History of the American Meritocracy.* New York: Farrar, Straus, and Giroux.

Long, James E., and Eugenia F. Toma. 1988. "The Determinants of Private School Attendance, 1970–1980." *Review of Economics and Statistics* 70 (May): 351–357.

Loury, Glenn C. 2002. *The Anatomy of Racial Inequality.* Cambridge, MA: Harvard University Press.

Loveless, Tom. 1999. *The Tracking Wars: State Reform Meets School Policy.* Washington, DC: Brookings Institution Press.

Lukas, J. Anthony. 1986. *Common Ground: A Turbulent Decade in the Lives of Three American Families.* New York: Vintage Books.

MacDonald, Jason A., Lee Sigelman, and Steven A. Tuch. 2000. "Not Black and White: The Racial Attitudes of American Youth." *The Responsive Community* 10, no. 4 (Fall): 76–81.

Margo, Robert A. 1990. *Race and Schooling in the South, 1880–1950: An Economic History.* Chicago: University of Chicago Press.

Martinez-Vazquez, Jorge, and Bruce A. Seaman. 1985. "Private Schooling and the Tiebout Hypothesis." *Public Finance Quarterly* 13 (July): 293–318.

Massachusetts State Advisory Committee. 1965. *Report to the United State Commission on Civil Rights: Report on Racial Imbalance in the Boston Public Schools.* January.

————. 1976. *Report to the United States Commission on Civil Rights: The Six District Plan: Integration of the Springfield, Massachusetts, Elementary Schools.* March.

Massey, Douglas S., and Nancy A. Denton. 1988. "The Dimensions of Residential Segregation." *Social Forces* 67 (December): 281–315.

————. 1993. *American Apartheid: Segregation and the Making of the Underclass.* Cambridge, MA: Harvard University Press.

Massey, Douglas S., and Zoltan Hajnal. 1995. "The Changing Geographic Structure of Black-White Segregation in the United States." *Social Science Quarterly* 76: 527–542.

McConahay, John B. 1982. "Self-Interest versus Racial Attitudes as Correlates of Anti-Busing Attitudes in Louisville: Is it the Buses or the Blacks?" *Journal of Politics* 44, no. 3 (August): 692–720.

McDermott, Kathryn A., Gordon Bruno, and Anna Varghese. 2002. "Have Connecticut's Desegregation Policies Produced Desegregation?" *Equity and Excellence in Education* 35, no. 1: 18–27.

McNeal, Ralph B. Jr. 1998. "High School Extracurricular Activities: Closed Structures and Stratifying Patterns of Participation." *Journal of Educational Research* 91 (January/February): 183–191.

———. 1999. "Participation in High School Extracurricular Activities: Investigating School Effects." *Social Science Quarterly* 80 (June): 291–309.

Meier, Kenneth J., Joseph Stewart, and Robert E. England. 1989. *Race, Class, and Education: The Politics of Second-Generation Discrimination.* Madison: University of Wisconsin Press.

Merrill, Charles. 1967. "Negroes in the Private Schools." *Atlantic Monthly,* July, pp. 37–40.

Mickelson, Roslyn Arlin. 2001. "Subverting *Swann*: First- and Second-Generation Segregation in the Charlotte-Mecklenburg Schools." *American Education Research Journal* 38 (Summer): 215–252.

———. 2003. "The Academic Consequences of Desegregation and Segregation: Evidence from the Charlotte-Mecklenburg Schools." *North Carolina Law Review* 81 (May): 1513–1562.

Mihelich, Dennis N., and Ashton Wesley Welch. 1981. "Omaha, Nebraska: Positive Planning for Peaceful Integration." In *Community Politics and Educational Change: Ten School Systems under Court Order,* ed. Charles V. Willie and Susan L. Greenblatt, pp. 260–297. New York: Longman.

Ming, William R. 1952. "The Elimination of Segregation in the Public Schools of the North and West." *Journal of Negro Education* 21 (Summer): 265–275.

Minow, Martha. 1990. *Making All the Difference: Inclusion, Exclusion, and the American Law.* Ithaca, NY: Cornell University Press.

Mitchell, Ross E., and Douglas E. Mitchell. 2003. "Student Segregation and Achievement Tracking in Year-Round Schools." Paper submitted for publication; originally presented at the Ninety-fourth Annual Meeting of the American Sociological Association under the title "Organizational Segregation of Student Achievement in Elementary Schools: The Influence of Multi-Track Year-Round Schools" (1999).

Moody, James. 2001. "Race, School Integration, and Friendship Segregation in America." *American Journal of Sociology* 107 (November): 679–716.

Morgan, P. R., and James M. McPartland. 1981. "The Extent of Classroom Segregation within Desegregated Schools." Unpublished manuscript, Johns Hopkins University, Center for Social Organization of Schools (August).

Morris, Lorenzo. 1979. *Elusive Equality: The Status of Black Americans in Higher Education.* Washington, DC: Howard University Press.

Myrdal, Gunner. [1944] 1962. *An American Dilemma: The Negro Problem and Modern Democracy.* New York: Pantheon Books.

National Association for the Advancement of Colored People. 1955. "Statistics." *The Crisis* 62 (August–September): 417–418.

———. 1962. *The Jim Crow School—North and West.* New York: National Association for the Advancement of Colored People.

National Catholic Educational Association. 1971. *A Report on U.S. Catholic Schools, 1970–71.* Washington, DC: National Catholic Educational Association.

New York Public Education Association. 1955. *The Status of the Public School Education of Negro and Puerto Rican Children in New York City.* New York: Board of Education Commission on Integration (October).

Newman, Dorothy K., et al. 1978. *Protest, Politics, and Prosperity: Black Americans and White Institutions, 1940–75.* New York: Pantheon Books.

North Carolina Superintendent of Public Instruction. *Biennial Report for 1950–52, 1958–1960, Part III, Statistical Report, 1951–52, 1959–60.*

Oakes, Jeannie. 1987. "Tracking in Secondary Schools: A Contextual Perspective." *Educational Psychologist* 22, no. 2: 129–153.

———. 1993. "Ability Grouping, Tracking and Within-School Segregation in the San Jose Unified School District." Unpublished paper, University of California, Los Angeles, Graduate School of Education (October).

Oakes, Jeannie, and Gretchen Guiton. 1995. "Matchmaking: The Dynamics of High School Tracking Decisions." *American Educational Research Journal* 32, no. 1: 3–33.

Orfield, Gary. 1969. *The Reconstruction of Southern Education: The Schools and the 1964 Civil Rights Act.* New York: Wiley-Interscience.

———. 1981. "Housing Patterns and Desegregation Policy." In *Effective School Desegregation,* ed. Willis Hawley, pp. 185–221. New York: Sage.

———. 1983. *Public School Desegregation in the United States, 1968–1980.* Washington, DC: Joint Center for Political Studies.

Orfield, Gary, Mark D. Bachmeier, David R. James, and Tamela Eitle. 1997. "Deepening Segregation in American Public Schools." Unpublished paper, Harvard Project on School Desegregation, Harvard University (April 5).

Orfield, Gary, and Susan E. Eaton. 1996. *Dismantling Desegregation: The Quiet Reversal of Brown v. Board of Education.* New York: New Press.

Orfield, Gary, and Nora Gordon. 2001. "Schools More Separate: Consequences of a Decade of Resegregation." Unpublished paper, Harvard University (July).

Orfield, Gary, and Frank Monfort. 1992. *Status of School Desegregation: The Next Generation.* Cambridge, MA: Metropolitan Opportunity Project, Harvard University (March).

Patterson, James T. 2001. Brown v. Board of Education: *A Civil Rights Milestone and Its Troubled Legacy.* Oxford: Oxford University Press.

Pearce, Diana. 1980. "Breaking Down Barriers: New Evidence on the Impact of Metropolitan School Desegregation on Housing Patterns." Unpublished report, Center for National Policy Review, Catholic University (November).

Peltason, Jack Walter. 1961. *Fifty-Eight Lonely Men: Southern Federal Judges and School Desegregation.* New York: Harcourt, Brace, and World.

Perlmann, Joel, and Mary C. Waters. 2002. *The New Race Question: How the Census Counts Multiracial Individuals.* New York: Russell Sage Foundation.

Perry, Pamela. 2002. *Shades of White: White Kids and Racial Identities in High School.* Durham, NC: Duke University Press.

Persell, Caroline H. 1977. *Education and Inequality: A Theoretical and Empirical Synthesis.* New York: Free Press.

Pettigrew, Thomas F., and Robert L. Green. 1976. "School Desegregation in Large Cities:

A Critique of the Coleman 'White Flight' Thesis." *Harvard Educational Review* 46 (February): 1–53.

Picott, J. Rupert, Stephen J. Wright, and Ellis O. Knox. 1950. "A Survey of the Public Schools of Durham, North Carolina." Bound manuscript "Prepared for the Durham Citizens by a Survey Committee" (June).

Plaut, Richard L. 1954. "Racial Integration in Higher Education in the North." *Journal of Negro Education* 23 (Summer): 310–316.

Quiroz, Pamela Anne, Nilda Flores Gonzalez, and Kenneth A. Frank. 1996. "Carving a Niche in the High School Social Structure: Formal and Informal Constraints on Participation in the Extra Curriculum." *Research in Sociology of Education and Socialization* 11: 93–120.

Reardon, Sean F., and John T. Yun. 2002. "Private School Racial Enrollments and Segregation." Unpublished paper, Civil Rights Project, Harvard University (June 26). Posted on the Web site for the Harvard Civil Rights Project, http://www.civilrightsproject. harvard.edu/research/deseg/Private—Schools.pdf.

Rebell, Michael A., and Arthur R. Block. 1985. *Equality and Education: Federal Civil Rights Enforcement in the New York City School System.* Princeton, NJ: Princeton University Press.

Reichert, Walter. 1977. "The Growth of Private Schools in Jefferson County following the Desegregation of the Public School System." Master's thesis, Indiana University.

Rice, Lorien, and Julian R. Betts. 2003. "Who Leaves and Why? An Analysis of School Choice Options in a Large Urban District." Unpublished paper, Public Policy Institute of California, San Francisco (November).

Rodgers, Harrell R. Jr., and Charles S. Bullock III. 1972. "School Desegregation: A Policy Analysis." *Journal of Black Studies* 2 (June): 409–437.

Rodgers, William M. III, and Michelle R. Ragsdale. 1999. "Racial Segregation in Extracurricular Activities: A Longitudinal Analysis." Unpublished paper, College of William and Mary (November 9).

Rosenbaum, James E. 1976. *Making Inequality: The Hidden Curriculum of High School Tracking.* New York: John Wiley and Sons.

Rossell, Christine H., and David J. Armor. 1996. "The Effectiveness of School Desegregation Plans, 1968–1991." *American Politics Quarterly* 24 (July): 267–302.

Rubinowitz, Leonard S., and James E. Rosenbaum. 2000. *Class and Color Lines: From Public Housing to White Suburbia.* Chicago: University of Chicago Press.

San Miguel, Guadalupe. 1987. *"Let All of Them Take Heed": Mexican Americans and the Campaign for Educational Equity in Texas, 1910–81.* Austin: University of Texas Press.

Sarratt, Reed. 1966. *The Ordeal of Desegregation: The First Decade.* New York: Harper and Row.

Schelling, Thomas C. 1972. "A Process of Residential Segregation: Neighborhood Tipping." In *Racial Discrimination in Economic Life,* ed. Anthony H. Pascal, pp. 157–184. Lexington, MA: D. C. Heath and Co.

Scherer, Jacqueline, and Edward J. Slawski. 1978. *Hard Walls—Soft Walls: The Social Ecology of an Urban Desegregated High School.* Final report. Washington, DC: National Institute of Education.

———. 1979. "Color, Class, and Social Control in an Urban Desegregated School." In *Desegregated Schools: Appraisals of an American Experiment,* ed. R. C. Rist, pp. 117–154. New York: Academic Press.

Schmidt, Amy B. 1992. "Private School Enrollment in Metropolitan Areas." *Public Finance Quarterly* 20 (July): 298–320.

Schneider, Mark, Paul E. Teske, and Melissa Marschall. 2000. *Choosing Schools: Consumer Choice and the Quality of American Schools.* Princeton, NJ: Princeton University Press.

Schofield, Janet Ward. 1979. "The Impact of Positively Structured Contact on Intergroup Behavior: Does It Last under Adverse Conditions?" *Social Psychology Quarterly* 42: 280–284.

———. 1982. *Black and White in School: Trust, Tension, or Tolerance.* New York: Praeger.

———. 1991. "School Desegregation and Intergroup Relations: A Review of the Literature." *Review of Educational Research* 17: 335–412.

———. 1995. "Review of Research on School Desegregation's Impact on Elementary and Secondary School Students." In *Handbook of Research on Multicultural Education,* ed. James A. Banks and Cherry A. McGee Banks, pp. 597–616. New York: Macmillan Publishing.

Schofield, Janet Ward, and H. A. Sagar. 1983. "Desegregation, School Practices, and Student Race Relations." In *The Consequences of School Desegregation,* ed. Christine H. Rossell and Willis D. Hawley, pp. 58–102. Philadelphia: Temple University Press.

Schuman, Howard, Charlotte Steeh, Lawrence Bobo, and Maria Krysan. 1997. *Racial Attitudes in America: Trends and Interpretations.* Cambridge, MA: Harvard University Press.

Sears, David O., Carl P. Hensler, and Leslie K. Speer. 1979. "Whites' Opposition to 'Busing': Self-Interest or Symbolic Politics?" *American Political Science Review* 73, no. 2 (June): 369–384.

Shagaloff, June. 1954. "A Study of Community Acceptance of Desegregation in Two Selected Areas." *Journal of Negro Education* 23 (Summer): 330–338.

Sieber, Timothy R. 1982. "The Politics of Middle-Class Success in an Inner-City Public School." *Boston University Journal of Education* 164: 30–47.

Sigelman, Lee, Timothy Bledsoe, Susan Welch, and Michael W. Combs. 1996. "Making Contact? Black-White Social Interaction in an Urban Setting." *American Journal of Sociology* 101 (March): 1306–1332.

Silberman, Todd. 2002. "Wake County Schools: A Question of Balance." In *Divided We Fail: Coming Together through Public School Choice,* by the Century Foundation Task Force on the Common School, pp. 141–166. New York: Century Foundation Press.

Smith, Walter. 1998. "Florida's Black Junior Colleges: Building Blocks for the 'Great 28.'" *Visions: The Journal of Applied Research for the Florida Association of Community Colleges* 1, no. 1 (Spring): 1–6. Posted on the Web at http://facc.org/visions98.htm, visited 10/31/03.

Solmon, Lewis C., Matthew S. Solmon, and Tamara W. Schiff. 2002. "The Changing Demographics: Problems and Opportunities." In *The Racial Crisis in American Higher Education: Continuing Challenges for the Twenty-First Century,* ed. William A. Smith, Philip G. Altbach, and Kofi Lomotey, pp. 43–75. Albany: State University of New York Press.

Southern Education Reporting Service. 1959. *Status of School Segregation-Desegregation in the Southern and Border States.* Atlanta: Southern Education Reporting Service.

———. 1961, 1965. *Summary, State-by-State, of School-Segregation-Desegregation in the Southern and Border Area from 1954 to the Present* (November 1961 and 1965–1966). Atlanta: Southern Education Reporting Service.

Southern Regional Council. 1960. "A Report on School Desegregation for 1960–61." Typescript (August 19).

St. John, Nancy. 1975. *School Desegregation: Outcomes for Children.* New York: Wiley.

Stephan, Walter G. 1986. "The Effects of School Desegregation: An Evaluation 30 Years after *Brown.*" In *Advances in Applied Social Psychology,* ed. Michael J. Saks and Leonard Saxe, pp. 181–206. Hillsdale, NJ: Erlbaum.

Sullivan, Mercer L. 1979. "Contacts among Cultures: School Desegregation in a Poly-ethnic New York City High School." In *Desegregated Schools: Appraisals of an American Experiment,* ed. R. C. Rist, pp. 201–240. New York: Academic Press.

Taeuber, Karl E., and Alma F. Taeuber. 1964. "The Negro as an Immigrant Group: Recent Trends in Racial and Ethnic Segregation in Chicago." *American Journal of Sociology* 69, no. 4 (January): 374–382.

———. [1965] 1972. *Negroes in Cities.* New York: Atheneum.

Taylor, D. Garth. 1986. *Public Opinion and Collective Action: The Boston School Deseg-regation Conflict.* Chicago: University of Chicago Press.

Teddlie, Charles, and John A. Freeman. 2002. "Twentieth-Century Desegregation in U.S. Higher Education: A Review of Five Distinct Historical Eras." In *The Racial Crisis in American Higher Education,* ed. William A. Smith, Philip G. Altbach, and Kofi Lomotey, pp. 77–102. Albany: State University of New York Press.

Thomas, Gail E., James M. McPartland, and Denise C. Gottfredson. 1981. "Desegrega-tion and Black Student Higher Educational Access." In Gail E. Thomas (ed.), *Black Students in Higher Education: Conditions and Experiences in the 1970s,* ed. Gail E. Thomas, pp. 336–356. Westport, CT: Greenwood Press.

Thompson, John M. 1976. "School Desegregation in Jefferson Co., Kentucky, 1954–1975." Ph.D. diss., University of Kentucky.

Tiebout, Charles M. 1956. "A Pure Theory of Local Expenditures." *Journal of Political Economy* 64 (October): 416–424.

Tierney, William G., and Jack K. Chung. 2002. "Affirmative Action in a Post-*Hopwood* Era." In *The Racial Crisis in American Higher Education: Continuing Challenges for the Twenty-First Century,* ed. William A. Smith, Philip G. Altbach, and Kofi Lomotey, pp. 271–283. Albany: State University of New York Press.

Tuch, Steven A., Lee Sigelman, and Jason A. MacDonald. 1999. "Race Relations and American Youth, 1976–1995." *Public Opinion Quarterly* 63: 109–148.

Tyson, Karolyn, William Darity Jr., and Domini Castellino. 2002. "Acting White, Acting Black, or Not Acting at All? Race and Curriculum Selection in North Carolina Schools." Paper presented at the Association for Public Policy and Management Re-search Conference (November 7–9).

U.S. Bureau of the Census. 1951, 1961, 1971. *Census of Population and Housing, Cen-sus Tract Reports, 1950, 1960,* and *1970.* Washington, DC: Government Printing Of-fice. Tables 1–3 (1950), tables P-1, P-2, and H-1 (1960), tables P1, P2, H1, H2 (1970).

———. 1975. *Historical Statistics of the United States, Colonial Times to 1970, Bicenten-nial Edition,* part 1. Washington, DC: Government Printing Office.

———. 2001. *County and City Data Book: 2000.* Washington, DC: Government Printing Office.

———. Various years. *Statistical Abstract of the United States.* Washington, DC: Govern-ment Printing Office.

U.S. Commission on Civil Rights. 1962. *Civil Rights U.S.A.: Public Schools, Southern States 1962.* Washington, DC: U.S. Commission on Civil Rights.

———. 1967. *Racial Isolation in the Public Schools.* Washington, DC: Government Printing Office.

———. 1973. *School Desegregation in Ten Communities.* Washington, DC: Government Printing Office (June).

———. 1977. *School Desegregation in Wichita, Kansas.* Washington, DC: U.S. Commission on Civil Rights (August).

U.S. Department of Education, National Center for Education Statistics. 1976. *Higher Education General Information Survey.* Washington, DC: Government Printing Office.

———. 1985. *The Traditionally Black Institutions of Higher Education, 1860 to 1982.* Washington, DC: Government Printing Office.

———. 1986. *Integrated Postsecondary Education Data System.* Washington, DC: Government Printing Office.

———. 1992. *Historically Black Colleges and Universities, 1976–90.* Washington, DC: Government Printing Office.

———. 1998. *Integrated Postsecondary Education Data System.* Washington, DC: Government Printing Office.

———. 2001a and 2001b. *See section on Electronic Data.*

———. 2001c. *Digest of Education Statistics, 2000.* Washington, DC: Government Printing Office.

———. 2001d. *Private School Universe Survey: 1999–2000, Statistical Analysis Report.* NCES 2001-330. Washington, DC: U.S. Department of Education (August).

———. 2002. *Digest of Education Statistics, 2001.* Washington, DC: Government Printing Office.

U.S. Department of Health, Education, and Welfare. 1976. *The Desegregation Literature: A Critical Appraisal.* Washington, DC: Government Printing Office (July).

U.S. Department of Health, Education, and Welfare, National Center for Education Statistics. 1970. *Digest of Educational Statistics, 1970 Edition.* Washington, DC: Government Printing Office.

———. 1973. *Statistics of Nonpublic Elementary and Secondary Schools, 1970–71.* Washington, DC: Government Printing Office.

U.S. Department of Health, Education, and Welfare, Office for Civil Rights. 1969, 1970. *Directory of Public Elementary and Secondary Schools in Large Districts, with Enrollment and Instructional Staff, by Race: Fall 1967, Fall 1968.* Washington, DC: Government Printing Office.

———. 1972. *Racial and Ethnic Enrollment Data from Institutions of Higher Education, Fall 1970.* Washington, DC: Government Printing Office.

———. 1974. *Racial and Ethnic Enrollment Data from Institutions of Higher Education, Fall 1972.* Washington, DC: Government Printing Office.

U.S. Office of Education. 1951. *Biennial Survey of Education in the United States, 1946– 48.* Washington, DC: Government Printing Office.

Valien, Bonita. 1954. "Racial Desegregation of the Public Schools in Southern Illinois." *Journal of Negro Education* 23 (Summer): 303–309.

Welch, Finis, and Audrey Light. 1987. *New Evidence on School Desegregation.* Washington, DC: U.S. Commission on Civil Rights (June).

Wells, Amy Stuart. 1995. "Reexamining Social Science Research on School Desegregation: Long- versus Short-Term Effects." *Teachers College Record* 96 (Summer): 691–706.

———. 1996. "African-American Students' View of School Choice." In *Who Chooses? Who Loses? Culture, Institutions, and the Unequal Effects of School Choice,* ed. Bruce Fuller and Richard F. Elmore, pp. 25–49. New York: Teachers College Press.

Wells, Amy Stuart, and Robert L. Crain. 1997. *Stepping over the Color Line: African-American Students in White Suburban Schools.* New Haven, CT: Yale University Press.

"White, Negro Undergraduates at Colleges Enrolling 500 or More, as Compiled from Reports to U.S. Office for Civil Rights." *Chronicle of Higher Education,* April 22, 1968.

Wiggins, Sam P. 1966. *The Desegregation Era in Higher Education.* Berkeley, CA: Mc-Catchan Publishing.

Wilger, Robert, and Reynolds Farley. 1989. "Black-White Residential Segregation: Recent Trends." Unpublished paper, Department of Rural Sociology, University of Wisconsin, Madison, and Population Studies Center, University of Michigan (August).

Williams, Robin M., and Margaret W. Ryan, eds. 1954. *Schools in Transition: Community Experiences in Desegregation.* Chapel Hill: University of North Carolina Press.

Willie, Charles V., and Susan L. Greenblatt, eds. 1981. *Community Politics and Educational Change: Ten School Systems under Court Order.* New York: Longman.

Wilson, William J. 1987. *The Truly Disadvantaged: The Inner City, the Underclass, and Public Policy.* Chicago: University of Chicago Press.

Wyckoff, James. 1992. "The Intrastate Equality of Public Primary and Secondary Education Resources." *Economics of Education Review* 11: 19–30.

Yinger, J. Milton. 1953. "A Memorandum on Negro-White Integration in the Cincinnati Public Schools." Unpublished report for the Ashmore Project.

Zoloth, Barbara. 1976. "Alternative Measures of School Segregation." *Land Economics* 52 (August): 278–298.

Court Cases

Adams v. Califano, 430 F. Supp 118 (D.C.D.C. 1977).

Adams v. Richardson, 351 F. Supp 636 (D.C.D.C. 1972, amended 1973).

Adams v. Richardson, 356 F. Supp 92 (D.C.D.C. 1973).

Adams v. Richardson, 480 F. 2d 1159 (C.A.D.C. 1973).

Alexander v. Holmes County Board of Education, 396 U.S. 19 (1969).

Belk v. Charlotte-Mecklenburg Schools, 269 F. 3d 305 (2001).

Berea College v. Commonwealth of Kentucky, 211 U.S. 45 (1908).

Board of Education of Oklahoma v. Dowell, 498 U.S. 237 (1991).

Briggs v. Elliott, 132 F. Supp. 796 (1955).

Brown v. Board of Education, 347 U.S. 483 (1954); 349 U.S. 294 (1955).

Capacchione v. Charlotte-Mecklenburg Schools, 57 F. Supp. 2nd 228 (1999).

Clemons v. Board of Education of Hillsboro, Ohio, 228 F. 2nd 853 (1955).

Delgado v. Bastrop Independent School District, Civil No. 388 (W.D. Tex.), unreported decision.

Freeman v. Pitts, 503 U.S. 467 (1992).

Gratz v. Bollinger, 71 U.S.L.W. 4480 (2003).

Green v. County School Board of New Kent County, 391 U.S. 430 (1968).

Grutter v. Bollinger, 71 U.S.L.W. 4498 (2003).

Hopwood v. Texas, 78 F. 3d 932 (5th Cir. 1996).

Keyes v. Denver School District No. 1, 413 U.S. 189 (1973).

McLaurin v. Oklahoma State Regents for Higher Education, 339 U.S. 637 (1949).

Mendez v. Westminster School District, 64 F. Supp. 544 (S.D. Cal.1945); 161 F. 2nd 744 (9th Cir. 1947).

Milliken v. Bradley, 418 U.S. 717 (1974).

Morgan v. Kerrigan (Boston School Committee), 401 F. Supp. 216 (D. Ma. 1975).

Moses v. Washington Parish School Board, 330 F. Supp. 1340 (E.D. La. 1971).

Newburg Area Council, Inc. v. Gordon (Board of Education of Jefferson County, Kentucky), 521 F. 2nd 578 (6th Cir. 1975).

People Who Care v. Rockford Board of Education, School District # 205, 851 F. Supp. 905, 1026 (1994).

Scott v. Winston-Salem/Forsyth County Board of Education, 317 F. Supp. 453 (1970).

Shelley v. Kraemer, 334 U.S. 1 (1948).

Spangler v. Pasadena, 375 F. Supp. 1304 (1974).

Swann v. Charlotte-Mecklenburg Board of Education, 402 U.S. 1 (1971).

Sweatt v. Painter, 339 U.S. 629 (1949).

United States v. Fordice, 505 U.S. 717 (1992)

United States v. City of Yonkers, 833 F. Supp. 214, 218 (1993).

University of California Regents v. Bakke, 438 U.S. 265 (1978).

ELECTRONIC DATA

Cutler, David, Edward Glaeser, and Jacob Vigdor. N.d. "Cutler/Glaeser/Vigdor Segregation Data." http://trinity.aas.duke.edu/~jvigdor/segregation/index.html. See also Cutler, Glaeser, and Vigdor (1999).

U.S. Bureau of the Census. 1973. *1970 Census Fourth Count (Population) School District Data.*

U.S. Department of Education, National Center for Education Statistics. 1989. *Common Core of Data, Public School Universe: 1987–1988.* Downloaded from NCES Web site: http://nces.ed.gov/ccd/pubschuniv.asp.

———. 1991. *Common Core of Data, Public School Universe: 1989–1990.* Downloaded from NCES Web site: http://nces.ed.gov/ccd/pubschuniv.asp.

———. 1992. *Common Core of Data, Local Education Agency Data: 1990–1991.* Downloaded from NCES Web site: http://nces.ed.gov/ccd/pubagency.asp.

———. 1998, 1999. *Integrated Postsecondary Education Data System (IPEDS): Fall Enrollment, 1986 and 1988.* ICPSR version. Computer file, distributed by Inter-university Consortium for Political and Social Research, 1999. Downloaded from ICPSR Web site: http://www.icpsr.umich.edu:8080/IAED-STUDY/02221.xml.

———. 2000a. *Common Core of Data, Public School Universe: 1998–1999.* Downloaded from NCES Web site: http://nces.ed.gov/ccd/pubschuniv.asp.

———. 2000b. *Common Core of Data, School Years 1993–94 through 1997–98.* CD-ROM from NCES Office of Educational Research and Improvement.

———. 2001a. *Common Core of Data, Public School Universe: 1999–2000.* Downloaded from NCES Web site: http://nces.ed.gov/ccd/pubschuniv.asp.

———. 2001b. *Private School Universe Survey: 1999–2000.* Downloaded from CD-ROM.

————. 2001c and 2001d. *See section on Printed Sources.*

————. 2001e. *Integrated Postsecondary Education Data System (IPEDS): Fall Enrollment, 1998.* Downloaded from NCES Web site: http://nces.ed.gov/Ipeds/ef9899/.

————. 2002. *Common Core of Data, Public School Universe: 2000–2001.* Downloaded from NCES Web site: http://nces.ed.gov/ccd/pubschuniv.asp.

U.S. Department of Education, Office for Civil Rights. N.d. *OCR Elementary and Secondary School Survey: 1968–1998.* CD-ROM. For more information, see http://205.207.175.84/ocr2000r/.

U.S. Department of Health, Education, and Welfare, National Center for Education Statistics. 1976. *Higher Education Opening Fall Enrollment, 1976.* 2nd ICPSR version. Computer file, distributed by Inter-university Consortium for Political and Social Research, 1998. Downloaded from ICPSR Web site: http://www.icpsr.umich.edu:8080/IAED-STUDY/07650.xml.

————. 1979. *Higher Education General Information Survey (HEGIS): Fall Enrollment, 1978.* ICPSR version. Computer file, distributed by Inter-university Consortium for Political and Social Research, 1998. Downloaded from ICPSR Web site: http://www.icpsr.umich.edu:8080/ICPSR-STUDY/02066.xml.

U.S. Department of Health, Education, and Welfare, Office for Civil Rights. 1978. *School Desegregation Trend Analysis, 1968–1976.* CD-ROM. Obtained through the Center for Demography and Ecology, University of Wisconsin.

Unpublished Data

Andrew W. Mellon Foundation. 2002. Unpublished tabulations based on the College and Beyond Survey, New York.

Charlotte-Mecklenburg Schools. 2002. "Charlotte-Mecklenburg Schools Monthly Membership at the End of Month 1" (September 23). Unpublished tabulation.

Denver Public Schools. "Estimated Ethnic Distribution of Pupils and Percentages" (May 1, 1962, October 15, 1964, October 15, 1965); "Student Membership by School, Grade, Ethnicity and Gender" (October 1, 2002). Unpublished tabulations.

Flint Community Schools. "Racial Distribution by Schools, K–12, 1950–1970." Unpublished tabulations.

Fort Wayne Community Schools. "Total Enrollments by Race 1950–51, 1962–63"; "Enrollment by Race" (October 1, 2002). Unpublished tabulations.

Jefferson County Public Schools. "Enrollment by Race and Sex, Elementary, Middle, and Secondary Schools, 2002–2003." Unpublished tabulation.

Pittsburgh Public Schools, Office of Technology. "Enrollment Numbers for the Years 1950–51 and 1960–61." Unpublished tabulations, transmitted by fax October 30, 2002.

Topeka Public Schools Demographic Services. "Racial Inventory of USD #501 Students, School Year 1955–56." Unpublished tabulation.

Wichita Public Schools. "Enrollment in Wichita Public Schools, 1952, 1960"; "Racial Enrollment by Attendance Unit, September 1997–September 2001"; "Official Enrollment, September 2, 2002." Unpublished tabulations.

* Index *

ability grouping, 4, 233n.32; in South, 138. *See also* academic tracking; tracking

academic achievement, 4–5; desegregation effects on, 187; narrowing racial gap in, 38; peer pressure and, 187; of private versus public school students, 101–102; regional disparities in, 30

academic performance: attitudes toward minorities and, 190–191; racial disparities in standards for, 227n.69; racial stereotypes and, 240n.21

academic tracking, 4, 9, 127–128, 198–199; discriminatory, 130–131; interracial friendships and, 189; legal challenge to, 128; minimizing desegregation impact, 182–183; opposition to, 232n.7; racial disparities in, 133; support for, 183; teachers' credentials and, 232n.9

achievement: under desegregation, 240n.9; desegregation effects on, 186–187; white-black gap in, 233n.32. *See also* academic achievement

Adams v. Califano, 237n.21

Adams v. Richardson, 156, 157, 165, 168, 237n.21

admissions policies, college, 199–200

advance placement classes: racial composition in, 126. *See also* honors classes

affirmative action, 149, 156–157

affirmative duty ruling, 26

African Americans, 51–52; achievement of, 186–187; anti-achievement orientation of, 187; attending all-black or majority black schools, 45–46; attitudes toward cross-race friendships of, 191; classroom segregation of, 129; college enrollment of, 154*t*; in colleges before *Brown*, 149–152; employment and educational opportunities of, 192–194; exposure rates for, 68*t*, 69; in extracurricular activities, 235n.64, 236n.70; in Harvard College, 148–149; impact of segregation on, 186; income trends for, 38; interracial rela-

tions of, 188–192; in majority nonwhite public schools, 56*t*; middle class, 150; as percentage of selective colleges, 236n.5; population trends of, 33, 36; proportion of in minority schools, 50–51*f*, 51–52; segregation of in 1940s-1960s, 71*t*; self-esteem in, 187, 240n.15; self-esteem in after desegregation, 240n.16; suburbanization of, 80–81; as teachers and administrators, 235n.53

Alabama, private school enrollment in, 113

Alexander v. Holmes, 26, 48, 103, 109

Allport, Gordon, 128; contact theory of, 3–4, 5

An American Dilemma (Myrdal), 14–15

American Friends Service Committee, 235n.58

Andrew W. Mellon Foundation, College and Beyond Survey of, 216

Anyon, Jean, 227n.69

apartheid, 14–15, 201

Arizona, segregated schools in, 18, 218n.17

Arkansas, early desegregation in, 23

Armor, David, 86, 93, 195

Ashmore, Harry, 19

Asian Americans: extracurricular activities of, 236n.70; growth of, 33, 35–36; in Harvard College, 148–149; in multiethnic metropolitan areas, 81; residential segregation of, 80; in Southern colleges and universities, 163; tracking assignments of, 138

assignment plans. *See* pupil assignment plans

Association of Independent Schools, 1969 survey of, 228n.18

association(s): bridging color line, 10; freedom of, 15. *See also* friendships; loose (weak) ties

athletic programs, integrated, 10. *See also* sports teams

Atlanta, Georgia: desegregation in, 24; metropolitan segregation index for, 231n.53

attendance rates, by socioeconomic class, 155, 237n.19

attendance zones, 51; adjustment of for racial balance, 32; in Cleveland, 221n.58; discriminatory, 197; gerrymandered, 18–20, 25, 51,

North (*cont.*)
152; hypocrisy of, 221n.67; interracial contact in before *Brown* decision, 46–47; lack of racial composition data on, 218n.12; percentage of nonwhite enrollment in, 163; private schools in, 103, 114; school segregation in before *Brown* decision, 17–22; segregated schools in, 219n.25

North Carolina: applications for transfer in, 220n.50; between-school segregation in, 147*t*; classroom-level data for, 11; classroom racial composition in, 132–135; classroom segregation in by percentage of blacks in, 136*f*; public colleges of, 161; pupil assignments in, 197–198; racial composition of schools in, 233n.33; segregation in colleges and universities of, 168–169; within-school segregation in, 147*t*, 185

North Carolina, University of, 169

Northeast: declining segregation in, 65; decreased within-district segregation in, 180; increased segregation in, 64; private school enrollment trends in, 103–104; proportion of black students in schools of, 207–208*t*; segregation in colleges and universities of, 170, 171; trends in higher education enrollment in, 166–167

Oakes, Jeannie, 137, 234n.52

Oberlin College, 237n.13; black enrollment in, 151

Office for Civil Rights: Desegregation Trends data of, 214; investigation of NYC public schools by, 130–131; *Racial and Ethnic Enrollment Data from Institutions of Higher Education* of, 216; *Racial Isolation in the Public Schools* of, 48–49; school-level interracial contact survey of, 45; survey data of, 27, 52, 81–82, 211–212, 215, 223n.13, 224n.31

Ohio: black colleges in, 152; school segregation in, 18–19

Oklahoma, University of, 150

Oklahoma City, 27

omitted variable bias: selection bias as one form of, 194; in statistical estimation, 194

open enrollment technique, 32

Orange County, California, "Mexican" schools in, 22

Orfield, Gary, 5–6, 10, 26, 48, 52, 55–56

Our Lady of Lourdes School, 100; racial composition of, 101

pairing (clustering), 31–32, 79–80, 84–85, 226n.44; dissimilarity index decline with, 85–86

parents: in academic tracking, 131, 233n.31; in school choice, 92–93; state and local governments accommodating, 9; withdrawing children from public schools, 84

Pell Grants, 155, 200

Pennsylvania, black colleges in, 152

People Who Care v. Rockford Board of Education, School District #205, 232n.12

perpetuation theory, 241n.40

Persell, Caroline H., 233n.23

Philadelphia, racial isolation indices for, 243n.5

Plaut, Richard L., 238n.30

policy, public, 4, 196–200; segregation as, 201

Pontiac, Michigan, school problems in, 93–94

population: racial composition of, 33–36; suburban migration of, 37

portable classrooms, 25

Powell, Lewis, 31

Powers, Daniel A., 232–233n.15

prejudice. *See* racial prejudice

primary metropolitan statistical areas (PMSAs), 231n.47, 231n.48

Prince Edward County, 103

Prince George's County, Maryland: black residential segregation in, 80; desegregation plans in, 27

private colleges/universities, 157; increased percentage of nonwhite students in, 239n.41; segregation trends in, 171–172

private foundations, 238n.28

private-public school disparities, 59–60, 74*t*, 231–232n.55, 231n.53

Private School Universe Survey (NCES): for 1997–1998, 235n.64; for 1999–2000, 211

private schools, 8–9, 184–185; academic achievement in, 101–102; blunting *Brown*'s effect, 67; economic models of demand for, 108; enrollment data on, 231n.46; enroll-

272

ment patterns of, 11, 102–104; exacerbating segregation, 122–123; exposure rates and enrollment in, 212; heterogeneity of, 100–101; incomes and enrollment rates in, 229n.19, 230n.36; increased interracial contact in, 180; increased segregation with enrollment in, 64–65; interracial contact in, 105–108; in Louisville, Kentucky, 229n.25; in measuring segregation, 116–122; minimizing desegregation impact in, 182; option of, 100–123; percentage of students in by region, 124t; proportion of white students enrolled in, 125t; race in demand for, 109–110; racial composition of, 100–101, 228n.12; regional enrollment trends in, 103–104, 105t; religious, 229n.23; religious and values-related factors in, 108–109; South's contrary trend in, 115–116; white flight and demand for, 108–116, 230n.41

proms: all-white, 1, 2; integrated, 1; racially separate, 139

propinquity, power of, 188–189

Proposition 209 (California), 236n.8

public higher education: in Border and Southern states, 160–162, 174t; enrollment trends in by region, 165; segregation trends in, 171, 174t

public housing projects, 19

public-private school disparities. See private-public school disparities

Public School Desegregation in the United States, 1968–1980 (Orfield), 5–6

Public School Universe. See Common Core of Data (CCD)

public schools: academic achievement in, 101–102; enrollment data for, 224n.31, 231n.46; increased interracial contact in, 179–180; per-pupil spending for by race, 15–16; racial composition of, 110, 228n.12; racially balanced, 213; social order in, 182–183; white flight from, 111–114

Puerto Rican Americans: increase in, 33; in New York City public schools, 20–21

pupil assignment plans, 224n.23, 242n.57; court-ordered, 242n.56; impact of, 197–198; nondiscriminatory methods of, 196–197; preventing racial discrimination in, 32–33;

racial segregation by, 131–132; random, 234n.40; separating from attendance zones, 32; techniques for modifying, 84–86

race: definition of, 217n.8; in private school enrollment, 109–110; school enrollment by, 70t

race relations, desegregation impact on, 188–192

Racial and Ethnic Enrollment Data from Institutions of Higher Education, 216

racial attitudes: interracial contact and, 190–191; segregation in schools and, 128–129

racial balance, 2; aggressive plan for, 49; backing off policy of, 9; classroom assignment and, 234n.40; with common racial composition in all schools, 211; costs and benefits of, 195–196; with court-ordered desegregation, 179; in extracurricular activities, 235n.58; judicial interventions in, 242n.54; in metropolitan areas, 57–67, 210, 231–232n.55; in private and public schools, 210–211; pursuit of, 39; weakening support for, 183–184

racial composition: calculation of, 201–202; regional patterns of after *Brown* decision, 48–57; residential housing patterns and, 76–78; tipping points of, 110–114; trends in, 33–36

racial discrimination: in academic tracking, 128; in tracking assignments, 137–139, 183

racial disparities, 11; across country, 233–234n.34; among individual private schools, 116; narrowing of, 38, 218n.11; national survey of, 29–30; in private versus public schools, 116, 210–211; between public school districts, 61–63, 116; within public school districts, 116; in school quality, 227n.69; within-region, 107–108

racial gap, narrowing, 38

racial groupings, 234n.41

racial incidents, 93–94

racial isolation, 5, 235n.64; calculation of, 243n.5; degree of change in from early 1960s to 1968, 55; extrapolating regional measures of, 205–206; by grade level, 46–47; measures of, 202; in metropolitan and non-